Lew Altfest Answers *Almost* All Your Questions About Money

Lew Altfest Answers *Almost* All Your Questions About Money

Lewis J. Altfest

Karen Caplan Altfest

McGraw-Hill, Inc.

New York San Francisco Washington, D.C. Auckland Bogotá
Caracas Lisbon London Madrid Mexico City Milan
Montreal New Delhi San Juan Singapore
Sydney Tokyo Toronto

Library of Congress Cataloging-in-Publication Data

Altfest, Lewis J.
Lew Altfest answers almost all your questions about money / Lewis J. Altfest, Karen Caplan Altfest.
p. cm.
ISBN 0-07-001274-1 (hc) : —ISBN 0-07-001290-3 (pbk) :
1. Finance, Personal—United States—Miscellanea. I. Altfest, Karen Caplan. II. Title.
HG179.A448 1992
332.024—dc20 92-2246
CIP

This book is printed on recycled, acid-free paper containing a minimum of 50% recycled de-inked fiber.

First McGraw-Hill paperback edition, 1994

2 3 4 5 6 7 8 9 0 DOC/DOC 9 8 7 6 5 4

ISBN 0-07-001274-1(HC)
ISBN 0-07-001290-3(PBK)

The sponsoring editor for this book was Caroline F. Carney, the editing supervisor was Jane Palmieri, and the production supervisor was Suzanne W. Babeuf. It was set in Baskerville by North Market Street Graphics.

Printed and bound by R. R. Donnelley & Sons Company.

To Ellen and Andrew
with all our love

Contents

Preface

How much of my salary should I save?

When should I refinance my mortgage?

Why should I use asset allocation?

How much life insurance is enough?

When should I start planning for retirement?

Lew Altfest Answers Almost All Your Questions About Money gives you in-depth, easy-to-read answers to money questions such as these. It responds to your need for a realistic book written by practicing financial planners—a book that requires no special financial training. The question-and-answer format provides genuine solutions to real problems. Whether you want specific answers to your key questions, hope to learn more about financial planning and how we do it, or both, we believe you will find this book useful and interesting to read.

We supply direct, concise, impartial information, similar to the advice we give clients in our fee-only financial planning practice, using anecdotes, simple rules, and easy-to-follow explanations. You can select just the advice you need or read the whole book as a way to understand the entire financial planning process. Although each answer stands on its own, a complete reading of the book can help you do much or all of your financial planning yourself. It can also save you a lot of money!

Every decade has its own identifying style. We believe the 1990s will be known as the decade in which a more knowledgeable public demands more concrete benefits for its money. We have therefore paid particular attention to what we call value-oriented money planning. Through value-oriented money planning we show you how to gain an advantage in all aspects of your financial life. We give value-oriented awards to strategies that offer particularly high benefits.

We have constructed this book in the same way we draw up a financial plan for a client. Each chapter covers a topic area in detail. First, we show you how to organize your finances and to save for your goals. Next, we explain investing and take you step by step through value-oriented investing techniques and modern investment practices. Both can help you improve your investment returns. Third, we suggest strategies for handling your finances at different stages of your life—living single, married, parenting, divorced, pre- and post-retired, widowed, and caring for the elderly. The chapters on relationship planning and caring for the elderly are particularly important today and, to our knowledge, are treated in detail for the first time in an overall money planning book.

In virtually every chapter we make recommendations on how to save in taxes and other costs. In each case we provide practical planning methods and actual real-life examples from our fee-only financial practice. The more than 160 questions are based on three things: (1) discussions we have had with hundreds of people who have consulted us about money matters, (2) questions raised at seminars before thousands of individuals, and (3) conversations with numerous independent financial planners over many years.

The final chapter brings all the material together. In it we describe our Money Ladder, which helps you focus on what is important to you and can lead the way to reaching your goals. We show you how to climb to the very top of your own Money Ladder. We believe this is the first time a book has given you a workable step-by-step approach to constructing your own financial plan.

If you are a financial services professional, *Lew Altfest Answers Almost All Your Questions About Money* can help you learn more about modern planning and investing techniques, gauging your client's concerns, and resolving them yourself. Our rules of thumb, tables, concepts, and practical examples should prove particularly useful. You can even use this book as a training tool for new employees.

We want to know which responses you find most helpful, and what questions remain after you have read this book. Please address your comments and your inquiries about our services to us at our offices: L.J. Altfest & Co., Inc., 140 William Street, New York, NY 10038 (212-406-0850).

We are fortunate to have had substantial expert help in the writing of this book. First, we would like to thank our editor, Caroline F. Carney, for all her helpful advice and encouragement. Special thanks to Frances Minters for her many constructive suggestions, and to our staff members: Michael Waldron for his valuable assistance throughout the book, and Peggy Roughton-Hester and Gale P. McEvilley for their contributions.

Finally, we wish to express our appreciation to our many colleagues who commented on various sections of the manuscript: Richard April, Steve Aronoff, Ken Ballin, Norman Barotz, David Blake, Donald Budnick, Joan Chasan, Peg Downey, Steven Enright, Louis Feinstein, Jay Gould, Gary Greenbaum, Randy Hedlund, Mike Kaufman, Mary Malgoire, Bob Maloney, Mike Martin, Neil Owen, Carole Phillips, Al Pollock, Alan Romm, Richard Rothberg, Vince Schiavi, Renee Schwartz, Margaret Scott, David Strauss, Bob Tansey, Henry Wendel, Noel Whearty, Carol Wilson, Kevin Wynne, and Paul Zuckerman.

Lewis J. Altfest
Karen Caplan Altfest

About the Authors

LEWIS J. ALTFEST, MBA, Ph.D., CPA, CFA, CFP, APFS, is president of L. J. Altfest & Co., Inc., a fee-only financial planning and investment management firm in New York City founded in 1982 and incorporated in 1984. He was formerly a general partner and director of research for Lord Abbett & Co. and before that was associated with Lehman Brothers, Wertheim & Co., and Peat Marwick Mitchell. He is active in the development of financial planning as a profession and has served on the Board of Directors of the National Association of Personal Financial Advisors. Lew is a director of the International Association for Financial Planning New York Chapter and has been admitted to the Registry of Financial Planning Practitioners.

Lew is associate professor of finance at the Lubin Graduate School of Business of Pace University. He writes extensively on financial planning and investments and frequently conducts seminars for professionals and the general public. He has served as an arbitrator for the NASD and the American Arbitration Association. He is often quoted in the national media, including *The Wall Street Journal, The New York Times, Los Angeles Times, Washington Post, Money, Fortune, USA Today*, and *Newsweek* and has appeared on CBS's *Wall Street Journal Report*, ABC, FNN, CNBC, and CNN.

KAREN CAPLAN ALTFEST, M.A., Ph.D., CFP, is vice president of L. J. Altfest & Co., Inc. She previously was coordinator of the Certified Financial Planner program, a training program for financial planners, which she originated at Pace University in White Plains, New York.

Karen teaches "On Your Own Financially," a course for financial novices at the New School for Social Research in New York City. She is a member of the National Association of Women Business Owners and speaks on financial planning issues to women's organizations and adult education groups. She is the author of a book and many articles and is a contributor to the *NAPFA News*, a newsletter for fee-only financial planners. She has been quoted in several publications, including *Financial Services Week.*

Karen devotes much of her spare time to charitable causes and has been interviewed in *The New York Times* and *Parents Magazine* because of her work. She was the founding chairperson of the Yorkville Common Pantry and currently serves on several community boards and committees.

Lew and Karen Altfest live in New York City with their daughter, son, and cat.

1
Managing Your Cashflow

Are you saving money each year or are you one of the people who doesn't quite have things under control? Do you always seem to be running to catch up with your bills? If so, you are not alone. When our clients first come to see us many are not saving, or are setting aside less than their parents did; our country as a whole saves only a fraction as much as our major trading partners do. Whatever your savings situation, don't worry. We will show you how to take charge of your finances.

Managing your cashflow is the key to successful financial planning. The result, savings (net cashflow), gives you choices. You can decide whether you want to invest the money, buy additional insurance, save more for your children, or spend some or all of it on living better now.

Your psychological makeup can determine your spending patterns, regardless of your level of income. Jonathan, a Wall Street executive, was making over $400,000 a year at age 32, and not saving a penny. He had no idea of where the money went and didn't feel he was living an extravagant lifestyle at all. Why, he and his wife ate at home five nights a week! We calculated that Jonathan's food bill alone, including purchases of takeout gourmet food five nights a week, came to over $25,000 annually.

We can't help but contrast Jonathan's situation with that of Harry, a 50-year-old department store worker we know whose wife Joyce gave up her career to raise their two children. On a salary of $28,000,

Harry and Joyce save over $5000 a year and still have money left over to put in Harry's pension plan. Harry's question to us was, "Am I saving as much money as other people in my income bracket?" Harry and Joyce were not interested in buying a lot of extra things that they did not need.

We notice, however, that most of our clients have no trouble at all spending more as soon as they earn more. This is not surprising, given the bombardment of goods and services we are offered on television and elsewhere. Temptation these days goes far beyond keeping up with your neighbors.

What *is* surprising is that you may not even appreciate that your increased spending has actually raised your standard of living. That is because you accept without thinking the upgrade in car, increased frequency of eating out, longer vacations, and better clothing that your higher income buys you.

We find that the more-money-better-standard-of-living spiral creates both a risk and an opportunity. The risk is that you will keep spending all that you earn and never achieve your long-term goals. Money will then be controlling you instead of the other way around. The good news is that since you don't highly value the increase in spending, you shouldn't have much trouble in restraining it. All that it takes is a bit of moderation.

It *is* possible to have it all. You can enjoy an attractive lifestyle, save to achieve your longer-term goals, and still be able to indulge in some extravagances occasionally without feeling guilty. All it involves is taking control of your cashflow. This chapter will explain how to do it in a relatively painless way.

What is value-oriented money planning and how can it help me?

Value-oriented money planning enables you to do the most with your money. Value does not mean cheap. You don't get value when you pay a sidewalk vendor $5 for a watch that quickly breaks. As the president of Sears Roebuck told me, "You get value by dividing quality by price. Either factor alone will not provide it." You are therefore just as likely to get value in a fancy French restaurant as you are in a fast-food one, depending on what you spend and what you get for your money.

The best way to get value is to spend time evaluating your options. For example, we found two insurance policies that seem identical in the amount of coverage and in the financial stability of the companies offering the policies. The only difference is that one cost twice as much, thousands of dollars more per year, than the other. Clearly, the less-expensive policy provides value that the more expensive policy does not.

Value can also come from avoiding commissions by buying a financial product directly rather than through a saleperson. In the investment arena, as a whole, value can come from independent thinking and acting. People often go through periods of optimism and pessimism that color their buying and selling decisions. By putting your cashflow to work when general opinion about a particular investment is negative, you can often improve your return on investment. One example is to buy a house during a recession as Eleanor and David did on our recommendation. They paid $140,000 for a house that had sold two years earlier for $240,000. Within 24 months, a similar home in their neighborhood was sold for $260,000, almost double their cost.

Value-oriented opportunities are available in many areas of your personal finances. We will highlight them throughout this book.

How much of my salary should I save?

Our first rule is to get into the savings habit. No matter what your income or your needs, you can do much to realize your goals now and in the future if you get used to putting some of your income away. Even a modest amount saved today can make a big difference in the future when you need it.

How much you should save will depend on your own circumstances, including your age, assets, income, current expenses, and goals. You will find it easier to save when you have a specific goal in mind. Begin saving now to meet your individual goals, whether they are short-term ones, such as buying a new car, or longer-term ones. Then decide which of your current funds could be used to meet your goals. When you get through satisfying all your immediate goals, generally the biggest one remains: retirement, or—in a broader sense—financial independence.

In our view, the average person should save 7 percent of pretax income when starting to save at age 25; 10 percent at age 35; 18 percent at age 45; and 35 percent if saving begins at age 55. Considering the sharp increase when you delay, you should begin saving as early as possible.

If your savings are behind where you would like them to be and your income is growing, we recommend that you make a deal with yourself. Each time you get a raise take your old salary, multiply it by 1 plus the projected yearly inflation rate, for example 1 + 0.05, and subtract that figure from your new, higher salary. For example, if you were earning $35,000 and now earn $38,000, your calculation would be:

$35,000	$38,000
× 1.05	−36,750
$36,750	$ 1,250

That will give you your additional savings pool of $1250.

If you are under 40, save one-third of that figure; over 40, save two-thirds of it. The rest can go toward your current living expenses. What you are doing is sacrificing a better standard of living now for a more secure retirement later. But if saving that percentage of your new increase in salary doesn't bring up your total savings in a reasonable time, consider saving the whole increase, and even cutting your living costs.

How will inflation affect my savings?

Inflation can reduce the purchasing power of your savings unless you take steps to cushion its effects.

Most people know about the steady price rises that have become a serious problem over the past two decades. Because these annual price increases are relatively small, it's easy to underestimate the impact inflation can have over a few years. We call this steady increase in prices "inflation creep."

Sarah and Ralph, who had an average income, were astonished to learn that they had inherited $200,000 from an elderly widow whom they had met on a family vacation. They asked us to include in our planning for them that all of the $200,000 inheritance be left for their two children after they passed away. Sarah and Ralph, who were in their late thirties, didn't want their two children to have to struggle as they had. They planned to use only the interest income from the inheritance. They were shocked to find out that should they live a normal number of years, say into their eighties, and should yearly inflation run at the 5 percent level—1 percent less than it has actually averaged over the past 25 years—the $100,000 at that future time for each child would be able to buy less than $10,000 worth of things now.

You may be surprised that the inheritance is expected to lose almost all its value when Sarah and Ralph don't plan to even touch the principal amount of $200,000. While inflation creep—the steady annual increase in the cost of living—is the basic reason, there is another factor, the compounding of inflation, at work here. Compounding, which literally is increase upon increase, magnifies any effect.

Think of compounding as a snowball no bigger than an orange that starts at the top of a mountain; by the time it finishes rolling it has grown to the size of a boulder. Why? Because the snowball grows and takes on a larger and larger size as it increases the amount of snow it picks up. Similarly, cost increases start slowly but through the snowball effect of compounding can become very large. Compounding can be either good (as in interest earned) or bad (as with inflation), but it is always powerful.

An example of compounding can be seen in the purchase of Manhattan for $24 worth of trinkets in 1626 by Peter Minuit, a director of the Dutch West India Company. Suppose the recipients had cashed in the $24, and deposited it in a savings account. Assuming that they received a 5 percent dividend on the original amount annually and didn't reinvest these dividends, they would have $462 today. But if the dividends had been deposited and reinvested, through compounding power the original $24 would be worth $1.3 billion now.

We tell our clients to consider inflation creep and compounding power in all their money plans, particularly the long-term ones. Think in terms of the *real* (inflation-adjusted) amount of money it would take to buy items at today's prices. Any financial calculator, including the Hewlett Packard 12C or 17BII, or a mathematical software program like Lotus 1-2-3, can give you future prices instantly. For your convenience, we have supplied calculating results in Schedule A-2 in Appendix A.

A handy rule of thumb that will help you figure out how long it takes for an item to double in price through compounding is the rule of 72. Just divide 72 by the inflation rate or rate of return. For example, if household costs rise at a 7 percent rate per year, it would take about 10 years for their expenses to double (72 divided by 7 = 10.3 years).

Can I protect myself against inflation?

The answer is yes. You can beat inflation by having your yearly savings grow by at least the rate of inflation.

Of course, this is sometimes easier said than done. Try breaking your expenses into things you must have—like food, clothing, and shelter—and discretionary items—things you don't really need but choose to buy with your extra cash. Under normal circumstances, the things you really need should increase in price by *less* than the inflation rate.

If you own a home and have financed a large portion of it with a fixed-rate mortgage, that is, one in which yearly costs don't change, the payments remain level. If there is not an unusually dramatic increase in inflation, even under a variable rate mortgage in which payments are altered according to changes in interest rates, payments are likely to become a lesser burden over time. Without a change in your standard of living, food and clothing should also climb less than inflation.

As for discretionary items, hard goods (for example, automobiles, televisions, and refrigerators), with some exceptions such as cars, are likely not to increase greatly in price. That is because new manufacturing techniques allow producers to make things at lower prices. Do you remember how expensive personal computers and video cameras were a few years ago?

Services will probably be the biggest problem area. That is because the largest component of services is usually labor, and costs increase as workers try—like you—to stay ahead of inflation. We don't think you can do much to escape a rise in service costs except to stay clear of this area as much as possible. Try to do your own servicing by using self-serve restaurants, self-serve gas stations, and so on, and by handling more of your own beauty needs, cleaning, and home repairs.

Another way to ease inflation's impact is to put your money into things that actually grow with inflation over long periods of time—for example, mutual funds of common stocks or real estate. (Read more about them in Chapters 3, 4, and 7.)

Finally, consider borrowing money to make money. We tell clients that it's harder to perform this neat trick now than in the late seventies and early eighties when interest rates (after adjustment for high inflation) were much lower. But it's still possible, particularly if you can deduct the interest from your taxes, as you can with home mortgage loans. (See Chapter 7 for a discussion of borrowing for investment in real estate.) Remember, this can be an aggressive strategy; use it carefully.

How should I plan for major expenses?

The first thing you need to do is to establish your priorities. If you have just one major expense in mind, such as buying a new car or a larger home, there's no problem. But when there are many such major expenses, ranging, say, from a trip abroad to putting your son or daughter through college, these expenditures need to be ranked by importance and then scheduled according to when the money will be needed.

Next, you should make a good-faith estimate of how much each item would cost if you were to buy it today. Then add an annual inflation adjustment factor from now until the time you actually intend to buy it. See how much it will cost you at that future time. Use your own estimate of inflation based on current conditions and how you think inflation will affect that particular item, or use our current estimate of a 5 percent rate of inflation per year. Next, break down the amount you have to save by year and then by month by dividing the total by the number of years until you need it.

For example, assume you are saving to purchase a car that costs $10,000 today. You plan to buy the car in four years. The amount you would need in four years at an assumed inflation rate of 5 percent would be $12,155, not $10,000. If you earn 5 percent interest after tax on your money, you would need to put away $2820 each year or about $235 a month from now until you buy the car.

You can ignore the income on the amount you are saving unless the purchase is more than five years off. If it is that far away, you can use Schedule A-2 in Appendix A.

For all but long-range planning, the discipline of regular saving is much more important than where you put the money. We advise our clients to avoid investments that move up and down very much, such as stocks, if they will need the money in less than two years. Instead, put your money into more conservative investments such as bank and mutual fund money-market accounts, U.S. government notes and bonds, or certificates of deposit.

We still remember Alice, a retired woman of 70, cautious in all her habits except for an occasional fling in the stock market when it looked particularly attractive. Once she asked us to manage her money in stocks for six months, after which time she planned to use the money as a down payment on a house for her daughter. Knowing that Alice's eagerness to invest reflected too much speculative enthusiasm in the market, we recommended instead that she roll her money over into a six-month certificate of deposit. This happened in the spring of 1987. Six months later the stock market dropped sharply, and with it the value of stocks plunged. It was evident that if Alice had acted on her emotions, her daughter would have had a considerably cheaper home!

Unless you are a highly disciplined person, focus on saving for the items that have the greatest meaning for you. By breaking the items into small monthly pieces, you can ensure that the amounts actually go into savings. Every six months add up all your savings and compare them with your targeted amount. If you are off just a little, the unplanned-for income from your investments may make up the difference. If you are greatly behind schedule and don't know the reason why, try a more disciplined approach, including changing your spending behavior. If you are at or ahead of where you expected to be, place any extra funds into another savings item or reward yourself with a small indulgence for a job well done.

What is the best way to save money?

Too often our clients put away money one month only to take it out the next, or, even worse, never make it to their savings account at all. Their cash on hand always seems to be just enough to meet their monthly expenses.

That provides a clue about savings: *the way to save is to treat savings as another mandatory expense.* Just as you pay your rent or your monthly mortgage bill, deposit your savings at the *beginning* of the weekly or monthly period in which you receive your paycheck. Better yet, have it taken out of your paycheck directly, if possible. The money should be deposited into a separate account and not touched unless there is an emergency.

Make an agreement with yourself that you will be depressed, highly depressed, if you do touch your savings before reaching your goal.

There are ways of saving that make it easier to leave the money where it is than to withdraw it. Depositing large sums into a pension plan can work if you truly don't expect to need the money; besides being difficult to make, withdrawals are subject to a penalty. If you need even more structure and can afford it, buy a whole life insurance policy when you want additional life insurance, or buy a large home substantially financed by an affordable mortgage—the loan will necessitate large monthly cash payments—if you think you will ultimately sell the house and recoup the amounts you have paid in.

Of course, the best way to save is not to spend. If our clients have problems not buying everything they see, we recommend they leave their credit cards in a drawer. Many times the card contributes to the problem because people don't feel that using it is the same as taking money out of their pockets. That's too bad, since if you are late with a credit card payment, you will run up excessive interest charges on your bill.

Patty made $60,000 a year as a lawyer right out of school but was on a $70,000-per-year spending habit fueled, in large part, by a love of new clothes. By leaving home without her credit cards, Patty was forced to think about whether she really needed that extra dress, and her personal expenses were brought down to manageable levels.

If you have a severe case of credit card overspending, we suggest that you lock your credit cards in a safe-deposit box and use them only for vacations and other unusual circumstances. In really extreme cases, we even advise people to cut up their cards and notify the issuer that they no longer want to be cardholders.

How can I keep track of my costs?

Clearly the way to keep track of costs is through a budget. However, what works best is to incorporate your budget in a broader document called a cashflow schedule. The *cash inflow* portion of the schedule should contain your income, including wages, salaries, bonuses, interest, dividends, alimony you receive, and other sources of income. The *cash outflow* section should include all major expenses, food, clothing, housing, medical care, vacations, entertainment, repayments of debt, and transportation costs. Be sure to include only those items that you actually paid for, not those you plan to buy or receive. Taxes, including social security, and income taxes, should be itemized in a separate section of the cash outflow portion.

You can try to identify last year's expenses using your checkbook. The figures you get will probably point to a greater savings than you actually had, because most people can't remember every one of their expenses.

If you can calculate your actual savings for last year, and if your estimates of savings (deducting cash outflows from cash inflows) are not too far off, just place the difference between the two savings figures in a miscellaneous column. If you don't know your savings, you can use the 10 to 20 percent of total expenses that we normally put in this column.

The following example shows a savings calculation for a family that earns $30,000 per year. They were able to identify only $23,000 of expenses. The $4000 miscellaneous figure represents the savings deposits they made for the year. The miscellaneous expense ($3000) is the difference between their preliminary savings calculation ($7000) and the actual amount they saved ($4000).

Cash inflows (income)	$30,000
Cash outflows (expenses accounted for)	23,000
Preliminary cashflow (savings)	$ 7,000
Miscellaneous expenses	3,000
Actual cashflow (savings)	$ 4,000

Once you set up your cashflow statement, you can use it to project your future years' cashflows. Remember to include any large, unusual expenses that you expect to have in the appropriate year—for example, remodeling your house, debt falling due, buying a new car, contributing to a child's wedding, or taking an expensive vacation.

As for income, one word of caution: you may want to be conservative about what you expect your income to be in the future. That could put less pressure on you to perform. We believe that it is good to be moderately conservative. However, make sure that your income is expected to grow at least at the rate of inflation. If it doesn't keep pace with inflation, even a strong saver will not be able to keep up as your expenses continue to grow. If you really expect your income to remain flat, you will probably have to cut back on your actual living expenses.

Your budget comes from the cash outflow section of your cashflow statement. It is a way to keep track of your expenses and to make sure that you don't exceed your target for spending. We used to downplay the need for a budget, but we have new respect for it now. Regardless of your income, a continuously updated budget forces you to compile figures and compare them with what you expected them to be. You can do this by copying Table 1-1 (Cashflow Statement) either on a piece of paper or on a simple Lotus 1-2-3 type computer spreadsheet.

Many people ask us what they should be allocating for each category of spending. This depends on where you live and your own preferences. Table 1-2 gives you the percentages other people are spending based on low-, intermediate-, and high-income groupings.

Here are some key things to watch when you prepare a budget:

- Spend the time to develop a realistic budget. Use last year's actual figures, if they are available, as a starting point.
- Break the yearly budget into small pieces, monthly or weekly, if you can.
- Compare your budgeted figures to your actual figures at least once each quarter (every three months). Be prepared for changes in both income and expenses, and make adjustments accordingly.
- One person can make a budget, but it's better to involve all your family members. By taking part in the process, they will have less trouble sticking to it.

Table 1-1. Cashflow Statement

	Monthly	Annually	Total annually
CASH INFLOWS			
Salary	______	______	
Bonus	______	______	
Business income	______	______	
Interest	______	______	
Dividends	______	______	
Other (alimony, etc.)	______	______	
Total cash inflows			______
CASH OUTFLOWS			
Continuing Monthly Payments			
Rent or mortgage	______	______	
Utilities	______	______	
Debt	______	______	
Other	______	______	
Total monthly payments		______	
Other Monthly Cash Expenses			
Food and beverages—eating in	______	______	
Household care	______	______	
Household furnishings	______	______	
Clothing	______	______	
Transportation	______	______	
Health care	______	______	
Insurance	______	______	
Education and training	______	______	
Eating out and entertainment	______	______	

Table 1-1. Cashflow Statement (*Continued*)

	Monthly	Annually	Total annually
Vacations	______	______	
Personal care	______	______	
Contributions and gifts	______	______	
Credit card not counted above	______	______	
Miscellaneous	______	______	
Total monthly expenses		______	
Total Living Expenses		______	
Taxes			
Social security tax		______	
Federal income tax		______	
State and local income tax		______	
Total taxes		______	
Total outflows			______
NET CASHFLOW (SAVINGS)			======
SAVINGS ALLOCATION			
For emergencies		______	
For short-term goals (1 year)		______	
For intermediate-term goals (2–5 years)		______	
For retirement—pensions, IRAs, 401(k), other		______	
For other longer-term goals (5 years or more)		______	
Reinvested interest and dividends		______	
Unallocated		______	
Total savings			======

Table 1-2. Consumer Spending Patterns (Percentage Breakdown by Income)*

Items	Lower budget, %	Intermediate budget, %	Higher budget, %
Food at home	13	11	8
Food away from home	6	7	8
Housing—shelter	19	19	20
Housing—furnishings and operations	15	15	15
Transportation	19	20	20
Clothing	6	6	7
Personal care	1	1	1
Medical care	8	6	4
Other family consumption	10	11	14
Other items	3	4	3
Total budget	100	100	100

*Taken from the Bureau of Labor Statistics.

- If your budget is higher than your income indicates you can afford, or if it always seems to come in over what you projected, change your practices. Our clients will often ask us to review their budget statements and suggest ways to cut costs. We limit ourselves to pointing out cashflow dangers and suggesting cuts in areas with above-average expenses. We tell clients we are not fiscal dieticians. They should decide on the actual items to be cut back because they know their priorities best. Separating the budget into fixed expenses (those that cannot be changed easily, such as mortgage payments) and variable expenses (ones that you have some control over, such as entertainment costs) can help you make cuts when necessary.
- Remember to pay off your credit card in full each month; this will present a more accurate picture of your expenditures for that month, lower your interest expenses, and, more importantly, force you to feel the bite of your living expenses. It will prevent you from accumulating debt without careful consideration, and from borrowing large sums of money that you cannot repay.

In our experience, nothing beats the budget for tracking and controlling your expenses. As a no-cost way to organize your financial affairs and to point the way to greater savings, we give the budget our first value-oriented money planning award.

If you are like most of our clients, you probably find a budget about as appetizing as a low-calorie diet—but since you are the one drawing it up, you can make it taste better. Be realistic, and you will find it easier to live with.

If you need a budget, whether you put it on a computer spreadsheet or on the back of an old envelope, there is one important thing to remember: stick to it! And reward yourself with occasional treats for good behavior. If, however, you have no desire to live with this somewhat rigid task and if you are able to save enough money without a budget, you can pass it up.

What records should I keep?

The importance of good and accurate recordkeeping was recently brought home by a story about a South African businessman who made extensive trips abroad and decided that, given his country's uncertainties, he would place his money in the more secure countries found in his travels. The only trouble was that he never recorded his transactions nor told his family where his money was. After his death his relatives could not locate his assets and experienced a substantial decline in their standard of living; at some point in the future, some foreign government is likely to benefit from this unintended windfall.

While your financial life may not be as complex, you should keep records of the following items in a safe yet easy-to-reach place:

1. Estate planning papers, including a validly executed will and any codicils to it, documentation of gifts given or received, information regarding any trusts, and living wills.
2. Insurance policies of all types (including homeowners, renters, automobile, life, disability, and health), receipts, and appraisals and photographs of furnishings, furs, jewelry, and collectibles.
3. Important contracts, such as corporate benefits, job-related salary contracts, stock options, profit-sharing accounts, partnership agreements, and social security benefits.

4. Investment papers, including bonds, stocks, bank, brokerage, and mutual fund statements. Every few years you should develop a listing of your current net worth (assets minus liabilities) or use an updated version of any financial plan done for you.
5. Ownership papers, including deeds to homes and automobile or other vehicle ownership papers. Make sure you have the year of purchase, cost, name of the seller, make and model of any vehicles, and all warranties.
6. Personal life-cycle certificates, such as birth or adoption, marriage, passport, military discharge, divorce, and death certificates of close relatives. Your social security number should be listed with these.
7. Federal, state, and local tax returns and supporting information. Keep returns, supporting documents, bank statements, and canceled checks for five years.
8. Important advisors. List names, addresses, and telephone numbers of important advisors including attorneys, accountants, financial and investment advisors, and insurance and investment brokers.
9. Miscellaneous. Keep track of loans outstanding, credit cards, their numbers and dates of expiration, as well as the disposition papers on legal claims, and warranties. Cut up and discard expired cards and ones you no longer use.

These records should be kept together in a safe place in your home, preferably one that is fireproof, or in a bank vault. Remember, however, that in many states safe-deposit boxes are sealed on the death of the box owner—even if the box is jointly held. Therefore, documents that will be needed soon after death, such as your will or burial instructions should be kept in another location, or should even reside with relatives you trust.

All records should be referred to in a summary sheet with clear instructions about where they may be found. Don't forget to let your heirs know where you keep the keys to your safe-deposit box and the location of any safes you have at home.

If you would like an excellent, relatively low cost method of helping you organize your records, you might consider Homefile, which is marketed principally to financial advisors for their clients. It can be purchased from Homefile, 3444-101 Ellicott Center Drive, Ellicott City, MD 21043-4153 (800-695-3453).

How much money should I have on hand in case of emergency?

The amount of money you should have on hand for emergencies depends on your personal situation. Money emergencies generally come in two forms: income cutbacks or elimination, often from the loss of a job; or the need for a sum of money for a special purpose. Of the two, the loss of income is probably harder to prepare for. That's because the expense outlay is often a one-time need while being out of a job can extend for a long period—even for years.

Because it is possible to lose self-esteem along with the job, when we meet someone who is out of work, we often stress emotional factors as much as the financial aspects of the emergency.

When John, a man of 52, came to us his face told the story. He had recently experienced what was for him a tragedy—he had been fired after 20 years of a strong relationship with one publishing family. We didn't recommend an immediate cutback in expenses even though that would have been justified because John was the sole breadwinner in a family with a fairly high cost of living. We felt the most important thing was to have him maintain his lifestyle and keep a positive attitude. Our only suggestion for retrenchment was to postpone an expensive vacation that he probably wouldn't have enjoyed at that time anyway. Our strategy paid off even sooner than we had expected. John found a job within six months and is now happy in his new career.

The emphasis would, of course, change for someone who failed to acknowledge the seriousness of the situation. Melissa was young, single, and had a checkered credit record and less than one month's savings in the bank. She had worked in advertising, where being laid off after an account is lost carries no stigma. Unfortunately, it can be some time before the next job turns up, particularly in a recessionary period such as the one we were experiencing at the time. Melissa, who would have burned her way through her savings in a short period, had to be bluntly told to get serious about her expenses and find some temporary, part-time, or free-lance work.

In general, we recommend you keep at least three months of household expenses in liquid accounts (accounts that you can quickly change into cash without losing your principal). That means placing the money in money-market accounts, certificates of deposit, or shorter-term government bonds or bond funds. When only one person in the household works, or when the upkeep is very high compared to unemployment compensation, we prefer that you have at least six months' reserve available. If you have a distinct possibility of being laid off, are in an unstable industry, or are over 50 years old, when finding a new job can take some time, we suggest you have as much as one year's expenses in reserve. In that case include high-quality bonds, particularly those with dates that are less than 10 years, among your investments.

If you know that you may be leaving your job soon, it is a good idea to reappraise what you have in your investment portfolio and consider raising the amount of liquidity by selling some of your holdings and putting the proceeds in money-market funds. You can think of taking out a home equity line of credit (a loan that uses your home as security) that could be denied to you later if you are between jobs.

If you have just been unexpectedly notified of a change in your position, don't panic. Your judgment is likely to be clouded for some time. Most important, don't liquidate well-established assets. Keep focused on your strengths and on getting a new job.

If your emergency has to do with new major expenses and is a nonrecurring problem, think of obtaining credit. There will be more about that in Chapter 2.

How do I know when I'm making enough?

This question could just as well be asked of a psychologist as of a financial advisor. Nonetheless, many people ask us this. In cases where financial and human factors are combined, some of our clients call us their "financial shrinks."

What is enough depends on the individual. Many of our clients keep the amount they make a closely guarded secret, known only by their spouse, and, if they have them, their accountant and financial advisor. New clients often ask us if their financial information will be kept confidential—which of course it will—or specifically ask us not to tell their spouse, their friends, or their relatives how much they earn or how much they have. To them, money defines status.

On the other hand, one of our clients, Rachel, has inherited a large sum of money from her family. She keeps her inheritance a secret so that her good fortune won't set her apart from her neighbors and coworkers.

On the behavioral side, some would say you're making enough when you have as much as the neighbors you admire. Others would say it's when you achieve inner fulfillment. The problem is that unless you are unusually self-fulfilled, "enough" becomes a moving target over time. Many of our most financially successful clients actually worry that they do not have enough to satisfy other people's expectations. Some people will never think they have enough. That is why the United States is known as a consumption-oriented society.

From a strict financial standpoint, you are making enough when you have sufficient funds to pay for your food, clothing, and shelter, and other essentials. What should you spend? The amount of the household budget you need depends on what part of the country you live in, whether in an urban or rural location, and the size of your family. For a three-person household in an urban area, use an average figure of $22,000 for low, $30,000 for medium, and $70,000 for high income as of 1992. Use the percentages given in Table 1-2 to obtain average outlays by type of expenditure. If you are single, you can cut that figure by 35 to 50 percent. If you have a two-person household, cut the three-person household figure by 15 percent; for four or more, raise it by about 10 percent. Adjust your figures for the relative cost of living in your region. If you live in a high-cost area, raise it by 20 percent; if you are in a rural or other low-cost area, subtract 15 to 20 percent.

If your goals are fairly realistic and you have many productive years left, write down the important objectives that you hope to achieve: type of home and car, frequency of vacations, years of college for your children, number of evenings out, and so on. Put a copy of the paper in a vault so that you can compare these goals with later changes. Estimate how much you should save for a comfortable retirement (see Chapter 9). Then approximate the total income you will need to attain these goals, using the budget established as the starting point.

When you reach the goals you have established, as many people do, whisper to yourself, "Enough!" and live within the target you have set. If you do, you will be a satisfied person.

On the other hand, if you have previously gone through this exercise and are into the tenth upward revision of your target lifestyle, don't be too hard on yourself; you have plenty of company.

How do I safeguard my money in case of recession?

Our clients' biggest concern in a recession usually involves household budgeting and investing. They often ask us what to do in such cases. The first thing you can do is recognize that your opinion on investments and sometimes on life in general may be unduly influenced by current circumstances. After all, it is difficult not to be influenced by the overall air of gloom and doom.

Think again. While we may not always be as lucky as we were after the 1982 recession, which was followed by relatively clear sailing, neither is our economy likely to be what one of our new clients said about his investment performance under his previous manager, "Down, down, and down." You may be tempted to move to safer investments, but it is unwise to make major investment decisions during a recession.

How can you predict the next recession? Our answer is, "With great difficulty." Except when they follow special shocks to our economic system, like an embargo or war, recessions tend to occur when prices have increased, factories are operating closer to capacity, and inflation is threatening to get out of hand. Often the medicine prescribed is for federal authorities to make it more difficult and expensive to borrow money. The administration may approve, or even encourage the Federal Reserve—the agency in charge of money in circulation—to act, but will never say so for fear that the American people will accuse them (correctly) of temporarily putting people out of work.

As a rule of thumb, when inflation and other economic factors indicate it, expect a recession to begin early after a presidential election or after mid-term voting two years later. That's because the new administration's goal is always to get the painful work of "fixing" things done as quickly as possible so that an economic rebound occurs well before the next presidential election.

Do you want a quick one-step forecaster of a recession? We believe the best short-term predictor of a recession is the stock market. It generally will predict a recession three to six months before it happens by declining sharply. The stock market not only reflects people's opinions on the future, but it also influences them—in this case its drop spreads a gloomy message and affects the wealth of investors who may cut back in personal spending. The only trouble is the stock market indicator makes too many predictions. Paul Samuelson, the economist, once said that the stock market predicted nine of the last five recessions.

In the same way, the stock market can also anticipate a strengthening in the economy by turning up substantially. That is another reason why we tell our clients not to switch their assets around during a recession. The end result can be a decision to sell stocks and real estate at the bottom of the market, just before they increase in price.

In addition, during a recession interest rates tend to decline sharply. You may be tempted to shift from money-market funds, shorter-term certificates of deposit, and short- and intermediate-term bonds to those with longer maturities (due dates farther in the future) in search of greater return on your money. Don't do it. When the economy gets stronger, interest rates will rise, which can result in losses if you don't hold your investments to maturity. A better time for you to move into longer-term maturities is six months or longer following the beginning of an economic recovery.

A recession can be a great time for some value-oriented investing as we will discuss in Chapters 3 and 4 (on investments) and 7 (on real estate).

During a recession, try to maintain your lifestyle and pattern of spending. However, if you feel your job is threatened, or if you have a large drop in your income, it may make you feel more comfortable to cut back on nonessential items such as vacations and eating out. If you are in great debt or otherwise particularly vulnerable, look for immediate sources of cash and then for ways to stay permanently out of that position. You will feel reassured if you have set aside savings for an emergency.

We find that just by thinking about your costs in a recessionary period your actual spending will decline. It isn't mental telepathy, just a greater focus on your spending habits. Try to take a longer-term view. Remember, most past recessions have ended in little more than a year; trying to alter your patterns to accommodate them often does more harm than good. In other words, in order to safeguard your money and your peace of mind, it can often be best to do nothing.

What about quality-of-life considerations?

This question usually comes from people who tell us they cannot save money because they are barely getting by as it is. Of course, they were barely getting by 10 years ago when many were making considerably less, even after adjustment for inflation. Nonetheless, this is a serious question. It is no good to earn money and not enjoy the benefits. Economists call these nonfinancial pleasures "psychic income." People who enjoy their jobs, have meaningful relationships, live in comfortable homes, are free from excessive pollution or noise, have low stress levels, and take regular vacations tend to have higher psychic income.

How much importance you should give to nonfinancial pleasures will depend on many factors. An economist might say that you reach the right balance between spending for today and saving for tomorrow when your pleasure in spending the next dollar is less than your satisfaction in saving the money to pay for your future cost of living. The balance between saving and spending is influenced by your stage in life. When you have a low salary or are raising children, you generally experience a more difficult period than when you are older and earn more. Unfortunately, some of our clients overemphasize their need for current gratification at all stages of life, buy more and spend more than they can afford, and find themselves rushing to catch up later on.

Then there are other clients who are too conservative. Harold and Estelle came to see us with a marital problem. Harold had buried himself in his work, while Estelle wanted to live a more balanced life. Harold said that he worked to achieve financial independence. Estelle said that future independence was coming at too high a cost—denial of even the simplest pleasures in life, such as eating out or owning a car. With our help, the couple reached an agreement, bought a car, and took their first vacation in more than a decade. Estelle has told us that every time Harold slips back into his old pattern she calls out, "Q of L!" which stands for "quality of life." That's their code. It signals Harold to reconsider his behavior.

We often remind clients that having a "good" quality of life depends on their progress toward achieving their own goals—social, family, religious, moral—reflecting their own personal values. It is made easier for most people by balancing physical, emotional, intellectual, and financial fitness, no matter what their earnings or income may be.

Even if you don't consider financial security as important to your ideal lifestyle as other factors, remember that freedom from financial worries makes accomplishments in other areas easier.

We will give you a handle on how to develop and achieve your financial goals throughout this book with special focus in the final chapter. Then you can integrate these goals with your personal quality-of-life considerations.

2
Handling Your Credit

Credit can work for you or against you. One or two generations ago people planned and saved for those things they wanted to have; they waited until they had the cash in their hands to actually purchase an expensive item. If they couldn't raise the money, sometimes they settled for less.

Today the trend is to buy now and worry about paying later. Why postpone enjoying things that are so attractive today? If you are young, have a good job, and not too many responsibilities, debt can seem painless.

When I was in charge of investment research for a Wall Street firm, I asked our staff economist how he projected consumer debt. He said he assumed consumers would borrow as much money as they were allowed, as opposed to as much as they could afford.

One young couple we know ran up over $50,000 in credit card debt—a whole year's salary for them—before their credit was finally cut off. For them, coming to a dead halt was a blessing. We were able to restructure their loans and help them set up a debt repayment schedule. If they keep to their schedule, they should be free of debt in time to plan for the children they hope to have in a few years.

While near-term considerations such as recessions and elections may temporarily change the focus, our government has shifted its longer-term emphasis from spending to saving. As a consequence, under most circumstances you will no longer get a tax deduction when you borrow money for anything other than a home.

The days when it was easy to borrow for investment purposes, when real interest rates (adjusted for inflation) were low and inflation was high, are gone. If you borrow today—particularly by using credit cards—it can cost you dearly. Therefore, you should use debt cautiously.

Nevertheless, there are still ways you can use credit properly to help you enjoy the good life—to enable you to buy an occasional expensive item or an attractive investment, to help you in an emergency, or to make a purchase more convenient. If you repay properly, it can even improve your credit rating.

Do you want to know more about the proper use of credit? Read on.

What is the lowest-cost way to borrow?

Lenders have the same attitude toward their money as we all do. When handing over their funds, they want to reduce the risk of loss and consequently they try to attract low-risk borrowers. They do so by offering a lower interest rate when there is lower risk. Having substantial assets as collateral for the loan—that is, assets that the lender can take if you don't repay the loan—generally results in a lower rate of interest. Also, when you have few assets or a poor credit history, using a cosigner with a better credit rating can get you a loan with better terms.

When you plan to borrow, shop around. Compare different lending sources on an after-tax basis. To do so, you'll have to know the pretax cost of interest and your own tax bracket.

Home Mortgage Financing. If you own your home, we recommend you consider home mortgage financing first. We believe it is by far the most attractive form of debt. Consequently, we give it our value-oriented money planning award. It is virtually the only method of obtaining a tax deduction on personal borrowing. In addition, interest rates are low because your home is considered high-quality collateral.

The tax deduction works this way: you are allowed to fully deduct the interest on borrowing the cost for the purchase of your principal dwelling and one vacation home, up to $1 million. The amount you can borrow is based on the original cost of your home plus improvements, not including ordinary repairs. In addition to those assets, you are allowed an additional loan of $100,000 which can be used for any purpose as long as your home serves as collateral.

As a consequence of this tax treatment, banks and other institutions have geared up their marketing to emphasize home equity loans and lines of credit, traditional second mortgages, and first-mortgage refinancing. If you are willing to pay a slightly higher rate of interest, a few of these institutions will provide you with no-income-check loans. Your ability to repay the loan will not be evaluated; instead, you will be lent money based solely on your credit history and the value of your home.

In our experience, this form of borrowing can be abused. For instance, too many people use their homes as a huge credit card and do not plan their debt repayments. And, if they don't keep up with the repayments, they ultimately could lose their home.

Harriet, who earned $30,000 a year, came to us with just such a problem. Her father had been a grocer of modest means who had raised her in a brownstone apartment above his store. After a time he was able to purchase the building for $25,000. Eventually the building's neighborhood became trendy and Harriet's brownstone grew in value to approximately $800,000. Harriet had taken out a no-credit-check mortgage of hundreds of thousands of dollars against the property, used the loan for living expenses, and had no idea of how to repay it. Unfortunately, her only way out was to sell the building. Harriet did receive some equity from the sale of her childhood home. Sadly, though, she lost the home that carried many fond memories for her.

On a more positive note, because it's so easy to get home mortgage financing, if you think things through carefully and keep to the terms of the agreement, this can be a great planning tool.

What are other ways to borrow?

If you don't own a house or an apartment, or if you are borrowing for business or investment purposes, you could consider one of the following loans. We have ranked them approximately in order of their attractiveness.

Investment Loans. Borrowing money against your securities (that is, using your stocks and bonds as collateral) can be a low-cost way to obtain funds. However, the government won't allow you to take a tax deduction for these loans unless they are used for personal investment or business activity.

Margin loan debt—the kind you get when you use these securities as collateral—usually has a highly favorable interest rate since the securities can easily be liquidated if you have trouble meeting your payments. Moreover, you can deduct the interest on the debt up to the amount of total taxable interest and dividend income you have for the year. Net capital gains income can also be used to offset margin loan interest but if you choose to do so you will be taxed at ordinary rates instead of at the maximum 28 percent federal rate on the amount of capital gains income taken as an offset. You are allowed to borrow up to 50 percent of the value of the publicly traded stocks and bonds on deposit.

You can borrow on your mutual funds at certain brokerage firms such as Charles Schwab & Company. Borrowing on mutual funds can actually be a better form of financing since these funds are more stable than individual securities.

Be careful, though. If the value of your debt is greater than 50 percent of the fair market value of your securities, you will receive a margin call. At that point either you will have to come up with more money or your securities will be sold. This can happen at just the wrong time, when security prices are dropping rapidly. We recommend that you use this type of financing only after careful consideration, and that you limit your borrowing to 25 percent of the value of your securities.

Certificates of Deposit (CD) or Passbook Loans. Certificates of deposit or passbooks can be used as collateral for loans. As with margin loans, you can deduct a CD or passbook loan to the extent of income you earn on those savings accounts and you may be able to get one at a low rate. Unlike individual securities and mutual funds, which have the potential for more rapid growth, CD income is likely to be well below the rate of the loan. Therefore, it is often more financially savvy to take withdrawals from the passbook account or to liquidate the CD, rather than to borrow against it. Note that if you pursue this course of action when the CD has not come due, you could lose three to six months' interest for prematurely cashing in a CD. If you have just a few weeks before the CD is due or if you will need the money for only a short period of time, it can make sense financially to wait.

Business and Investment Loans. You can deduct any loans that you use to finance a business or to purchase an investment from your taxes. Clearly, then, a loan against business or investment interests can be more desirable than other non-tax-deductible personal loans if it's appropriate for you. Investment loans, including margin loans, will in some instances be deductible only to the extent of income; the part not currently deductible can be deferred until more income is generated, such as a profit on sale of the asset.

Life Insurance and Pension Loans. Borrowing against the cash value of your life insurance used to be possible at very low rates, usually 5 or 6 percent. In newer policies, loan rates are much higher. If you plan to borrow against your life insurance, make sure that you aren't getting a rate of return that is lower than the market rate during the period of the loan. It can make borrowing from this source unattractive.

Loans against 401(k)s or profit-sharing plans, where permitted, have a distinct advantage—the interest rate charged on your personal loan generally is deposited directly to your pension account. Pension loans are limited to 50 percent of the value of your account or $10,000, whichever is higher, with a maximum under any circumstances of $50,000. Recognize, however, that you won't be able to deduct the interest from either loan.

Auto Loan. Since a tangible asset—your car—is involved as collateral, the rate on an auto loan is relatively low on a pretax basis; but it isn't tax-deductible. On an after-tax basis this type of loan is likely to be more expensive than a home equity loan unless you have great costs in taking out a *new* home equity loan or if a car dealer offers you an extremely low borrowing rate so you will buy a new car from him. (In that case, you probably would be better off negotiating for an even lower cash purchase price.) As a general rule, while it may sound illogical at first, you should use a tax-deductible home equity loan to finance your car. But discipline yourself to pay off the amounts due over the same time period you would repay a traditional auto loan: three to five years.

Credit Union Loan. The cost of credit union loans can sometimes be lower than other forms of debt, such as commercial bank loans. If you are a member of a credit union, it is a good idea to investigate its offerings before going to a bank.

Unsecured Commercial Bank, Savings and Loan, and Mutual Savings Bank Loans. "Unsecured" means no asset is required as collateral. Therefore, the rates on these loans are higher, and they aren't deductible. The commercial bank rates in some cases may be lower than those of the savings and loan and mutual savings banks. If you have an account that allows you to write checks on more than you have in your checking account, the interest rate is likely to be considerably higher.

While doing financial planning for Gail and Ian we noticed they had a personal loan outstanding for $50,000 at a 15 percent interest rate, which they had taken to remodel their home. By transferring the personal loan to a tax-deductible home equity loan at a lower pretax rate of interest at that very same bank, we were able to reduce Gail and Ian's out-of-pocket costs after taxes by more than 50 percent.

Consumer Finance Company. Advertising jingles notwithstanding, consumer finance loans are similar to unsecured bank loans but cost more because the finance companies themselves may be borrowing from the banks. Avoid these loans if you can.

Credit Card Debt. This four-star no-no receives our value-oriented rejection. The interest rates are unreasonable, ranging from 12 percent to the low twenties, just inside of usury laws. As we've said before, for many people credit card purchases are the most convenient way of borrowing, and somehow you won't feel that your purchase has reduced your cash. But that good feeling carries a high price tag, as we show here:

	Credit card loan	Home equity loan
Amount	$6000	$6000
Interest rate	18%	11%
Pretax cost	$1080	$ 660
Tax deduction (assumed 28% rate)	0	(185)
Net cost	$1080	$ 475

It costs less than half as much to borrow from a home equity line of credit; the difference of about $600 per year could finance a major purchase for you.

To avoid credit card debt, all you have to do is pay your bills each month. You might try using a debit card; it looks like a regular credit card, but it enables your bank to deduct expenditures directly from your bank account. Or just carry around your checkbook. Direct payments for purchases may be a little more painful, but that holds some benefits as well.

If you aren't persuaded to forgo credit cards altogether, at least switch to a card that charges a lower interest rate. You can investigate your options by sending $4 to Bankcard Holders of America, 333 Pennsylvania Avenue, S.E., Washington, DC 20003 (800-553-8025). They will send you their quarterly list of 50 bank cards, interest rates, and annual rates. Or try Ram Research at 800-344-7714; for $5 they will give you their monthly list of 500 credit card rates.

Borrowing from Friends or Relatives. Notice that we mentioned this form of borrowing at the bottom of our list. Many people think of borrowing from people they know as a low- or no-cost way to get a loan without the hassle of going through credit screens and filling out complicated forms. And often we do hear about friends who grew up together, would do anything for one another, and are willing to show it by lending each other money.

The problem is that there can be poor communication between the parties to such a loan. Mixing business and friendship can discourage people from establishing clear rules in what is really a business transaction. What one party intends may be a short-term loan; the other may hear, "Pay it back whenever you can afford to." The parties involved often neglect to discuss interest rates for the loan, and while the lender usually wants to be paid a market rate, the borrower may expect to have use of the money for free. We often are told, "My friend can afford it, I can't!" The resulting misunderstanding can jeopardize the relationship. That's why we don't recommend this form of debt.

One exception is borrowing money from parents for a starter home. Here the outlay can be looked on as a last financial transaction after leaving the nest. You can take a deduction if you record this mortgage properly. Whether you do or not, your parents will be taxed on the income they should have or did receive.

Handle any loans from friends or relatives at arm's length, with all terms put in writing so that there are concrete conditions instead of fading memories. Clearly state the scheduled dates for repayment. Set the interest rate somewhere between the rate of return on conservative investments and the current bank borrowing rate. Then call on this agreement whenever there is a conflict between the parties involved. With everything agreed to beforehand and set down in black and white, neither you nor your friend or relative need feel taken advantage of.

How can I compare borrowing costs on a consumer loan?

To compare borrowing costs, look at the annual percentage rate (APR) charged by the lender. Comparison is made much easier by the Truth-in-Lending Law established in 1969 which requires all lenders to disclose their APR and total amount of interest charges. The APR is your annualized finance charge divided by the weighted yearly average of debt outstanding.

Calculating the interest rate you are paying can be a problem. For example, if you borrow $1000 and pay it off in straight monthly installments over a year, including $100 in total interest payments made during the year, you are paying at a rate of 10 percent. Right? Wrong. Since you paid back the amount equally over the year, you had an average debt outstanding of $500 and your rate is approximately double that, around 20 percent.

Always look at the APR. The APR enables you to evaluate costs on a comparable basis. Armed with this knowledge, look carefully at institutions in your area; you may be surprised that the interest rates of different institutions can vary substantially. Look for a bank or other institution that has placed its rates on sale because it temporarily has a large amount of cash it needs to lend out.

How can I find out what my credit rating is?

A good credit rating is an asset, yet few people even know how they are regarded by the agencies—that is, until they are rejected in an application for a loan or credit card. Max and Helen, who made over $250,000 a year and had substantial assets and no meaningful debt outstanding other than a mortgage on their home, had their application for a Sears credit card rejected. The couple had a history of late payment of bills. It wasn't that they didn't have the cash available, they just lacked the discipline to pay bills on time.

Max and Helen didn't like being rejected for one credit card; it was an inconvenience and a minor blow to their self-esteem. If, however, they had applied for a mortgage to finance a property, they would have faced more serious consequences. They might have had to pay a higher interest rate costing thousands of dollars more over the life of the loan, or might even have been rejected altogether. The moral is obvious: repay your debts when they are due, and check your credit rating from time to time.

Tony did pay his bills on time, and had no reason to suspect that his credit rating was unfavorable. When he was turned down for a credit card at a new neighborhood store he found that the national credit agency was reporting his credit rating as poor. They also listed Tony, who had a common last name, with an incorrect social security number, at the wrong address, and as unemployed although Tony had held the same position for 12 years. After several letters and many months, Tony was able to make the appropriate changes to his credit file.

When deciding whether to extend you credit a company will look at your age (the older, the better, as long as you aren't retired), your family income, possibly your assets, how long you have held your job, and how many loans and credit cards you have outstanding. And, of course, they will examine your history of paying on time.

Credit agencies are required to send you information on your credit history if you request it. The cost of the credit report ranges from $0 to $50. The three principal credit agencies are TRW (P.O. Box 749029, Dallas, TX 75374), Equifax (P.O. Box 740241, Atlanta, GA 30374), and Trans Union National (25249 Country Club Blvd., P.O. Box 7000, North Olmsted, OH 44070). If an error has been made, the agencies are required to rectify it upon your written request. If you are denied credit or charged more for credit, by all means investigate your credit rating. If your application for credit has been turned down, the lender is obligated to explain why.

If there is a disputed fact about your credit report, send your version of the incident to the credit agency. At least, this document will be kept in your file. Moreover, we believe credit agencies are becoming more receptive to correcting problems. We recommend that you request a copy of your credit record at least once every three years.

How much debt can I afford?

One good way to answer this question is to look at your household as a form of business. You have current and projected income, you have monthly and annual expenses, and you have a resulting current and future free cashflow. If your prospects for growth in income are good and your position is a fairly stable one, you can afford to assume greater debt than you can if, for instance, you are about to retire and the assets you have accumulated are modest.

To decide how much debt you can afford, list your own projected income and expenses. Then factor in the interest and principal payments on different loans. As a general rule of thumb, your monthly installment debt repayments, excluding mortgages, should not exceed 20 percent of your take-home pay for that period. If you have significant home mortgage debt outstanding, your payments should be considerably lower than that. Because these loans are not tax-deductible—which makes installment debt more expensive than it used to be—the average person should set a 15 percent limit.

We consider home mortgage debt separately because the purchase of a home enables you to save rental costs. The rules of thumb in this area vary, but we believe that 30 percent of gross income on real estate taxes, insurance, interest, and principal repayments are okay in general. (Banks usually use 28 percent.) When dealing with high real estate costs in large cities in the Northeast and on the West Coast, the figure can amount to 40 percent and still be acceptable providing you have a good credit record and a secure job.

How do I get out of debt?

Too many people we meet are asking us that question now. Some have had higher-paying jobs that have disappeared. Others borrowed too much money and realized they had more debt than they could repay.

The first thing you should do to get out of this situation is to make a budget that includes a debt repayment plan and live by it. We explained how to do it in Chapter 1. Make budgeted debt payments as soon as you receive your income check. Pay off your loans with the highest after-tax interest costs first. If you have problems meeting the called-for debt repayments, speak to the institutions. Many will lower and extend the debt repayments if they are impressed with the seriousness of your situation and believe that you really want to repay. See if you can get a lender to provide funds to consolidate all your loans into one. That will reduce your stress and often your interest charges as well.

If you have a Federal Housing Authority (FHA)–insured or Veteran's Administration (VA) loan and are unemployed, you can get a reduction in or a suspension of the loan for up to three years. If you have trouble disciplining yourself or prefer some help, you can call on professional credit counselors. These organizations—many of which are not-for-profit—sometimes provide free counseling or low-cost services, can help you plan cashflow, and often arrange debt restructuring or consolidation. The address of your local organization can be obtained through the Consumer Credit Counselling Service National Referral Line (800-388-2227), your local chamber of commerce, or Better Business Bureau.

Should I consider bankruptcy?

The number of individuals filing for bankruptcy, as well as the number of businesses doing so, has grown at a rapid pace. For years ending June 30, in 1985 298,000 individual people filed for bankruptcy in the United States; in 1990, 661,000; and in 1991, 811,000—up about 40 percent in 2 years and more than 2.5 times what it had been less than 10 years earlier. For some, the cause was spending in the free-spirited optimism of the eighties. For others, it was an investment that went sour, the loss of a job, or massive medical costs not covered by insurance. Consequently, bankruptcy is beginning to lose some of the stigma that it once had.

For individuals, there are two types of bankruptcy usually used. A Chapter 13 filing works out an orderly plan of debt repayments over a period of three to five years under court auspices, sometimes at less than their full value. Under a Chapter 13 filing, a budget is formulated and your creditors get your income above the budgeted expenditures. You may be able to keep part or all of your assets. A Chapter

7 filing is a straight bankruptcy that will liquidate most of your assets and free you of debts. According to federal guidelines, under a Chapter 7 filing you may get to keep the equity in your home, your car, and smaller amounts in household goods, jewelry, and probably all your professional tools and books. Some states have more liberal bankruptcy exemptions than the federal ones, and you may be able to choose to file under their exemptions.

People can receive a discharge from their debts under the bankruptcy code only once every six years. To file, you can buy a bankruptcy kit and petition the federal court yourself. It is a good idea to see a bankruptcy lawyer, however, particularly if the bankruptcy is complicated.

Bankruptcy is a step that you should consider only in the most serious circumstances. People sometimes come to us owing only a few thousand dollars, yet wanting to be relieved of their debts. Typically they are depressed, many times from things other than the debts directly, such as from loss of a job. What they often need is some credit counseling, a debt restructuring, and some reassurance that what looks so bleak now won't seem so in the near future. Alex came to see us about declaring bankruptcy. His business wasn't doing well, he couldn't pay his son's college fees, and his wife, Wendy, had recently lost her job. Alex was fearful about this cut in the family's income, but Wendy didn't want to declare bankruptcy. We examined Alex's debts and found that they were manageable. We encouraged him to apply for aid at his son's college (which he got), and to wait out the period until his wife found a new job. We encouraged him to help his wife with her résumé and with calling their contacts. After five months Wendy took a new job (though at a small decrease from her previous salary), the worst had passed, and Alex was very glad that he hadn't taken that major step.

Bankruptcy does not promote self-esteem and will leave a black mark on your credit record for 10 years. It can make getting or refinancing a mortgage very difficult. If you believe that your debt is insurmountable or that it would restrict you emotionally and financially for many years, bankruptcy can have its place. In that situation, wiping the debt slate clean can give you an emotional uplift. Surprisingly, some firms will extend credit to bankrupt people under the theory that a further bankruptcy is not possible for another six years.

If you are considering filing for bankruptcy, confide in someone who is understanding and sophisticated in business matters. And, if possible, wait a few months before taking action. Things often look better over time.

When should I prepay my mortgage or college loan?

Repaying a loan before you are required to can be considered a form of prepayment. How do you decide when to prepay?

Your college loans were extended at various interest rates, generally ranging from 5 percent to current market interest rates. They often have liberal repayment terms. When interest was deductible, college loans were an inexpensive means of obtaining funds. Now they are less attractive. For example, a college loan that you take at 7 percent is equivalent to about a 10 percent tax-deductible home mortgage loan for a person in the 28 percent federal tax bracket.

Taking your time to repay a college loan may make sense when you either do not have the funds or need your money for other purposes. Holding on to such loans long after you need them serves no purpose. Sheila, who didn't work outside the home, and her husband, Bruce, who made hundreds of thousands of dollars every year, came to our office for overall financial planning advice. We noticed that Sheila, then in her mid-thirties, had an outstanding $8000 college loan. Strangely enough, we figured out that she was reluctant to repay the loan because she used it to retain ties to her college days. She was paying 8.5 percent interest to keep in touch. Obviously, we could see no financial reason to maintain the relationship in this manner. So, we advised Sheila to pay off the loan in full and join her alumna association.

"When should I prepay my mortgage?" is really part of a broader question, "When should I prepay my loan?" Whatever the form of debt, when you have surplus cash, rank your loans in order of their after-tax costs. Be sure to take into account any prepayment penalties. Also, recognize that while your monthly payment may remain level as your installment loan or home mortgage loan progresses, more of it goes for principal payment and less for interest. Therefore, an older loan may have a relatively low tax deduction for interest. Look at a recent payment stub or call your lender. Before prepaying the loan with the highest after-tax cost, compare it to the after-tax return on investing the proceeds. If you are a conservative investor, you may be surprised to find that you are better off prepaying the debt.

In deciding whether to prepay your debt, consider liquidity—that is, the ability to get your hands on cash for emergencies or for investments in the future. Repaying your debt instead of leaving the money in publicly traded securities can reduce your liquidity. If you repay substantial amounts of your mortgage, keep in mind that once it is paid down you lose the tax deduction for additional sums borrowed on your home except for home improvements and a maximum of $100,000 for any other purpose.

In general, however, we encourage prepayment of debt, particularly if you are a conservative investor. If you have a large amount of nonhome debt outstanding, you can skip the comparison with investments and put the check to the lender in the mail.

Should I take out a 15-year or a 30-year mortgage?

Often our clients take out long-term mortgages because they think that they will be under less pressure to repay. But many of them have trouble managing a free cashflow (savings) and could use the discipline of a shorter repayment period. We recommend that most clients, particularly those who are conservative investors, take out a 15-year instead of a 30-year mortgage.

The results can be surprising. For example, a 30-year loan of $100,000 at 10 percent will require a monthly payment of $878, or $216,000 of interest payments over its term. Notice that the interest payments are more than twice that of the principal payments. And after 15 years you will have paid off less than 20 percent of your loan amount.

The same $100,000 loan paid over 15 years has $1075 in monthly payments. The monthly payments for the 15-year loan are only 22 percent or $197 greater than the 30-year loan. The total interest charges over the 15-year term are only $93,500, a saving in interest of over $122,000 compared to the 30-year mortgage. And your loan is paid off in half the time. The total principal and interest payments over a 15- and 30-year life are shown in Figure 2-1.

You can get the same kind of results if you have already taken out a loan by paying more than the monthly amount due. If you remitted one extra monthly payment each quarter, you would save $120,000 in interest charges over the life of the loan and be paid up in 14 years. The result can be a house that is fully paid and a step up in free cashflow when you need it.

Which is more attractive, a fixed or variable interest rate mortgage?

The answer to this question depends on whether you are an optimist or a pessimist, and whether you like the security of a level payment. A fixed-rate mortgage is the simpler of the two; you pay the same interest rate and cash payment each month over the life of the loan. The variable rate is more complicated. Your payment depends on your interest rate for that period. There is an initial low come-on rate for the first year followed immediately by or escalating steadily to the market rate.

It never fails to amaze us how many people select their mortgages based on a comparison of the initial rates. There are only a few occasions when the initial rate should count, such as when you intend to move in a relatively short period of time or when you cannot afford

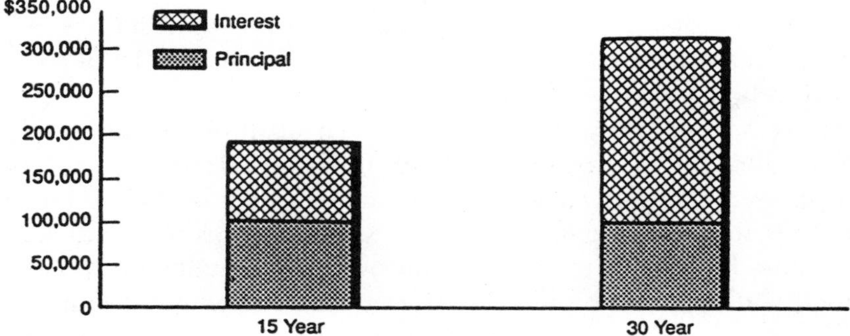

Figure 2-1. Total Payments Over Life of $100,000 Loan.

the current market interest rate but are confident that your income will rise sharply in the near future. Otherwise, you can find yourself overpaying for 29 years in exchange for some benefits that you capture for only 1 year.

The variable rate is usually based on some independent benchmark interest rates. Measures that are commonly used are the Federal Home Loan Board cost of funds rate, and the U.S. Treasury interest rates usually ranging from three months to maturities of three years, although maturities can be even longer. We prefer the Federal Home Loan Board rate because it tends to fluctuate (shift up and down) less, although you will have smaller variations monthly. If you use the Treasury rate as an index, the longer the benchmark maturity, the better, for the same reason. The worst measure can be the bank's own cost of funds since there may be some room for fudging there.

Even more important is the relationship of your rate to the index (known as the margin). We had one client who fell for a come-on 5 percent initial rate and subsequently paid 11 percent (3 percent over the three-year Treasury rate). He could have done much better at another institution in his area that offered variable rate loans with an initial 8 percent rate, but thereafter settled at 9 percent (1 percent over the three-year Treasury rate).

When you choose an adjustable rate index, immediately ask what the rate would be without the initial bargain rate (called the "fully indexed rate"). Then compare all variable rates with each other and with fixed-rate mortgages. Also take into account any limits on step-ups in rate and how often rates are adjusted (adjustment "caps"); for example, an increase or decrease limited to 2 percent per year can smooth out fluctuations in rates. Finally, consider life "caps"—that is, limits on how high mortgage rates can go if market interest rates suddenly increase to high double-digit levels. Obviously, a 14 percent life cap is better than an 18 percent one.

Stay away from mortgages that have no cap at all. Your interest payments could really skyrocket in a highly inflationary environment. In some cases the monthly payment will remain level but, when interest rates rise, the loan negatively amortizes. This means that your payment stays level but the amount you owe can actually go up even though you make all required payments. We recommend that you avoid mortgages that negatively amortize because of the potential of open-ended debt over time.

Variable rate mortgages have some advantages over fixed-rate ones. They allow you to benefit from declines in rates without having the inconvenience and cost of refinancing a fixed-rate mortgage. Moreover, when interest rates are clearly high, such as when they are well into the double-digit area, you can buy a home with a low initial variable rate that you wouldn't be able to afford otherwise. On the other hand, variable rate mortgages can confuse your budgeting efforts over time. Most of our clients prefer the certainty of a fixed payment to what appears to them as open-ended uncertainty. And in most instances we agree. A contract that carries an upper rate limit (in this case, a fixed interest rate), with your option to get out through refinancing if rates decline, has real value.

If you expect to move within a few years, a variable rate mortgage with a particularly low come-on rate can be attractive. If you can reasonably expect to move within five to seven years, consider a hybrid fixed-variable rate loan that after five to seven years gives the lender a one-time option to change rates to prevailing market rates at that time. This type of mortgage is often provided at a lower interest rate than other fixed-rate loans until the lender's option period is up, and is frequently higher than market interest rates thereafter.

If you expect to be in the house for a longer period than five to seven years or are not sure how long you will remain there, we recommend comparing the current cost of fixed-rate mortgages with the fully indexed variable rate. To receive this indexed variable rate, just ask the lender to give you the rate that would apply currently if there were no "come-on" rates and no restrictions—just the pure current market rate. When three conditions are met—when the difference between the fixed rate and the full market indexed rate isn't great, the rates for mortgages are under 11 percent, and our clients aren't strongly optimistic about a near-term drop in rates—we recommend taking fixed-rate mortgages and refinancing if rates decline.

How can I compare interest rates on financing my home?

A quick way to compare rates is to skip the advertised rates and look for the annual percentage rate (APR) that each lender is required to supply. The APR includes the interest rate and the points spread out over the life of the loan, even though you pay the points up front and your monthly payments are based on the listed interest rate only. However, in this case, in contrast to other consumer loans, the APR doesn't tell the whole story.

One factor the APR doesn't include is other costs that accompany a loan besides interest, such as points and other closing costs. Points are the percentage that is normally deducted from the loan to "reimburse" the bank for costs associated with the transaction. Points range from 0 to 5 percent. Closing costs include bank charges such as appraisal costs, credit check costs, and bank attorney charges. The important thing to know is that bank charges and points can vary considerably among lending institutions. Other closing costs such as title insurance and mortgage costs do not usually differ considerably.

Also make sure you compare fixed- and variable rate loans separately. And as we mentioned earlier, don't ever use the come-on first-year rate on a variable rate loan as your benchmark.

When comparing costs of a loan, it helps to make a broad checklist of all associated expenses. Frequently you will be offered a lower interest rate for a loan with higher points. For example, you might be able to select from two $100,000 fixed-rate mortgages: one at a 10 percent rate with 1 point and the other at a 9¾ percent rate with 2 points. As a rule of thumb a 1-point decline in the points charged can be traded off against a ¼-point increase in the interest rate over the life of the loan. If you take the time to set all costs down in a few columns, you will be able to compare the loans more easily.

Assuming you don't want to speculate on interest rates, the one you should take will depend on the period you expect to live in the house. Financially, you will break even from a cash standpoint after about five years. Adjusting for a return on the monies deposited for the points currently, you would break even in four years. Therefore, if this is your first home or you think you will have to move before too long because of your job, take the higher interest rate. Try to get an assignable mortgage that you can transfer to your buyer when you sell your house. It makes your house easier to sell, possibly at a higher price if rates rise in the interim. However, if you expect to live in the house for many years, take the higher points and lower interest rates. You can save a material amount over an extended period of time.

By looking aggressively at rates for institutions in your area, you can end up saving a great deal of money. HSH Associates (800-873-2837) can make the job easier by supplying you with current interest rates and terms for many lenders in several areas of the country.

If you want to have help with the process or expect difficulties obtaining a loan, consider a mortgage broker. A good mortgage broker represents and can select from many lending institutions based on cost and terms and should be compensated by the institution you choose. Make sure the broker is licensed, and don't pay more than $500 up front for processing, credit check, and appraisal. However, because there are some unethical and even fraudulent individuals who represent themselves as brokers, it is wise to take precautions. Check to see that the financial institution you deal with is reputable and that your agent is licensed to represent it. For a referral, ask your financial planner, accountant, or real estate agent, or contact the National Association of Mortgage Brokers (602-992-6181). It is also a good idea to check the mortgage broker's recommendations against the rates and terms of lending institutions given in your local paper or by HSH Associates.

When should I refinance my mortgage?

Suppose interest rates have dropped. They are now below the rate that you are paying on your mortgage. Should you refinance it? This question pertains principally to fixed-rate mortgages. If you have a variable rate mortgage, unless you are stuck with unattractive terms or you want to lock in a fixed-rate loan, the fact that your interest charges will decline in response to the drop in rates should be a sufficient adjustment.

If you have a fixed-rate mortgage, there are a number of factors we take into account in deciding whether to recommend refinancing it. On one side, we look at the savings in interest costs over the remaining life of the original loan. On the other side, we find out the costs involved in closing the new loan and any prepayment penalty. On a $100,000 loan these can amount to $2200, or 2.2 percent of the loan excluding points, with expenses considerably greater in high-cost areas, particularly those in the Northeast.

Sometimes your original lender will reduce the closing costs if you refinance with the same company, which can make them your refinancer of choice if their rates are competitive.

Consider that you will not get a current tax deduction for new closing costs. They are to be spread over the life of the mortgage.

Next estimate how long you are going to live in your home. The average American lives in a home for seven years. It generally won't pay to refinance if you are planning to live in the home for less than a few years.

If you fancy yourself a predictor of interest rates, you will want to wait until rates have bottomed to refinance. We don't recommend this because most people cannot predict mortgage rates accurately. They just end up incorrectly projecting a further decline when rates are dropping and a further increase when they are rising.

If you take out a larger mortgage, the refinancing option is more attractive because fixed closing costs have less impact. Refinancing becomes progressively less profitable the longer you have held the mortgage because over time smaller parts of your mortgage payments go for interest and larger portions go to prepay the principal. As we mentioned, in most circumstances it isn't beneficial to refinance when you have just a few years left on your mortgage for two reasons. First, the portion of your payment that goes for interest is so small that the savings in interest cost is negligible. Second, you have fewer years of interest savings to offset the outlay for fixed closing costs.

Whatever the number of years left on the mortgage, be careful when comparing the monthly payment on the old and new mortgages. Don't fall into the trap of having most of the reduction in payments on the new mortgage come from a longer maturity date—as it would, for example, if you exchanged a mortgage with 8 years left for one with 15 years to go.

As a rough rule of thumb, we recommend that it is worthwhile to refinance when you can get a present rate that is 2 percent lower than the one you are currently paying.

3
Investing Wisely: The Basics

When I was director of research and partner at a leading Wall Street investment management firm, I had access to many of the best minds in the investment community. I had breakfast with Henry Kaufman, lunch with Milton Friedman, and dinner with Leon Cooperman. Each of these men had at one time or another been thought to possess the keys to the financial kingdom; that is, Wall Street believed they could predict what would actually happen in the stock market. The fact that two of the three currently run successful investment firms themselves and the third won a Nobel prize in economics makes us think that they never believed they had a crystal ball. The really successful investment people we know have gotten there through hard work, sharp minds, and an ability to think independently.

You too can invest successfully. But first you have to forget about the magic bullet, the pot of gold, the secret formula that will make you instantly rich. The real secret is that there is no secret.

You have to acquire some basic knowledge of the role and risk of various types of investments and, just as important, learn to understand your investment temperament. This chapter and the next will share some practices used by the experts and show you how to substantially improve your investment returns.

First we'll look at two of the main types of investment: stocks and bonds.

What is the difference between a stock and a bond?

When you invest, you can be either a lender or an owner. It is generally safer to be a lender. If you have your money in bonds or bond-like investments, you are a lender. You are, in effect, lending your cash to a business or a government. Borrowers pay you interest on the money you lend them and promise to pay back your original loan. In many cases, the agreed-upon amount is repaid at maturity (the repayment date).

If you lend money to high-quality borrowers, there shouldn't be any problem with repayment. The real risk is if you sell before maturity when interest rates are high. If interest rates have gone down since the purchase date, the value of your investment will go up; if interest rates have gone up, your investment will go down. The longer the agreed-upon time until your investment is repaid, the greater the chance of a movement in the value of your bond because of changes in interest rates. Usually, the further away the maturity date, the higher the interest rate offered in the marketplace.

Some bonds—such as U.S. savings bonds—pledge to repay your original investment at any time, no matter where market interest rates move. There may be a slight penalty for early withdrawal.

Stocks, which are also called shares or equities, are a different matter. When you invest in stocks or in real estate, you are an owner—of shares in a business in the one case, of buildings and land in the other. This type of investment is riskier than being a lender. Over time, though, it offers greater money rewards. High-quality stocks pay owners dividends, which are cash returns on their investments. Dividends should increase over time. Also, the value of your holdings should rise as other investors recognize the increasing worth of your stocks, buy some of the stock for their own portfolios, and the growing demand for the stock further increases its price.

Which investments combine safety and high income?

High income is like apple pie: practically everyone wants some. But there are many different recipes for the pie. The key factor in making your investment choices is safety. Ask yourself, "What is safe to me?" If your idea of safe is virtually no chance of loss—no matter when you want to sell—then you should restrict yourself to money-market funds, Treasury bills (T-bills), Series EE bonds, or certificates of deposit. If you take our advice, however, you will broaden your horizons by also purchasing bonds that change in price, based on current interest rates.

As Michelle, one of our clients, said, "It makes me nervous to think my investments go up and down every day, but if it will increase my returns, I can handle it." Then, after thinking about what for her was a radical decision, Michelle added, "Just make sure I can get my money back at the expiration [maturity] date."

Your investment income choices are indicated below. In each case you can anticipate getting your money back at maturity or before, except for utilities, which, like other common stocks, have no maturity.

There are a growing number of investments that you can purchase principally for income, or yield:

U.S. Treasury Bills (T-bills). T-bills are the champions of risk-free investments. They have average maturities of up to one year, and are state and city tax free. They sell at a discount—interest is included when they are paid off at maturity. Above the minimum of $10,000, you must buy in increments of $5000. You can buy them through a broker or bank, or you can save the transaction charge and buy these and other Treasury issues—such as U.S. government notes and bonds—by setting up a Treasury Direct account. Contact your regional Federal Reserve office.

Bank Money-Market Accounts. A money-market account provides a current rate of interest and allows you to make withdrawals at any time. In money-market accounts managed by banks, the first $100,000 is guaranteed by the Federal Deposit Insurance Corporation (FDIC). The accounts are convenient to open, and you can sometimes combine them with full checking privileges. But your yield will generally be below the income you'd get from a mutual fund money-market account.

Mutual Fund Money-Market Accounts. A mutual fund is the pooling of money by investors in order to receive the benefits of ongoing investment management. As a group, mutual fund money-market accounts are noted for yielding higher short-term returns than banks' money-market accounts, but the rates and quality vary from fund to fund. The accounts are not guaranteed; in fact, some funds have had relatively minor losses which have been absorbed by fund management without the investor being penalized. If you're concerned about this, choose U.S. government money-market funds at a moderately lower rate of return.

If you are a serious money-market investor, pay attention to overhead costs. Funds that are well managed can provide as much as ½ percent higher returns each year. Give preference to larger-fund families that have the deep pockets needed to cover any potential future losses.

Bank Savings Accounts. The first $100,000 in a bank savings account is guaranteed by the FDIC. The accounts are convenient to invest in but generally pay a low rate of interest. Their name is appropriate because it is *the bank* that literally saves money in interest paid out every time you make a deposit into your account. You can bet that when we get a client with one of these accounts, we suggest a simple transfer to a money-market account.

Certificates of Deposit (CDs). CDs are debt obligations issued by banks. They are FDIC-guaranteed for the first $100,000 with a penalty for early withdrawal. The money you have invested (the principal) does not fluctuate and can be redeemed at any time. The rates on CDs recently have become less competitive, probably because banks have not been as aggressive in lending money and many of the problem banks that paid high yields have been closed. Shop around for the best rates before you settle on a CD. Doing so has sometimes enabled us to improve yields by as much as 2 percent annually.

U.S. Government Notes and Bonds. Government notes and bonds are of the highest quality. They customarily pay higher returns than money-market accounts, and lately they have paid more than CDs. In addition, these notes and bonds are free from state and city taxes, which increases your after-tax income. A drawback is that you can't cash in a government note or bond before its due date. Instead, in this and all other categories that follow (with the exception of Series EE bonds), you will have to sell it on the open market.

Since the value of the bond fluctuates depending on current interest rates, you cannot be assured of achieving a particular selling price.

Government National Mortgage Association Instruments (GNMAs). Because the mortgages are guaranteed by the U.S. government, Government National Mortgage Association Instruments, or "Ginnie Maes" as they are commonly called, are of high quality. They provide higher returns than do U.S. government bonds, but unlike U.S. government bonds they are subject to state and local income taxes. When you buy a Ginnie Mae, you become a shareholder in a group of family home mortgages. You don't receive all your money back at a fixed maturity date. Instead you receive a return of your principal when people change homes or when a decline in market rates encourages refinancing of their mortgage. Since people refinance when interest rates drop, you will have the worst of both worlds; you'll get a greater return of principal when interest rates are low and you don't want to reinvest the money, and a substantially lower return of principal (and a drop in the value of the GNMA) when interest rates rise and you could reinvest and benefit from the returns on your money. Nonetheless, Ginnie Maes can be attractive investments because of their higher yields, safety of principal, and lower price movements compared to other bonds.

Series EE Bonds. These are high-quality bonds issued by the U.S. government that can be cashed in at any time after six months from the issue date. The bonds have a moderate tax benefit; taxes on the interest earned can be postponed until the bonds are redeemed. On the other hand, the rate of interest on the bonds is 15 percent below that of regular U.S. bonds, which are payable in five years. Safety, in the form of no fluctuation in price, is Series EE's strong suit. You can also cash in your money whenever you like, although doing so within the first five years will result in a penalty in the form of a lower interest rate earned. Normally, the after-tax yields can be beaten by other conservative investments like municipal bonds that have long-term maturities.

Collateralized Mortgage Obligations (CMOs). CMOs are mortgages that have been split up into various parts (delayed payment streams). In that way, investors can choose the projected maturity and yield they are most interested in. Each part or payment stream is called a "tranche." In the more basic and popular, sequential type of CMOs, think of the tranches as glasses arranged in a row in a slightly sloping sink. When you turn on the tap, the second glass receives water when the first glass overflows, and so on. As with GNMAs, in CMOs the repayment streams will vary depending on interest rates. If you own the last glass, called the Z tranche, your date of maturity can vary from 2 years to 20, depending on the course of interest rates.

Does this sound complicated? It is. Even investment professionals have a hard time getting a good handle on these instruments.

The quality of CMOs depends in part on who issues the original security. When the issuer is the Government National Mortgage Association, the CMOs are high quality because there is virtually no risk of nonpayment at maturity. Yields vary. The longest maturity tranches tend to advertise that they have high, attractive yields. Yet in many instances these are the same instruments that professional investors have declined because of their unpredictable cashflows due to changes in interest rates.

Pass on these investments unless you or your advisors have been assured of a high-quality backing (as in GNMAs) or relatively stable cash payments regardless of interest rate, and unless you don't care about maturity dates.

Zero-Coupon Bonds. The U.S. government is the primary issuer of the highest-quality zero-coupon bonds, commonly known as "zeros." Yields vary but on average are modestly higher than equivalent regular U.S. government bonds. Zeros pay all interest and principal on the maturity date—and nothing till then. Since you receive no cash returns until well into the future, the bonds tend to fluctuate greatly with any change in interest rates. With most zeros, you must pay taxes on the interest the government says you earn, even though you don't receive any money until maturity. This makes taxable zeros most appropriate for tax-deferred accounts such as IRAs and pensions. Nontaxable zero-coupon municipals, which are harder to find, can be useful for college savings; their maturities can be targeted to actual college payment dates.

Use zeros only if you have divine information that interest rates will decline or you are confident that you will be able to hold them to maturity.

Municipal Bonds. Municipal bonds generally provide the best return of all long-term, high-quality bond investments—provided you are in a 28 percent or greater tax bracket. If you have an income tax in your state, it might be advantageous to buy the bonds of your home state since they are free of federal, state, and local taxes. Stay away from unrated municipals, those below an A rating. Taxable municipals (yes, there are such things) can be attractive if you are in a low 15 percent bracket because they are still free of state and city taxes. Concentrate on your state's general obligation bonds (those issued and guaranteed by the state) if you are just beginning to purchase municipals.

Corporate Bonds. As you might expect, the quality of corporate bonds depends on the corporation issuing the bonds. The highest-quality corporate bonds, rated AAA by rating agencies such as Standard & Poor's and Moody's, pay modestly more than do U.S. government bonds. If interest rates drop, the corporation may call in its bonds and give you the cash amount (call price) promised when issued. (Most bonds other than federal government bonds generally are callable.) The cash amount received can be higher or lower than what you paid. This process is called redeeming the bonds. It can stop you from holding a high-interest bond when rates have dropped. Therefore, we prefer U.S. government bonds—most of which are not callable—to high-quality corporate bonds unless the latter type yield at least 1 percent more than do the former.

Utility Stocks. Utilities include telephone companies, electricity companies, and other corporations whose profits are strictly regulated by the government. As investments, utilities are midway between bonds and stocks in terms of desirability, combining a bond's above-average yield with a stock's growth in value. But utilities tend to be safer than regular stocks because the companies have little competition and regulators generally allow them to raise prices to earn a satisfactory return. Compared with bonds, utility stocks produce lower current yields and have higher risk because they are affected by stock market fluctuations.

Utilities can be a good compromise if you are a conservative investor who wants current income and a modest inflation hedge.

Which income investments are best?

On balance, you might invest in Treasury bills or money-market funds for liquidity. Put the emphasis on municipal bonds if you are in the 28 percent federal bracket or above, and use U.S. government bonds and GNMAs if your interest income will be taxed at a rate below that. Buy utilities for the adventurous side of a conservative income-based investment mix.

One strategy that's interesting if you are very conservative (risk-adverse) and believe that interest rates are more likely to drop than to rise is to buy a certificate of deposit with a very long maturity. If you are correct, you have locked in a high rate. If interest rates move up sharply, you can simply cash in the certificate, pay the penalty, and reinvest the money in a new certificate or bond.

Should I search for highest yield?

Yes and no. If searching for highest yield means that you'll end up buying junk bonds, nonpublic mortgage obligations, or other securities that you don't fully understand except for their advertised yield, the answer is a resounding no for all but the most sophisticated investors. Heavily advertised high current yield is the bait that often snares the unsophisticated investor.

The law of modern investment theory (which we will explain later in the chapter) usually rings true here—the higher the expected return, the higher the risk. Not too long ago, there was a flurry of activity in new Real Estate Investment Trusts (REITs) that invested in collateralized mortgage obligations (CMOs). The public was attracted to the unusually high double-digit yields offered, but didn't really understand what the instruments were or how returns were generated. The returns were received in part through use of borrowed monies. When interest rates changed, the income the REITs generated turned to losses, and some of these "safe" investments went bankrupt.

Higher risk, however, does not always guarantee higher returns. You may be familiar with the story of junk bonds. Junk bonds are bonds that the agencies rate below BBB, the lowest investment grade category. The rating agencies give them low ratings because there is no assurance they can repay when due. Their good performance in the early to mid-1980s was followed by a string of poor results later in the decade. By 1990 junk bonds actually had lower cumulative returns than higher-quality, lower-risk investments—a violation of a strict interpretation of modern investment theory.

Junk bonds are really a mixture of equities and bonds. As with other bonds, junk bonds are influenced by changes in interest rates. They also respond to shifts in investors' sentiments about stocks. How junk bonds perform in the nineties depends on the exact number of bankruptcies and restructurings that are likely to occur. Each bankruptcy and restructuring in most instances represents a partial or full loss of your investment. Compare these projected losses with the benefits you receive from their higher-than-normal current yield. You are right if you think this is too complicated to deal with. Pass.

If you limit your search for higher yield to high-quality investments, go ahead. How can you do this? You can often receive higher yields by extending maturities, for example buying 10-year Treasury bonds instead of 6-month Treasury bills. But be careful of placing too much of your money in longer-term maturities with higher-than-normal extra yields; the extra yield can be a trap if interest rates rise. When they do, the value of your investment goes down, catching you with losses on your investment.

Remember that municipal bonds can provide higher after-tax yields if you're in a high bracket. Watching the cost structure for mutual funds also brings about higher returns.

Shop around for best yields on certificates of deposit. If the banks in your area seem to be asleep yield-wise, consider buying the highest-yielding out-of-town certificates of deposit as listed in *Barron's* or your local paper; the FDIC guarantee for the first $100,000 will limit your risk. Don't forget to shop among brokerage firms for the best sales price when you sell a bond before it matures. We remember one circumstance when a little comparison shopping resulted in a 15 percent increase in the sales price of a plain vanilla bond for one of our clients.

What are my growth alternatives?

People who want their investments to grow rapidly usually end up with a portion of their money in stocks and stock mutual funds. And no wonder. Over the past 65 years the average stock has increased 10 to 12 percent a year compared to long-term U.S. government bonds which have increased about 5 percent a year over that same period. Through compounding power, $1000 invested in the average bond in 1926, the first year accurate results are available, was worth $21,000 at the end of 1991, while $1000 invested in stocks amounted to more than 30 times that amount at $675,000 over the same time frame.

Your common-stock alternatives are separated into major categories, which are described below in increasing order of risk.

Utilities. These are appropriate to put under both income and growth categories. They combine high income and modest growth of principal. As we mentioned previously, what makes utilities lower risk is steady demand and government regulation which limits anyone trying to compete with them. They are an excellent way for beginners to dip their toes into the common-stock waters.

Blue Chips. These are large-sized, high-quality companies with strong positions in their various industries. In most instances, these industries are fairly mature and the companies pay a dividend yielding 2 to 3 percent annually or more. Some blue-chip companies—such as food and beverage companies—provide relatively steady sales regardless of the state of the economy. If, on the other hand, the company is part of an industry that is influenced by economic conditions, like department stores or automobiles are, it is considered cyclical. Since investors tend to anticipate future results in establishing current prices, cyclical companies should be bought when the economy is weak, earnings are depressed, and expectations are negative.

Growth Companies. These companies are the all-stars of the investment world. They have strong positions in industries that are growing rapidly, or they are in more mature industries but are gaining many new customers. Current industry examples include biotechnology and waste disposal markets, both of which are believed by many to have strong growth characteristics. They carry risk as well as opportunity, since yesterday's growth markets can be today's stragglers and new competition often goes after the industry leader's business.

Smaller Companies. These companies are more nimble than their larger siblings and can be outstanding performers over long periods of time. We define smaller companies as having under $300 million in total stock market value, although we prefer those that are less than half that size. Unfortunately, these companies can be volatile, and owning just a few that have setbacks can rapidly put you in the poorhouse. Make sure you watch these investments carefully and diversify: purchase at least eight of them in different industries to receive their benefits.

Speculative Companies. These are the highest risk because the companies usually have few assets and lack competitive positioning. Practically any company that is operating at a loss for a number of years, no matter how great the outlook seems to be, is a speculative company. Yet, investors are attracted to the possibility of large profits on their investment. Lawrence yawned when we told him his investment portfolio of unknown stocks looked like a disaster waiting to happen. However, putting good sense ahead of excitement, he took our advice and traded 90 percent of his speculative portfolio for a balanced growth one. The remaining 10 percent was deliberately left invested in speculative assets—a gamble that Lawrence wanted to take. From our standpoint, he might have risked even more money in Las Vegas, where he vacationed, if we had restricted him further. We often make similar deals with clients who like to take high risk. If you are attracted to these sorts of assets, just make sure you can afford a total write-off of your investments in the speculative stocks.

International Stocks. These are stocks that take advantage of opportunities abroad. They can provide true diversification and faster potential growth. They add a new element of risk: foreign exchange exposure. Global currencies are constantly fluctuating against the value of the dollar. When you decide to trade these stocks, you might find that the exchange rate has moved against you.

Despite the risk and complexity of these investments, some of our clients' best returns have been in the international sector. Invest in these markets through international mutual funds. That way, you'll reap the rewards with much less risk.

Should I buy the best-performing stocks?

That's exactly what you should *not* do. If you buy stocks that are very popular, greater expectations are already built into their high valuations—you are paying more for their worth. You'd be surprised how many people buy stocks like this just because it gives them a feeling of confidence. They like being associated with investments that have been winners.

The only trouble is, this is exactly the opposite way of doing well in the stock market. The key to success is to strip away your emotions from your investments.

Don't buy a company just because another company in that industry has had outstanding success. Investigate to see if they can make it on their own merits. Remember, for every successful McDonald's there are 10 other fast-food chains that looked just as good at the starting gate but didn't finish with the same flourish.

Companies that are universally beloved carry a specific burden: good results are expected and therefore don't influence stock prices (the prices remain relatively flat), while any negative surprises can have monumental effects on prices. I learned that fact about 20 years ago when I was an analyst specializing in entertainment industry stocks.

After a string of successful recommendations, I developed an inflated sense of my abilities. My next recommendation was a company that had rapid growth in earnings, a seemingly flawless financial future, and a valuation as lofty as its supposed position. Despite its misleading claim that future earnings would be good, the company took a one-time tax writedown, which reduced earnings considerably. The shares dropped 75 percent, from $40 to $10 each, even though the company's fundamental position and true earning power were unchanged.

In fact, my analysis of the company was correct—it is still a leader in the industry some two decades later. My error was to ignore the high expectations that made the company vulnerable to negative surprises. I can still hear the voice of the salesman who came in during the stock's descent to ask what a client who owned the stock should do. I glibly replied, "Double up" [his shares of the stock]. He replied, "Lew, my client is already doubled up" [in pain].

After that experience, I vowed to stay away from popular stocks.

How do you decide which stocks to buy?

We combine modern investment theory with a value-oriented approach to investing. We believe that by joining the two you can substantially improve your investment performance in stocks and other assets. We will explain modern investment theory here and value orientation in the next question.

We use modern investment theory in three ways: (1) to gauge the risk of individual stocks, mutual funds, and other investments, (2) to measure their past performance, and (3) to blend individual investments into an overall portfolio. Modern investment theory was developed by four professors, all of whom won Nobel prizes in economics for their work. Among other things, the theory says that you can't measure how well your investments have done without taking into account the risk that you took to get there. Neglecting the risk factor would be like having an auto race in which one car took the highway and cruised to the finish line and a second car took the back roads, exceeded the speed limit, jumped a few lights, and barely missed getting hit by a train. The second car won, but would you want to bet your money on the result next time?

Leo's wife, Millie, asked us to review the couple's investment portfolio about which she was nervous. Leo, on the other hand, didn't understand why a review was necessary. Why, his selections of stocks had outperformed the market for the past three years. When we looked into it, we found that every stock was a high-risk investment. Most didn't earn any money, and none paid dividends. Using modern investment theory concepts, we adjusted their past performance for risk and found that for each stock the performance was poor. Leo didn't know how his "great" performance could have been negative, and didn't want to make adjustments. Unfortunately, a few months later Millie and Leo received a practical lesson in modern investment theory when their investments hit the equivalent of a head-on collision with a speeding train—the crash of 1987. It was at that market low that Leo, continuing his head-in-the-sand style of investing, chose to liquidate virtually all of his holdings.

We don't believe that modern investment theory concepts work in every instance. For example, modern investment theorists believe that you cannot have better-than-average results in the stock market. There are many examples tested by good theoreticians that dispute this contention. One of the approaches that has qualified is—you guessed it—a value-oriented strategy which we will discuss next.

By using a logical theory and computers, modern investment theory has brought investing closer to a science from what sometimes used to seem like witchcraft. We will use modern investment theory concepts and practices throughout this and the next chapter when it is appropriate. Appendix 3-1 will show you how you can use it to measure your own investment performance.

How can I use a value-oriented investment strategy to improve my performance?

In Chapter 1 we discussed value-oriented money planning and how you can benefit from it. The value-oriented idea can be applied to investments as well. What does that mean? Broadly speaking, it means investing in something that gives you an edge. It can save you investment costs or generate higher investment returns directly. To many professionals it means that, without sacrificing quality, you look for investments that are selling substantially below their fair price. Quality stocks that are currently *unpopular* with investors can be excellent value-oriented purchases.

Think of your investments just as you would a business. You wouldn't buy a business without inspecting it and calculating its cashflow. Neither should you buy a stock based on dreams instead of current realities. Stocks are often called "merchandise" by the firms that market them. The easiest merchandise to move is the current fashion, the fad of the day. But when the fashion changes and the investment herd has moved on to something else, you will be left holding the bag.

Some years ago, I had a meeting with the president of Twentieth Century Fox in his corporate office. It looked like a Hollywood set, complete with animal skins and a couch that must have dropped one foot when I sank into it. I asked him why his company's stock was up sharply when the overall market was weak. With unusual candor that made me gain new respect for him he said there was no fundamental reason but, "Lew, the promoters are taking the stock higher."

Those investors who bought Twentieth Century Fox stock based on the promoters' concept of untold wealth were left with large losses when the investment mood soured on film production companies' future potential.

A value-oriented investor selects from investments that have below-average valuations—that is, their price is cheap in relation to one or more of the following: their earnings, their cashflows, their assets, or other positive factors that are not reflected in the current price. You might think that this type of investment is risky. Actually, the risk is often below average because expectations for undervalued stocks are not high and they are less costly than other stocks. If the earnings are better than anticipated, the shares are likely to be excellent performers.

Taking a value-oriented approach can protect you from the ebbs and flows of the stock market. Over short periods of time, the market can be guided by emotions and other unpredictable factors. Value-oriented investors seek longer-term goals rather than quick, speculative transactions. If you have enough patience to wait until the fashion cycle shifts in your direction, you should have unusual opportunities.

Remember back in the early 1980s when everyone was saying that the energy shortages would last into the next century and that oil prices, then $35 a barrel, would move steadily higher? Many investors were buying oil shares. Value-oriented investors were selling theirs. They were proved right when the price of oil crashed due to conservation and a weak economy.

Then there was the time not too long ago when municipal bonds briefly yielded more than U.S. government bonds on a pretax basis. There were all kinds of seemingly logical reasons, such as a change in the tax law for banks and lower income tax brackets for individuals. But you didn't have to be a professional investor to recognize that it was illogical for high-quality tax-free bonds to yield more than taxable bonds even before their tax advantage. The market adjustment that followed created above-average returns for buyers of municipal bonds.

By using a value-oriented style, you can position yourself ahead of the crowd. Since value-oriented investing is really the investment extension of value-oriented money planning, it should come as no surprise that it receives the money planning award for this chapter.

Can you give me some examples of value-oriented investing?

You can apply a value-oriented strategy to all areas of investing, including stocks, bonds, and real estate. Here are some current opportunities that will provide you with the edge that value-oriented investors seek:

Buying Closed-End Mutual Funds Selling at a Discount. Certain mutual funds are offered at discounts of 10, 15, or even 20 percent to the market value of the investments they hold. In essence, you can purchase a dollar's worth of assets for as little as 80 cents; if the fund's investments have a current yield of 5 percent, you will get a cash return of closer to 6 percent—an extra 1 percent. Then, should the discount narrow or be eliminated due to a temporary or permanent return to popularity, as it has many times in the past, your return will be even greater than normal.

Buying Municipal Bonds. Municipal bonds can be an exception to the theory that the greater the risk taken, the higher the return achieved. High-quality municipal bonds have relatively low risk, yet provide after-tax returns that are superior to other bonds for people in the 28 percent or higher tax bracket.

Buying Bonds at New-Issue Date. Most bonds (other than those of larger corporations) are not traded on the New York Stock Exchange or any other listed exchange. They are traded over the counter, where prices can be murky and sales commissions, which are not separately itemized, can vary. For example, virtually all U.S. government and all municipal bonds are traded over the counter. When you buy bonds at the time they are originally issued, the company issuing the bonds pays the commission, not you. Also, you pay the same price as the big investors, thereby raising your yield beyond what you would pay after the bonds have been issued.

Using No-Load Mutual Funds. If you are comfortable doing your own fund selecting, no-load (sales commission–free) mutual funds provide a cost savings for mutual fund investors by bypassing the sales agent.

Buying Your Own Real Estate. Don't believe the naysayers; good-quality, well-situated real estate bought in a value-oriented manner, whether commercial or residential, will always reward patient holders. Buy it when sellers believe the market is going down or when they are compelled to unload their property. The largest rewards will go to those who do their homework and invest and manage the holdings by themselves or with a small group of like-minded investors.

Buying Value-Oriented Stock Funds. If you're uncomfortable buying stocks yourself, there is a simple solution. Let a mutual fund manager with a value-oriented philosophy and a good past record of performance choose your stocks for you. Read more about it in Chapter 4.

Aside from stocks and bonds, what other types of investments are attractive?

One attractive investment is real estate—we talk about that in Chapter 7. Aside from the three types mentioned—stocks, bonds, and real estate—there aren't many types of investments that we consider attractive. To us, an attractive investment is one that gives you income now or that you foresee as generating income in the future. It is the growth in income that makes traditional investments increase in value over time. Many alternative investments—collectibles, commodities, gold, options, and futures—don't provide income at all and depend on limited supply, increasing consumer demand, and a fair shake from the salesperson to provide profitable opportunities.

Let's take a closer look.

Collectibles. Collectibles such as art, antiques, baseball cards, antiquarian books, comic books, stamps, or coins are good examples of investments with blemishes. While they have historically been good hedges against inflation, their value depends on consumer demand. Any shift in demand caused by the economic climate can result in wide fluctuations in price, while a fundamental change in taste can be disastrous.

Just as important, the spread between purchase and sales prices can be enormous. Our 11-year-old son collects comic books. He checks a comic-book guide for selling prices. During a recent visit to a comic-book store, we asked the manager what he would pay for an average comic book that the guide said sold to the public for $10. His answer was $3.50. Assuming that comic books increase in price at a rate of 10 percent a year and taking inflation into account, 22 years from now—about the time his own child may be collecting comic books—our son will be able to get his money back. He will, that is, if his collection is still popular, unlike our old favorite, Captain Marvel, who—except for fond memories—appears to be as dead as a doornail. Of course, besides wanting to make money, our son loves reading his comics and enjoys selecting and maintaining his collection.

You should collect items that you know something about and enjoy having. Realize that most collectibles provide you not only with an investment, but also with a time-consuming hobby. Establish that there is a ready market for both buying and selling with reasonable markups—lower than the one on our son's comic books. Even then, you should give collectibles only a limited role in your investment strategy, and you shouldn't consider them investments at all if you never intend to sell.

Commodities. Commodities are the country's raw materials, like food, oil, metals, and so on. Prices are often set on commodity exchanges, such as those in Chicago. In theory, commodities are excellent hedging devices because they aren't affected by the same factors as stocks and bonds and could increase when your other investments are plunging. However, they are extremely risky and have very high costs associated with hiring professionals to manage accounts for you. Avoid them.

Options and Financial Futures. Options and futures aren't basic assets. They are contracts giving you the right to buy or sell stocks or commodities at a certain price within a certain time. There are occasions when they can be used to reduce risk, but for the purposes of the average investor their risks far outweigh their benefits. We don't recommend them. Even so, we've met many otherwise sensible investors who bought them thinking they would get rich quick.

"Don't worry. If something goes wrong I can get you out in time," Jerry told us his broker had said. Three weeks later he had nothing left of his $10,000 investment. Stay away.

Gold. Gold is a commodity of last resort. It usually becomes popular and its value tends to increase in times of inflation and fears about international stability. At other times, gold can have a modest place among your investments through your purchase of actual gold bars or coins or, more likely, through mutual funds consisting of gold stocks. You might think of it as a hedge against disappointing results among your other investments. In any case, don't buy this investment aggressively.

Venture Capital. This is a high-risk/high-return proposition. Essentially you buy an investment, for example, a part of a business partnership, in which you can make many times the sum you put in, if things work out. But as professionals we know that for every business that works out, many more fail. Don't invest in this area unless you can stand the risk and have enough money to take a full loss.

To sum up, we advise you, as we advise most of our clients, to restrict your interest to more traditional areas, where it belongs.

How can I choose investments that are right for me?

No matter how attractive an investment may appear, there is no sense in buying it unless it suits your personality. To choose investments that are right for you, the most important factor is to know your tolerance for risk. Do you feel uncomfortable if you can't be sure of making a profit? Or, on the other hand, are you thrilled by the prospect of making a killing, even though you know you are taking the chance of losing a bundle?

One of the biggest mistakes you can make is to choose investments that go beyond your normal risk tolerance. What might happen next is that you'll become uncomfortable and sell at the wrong part of the investment cycle, when your shares have temporarily decreased in value. The result would be an unnecessary loss. So be honest with yourself.

Risk Profile Quiz

Answer the following questions with ratings from 1 (strongly agree) to 5 (strongly disagree).

1. Short-term fluctuations in the value of my assets do not bother me.
2. I tend to buy and sell securities at the right time.
3. Having high current investment income is not important to me.
4. If an investment could not be sold quickly without a substantial financial penalty, it would not disturb me, provided the longer-term returns on the investment were favorable.
5. It would not bother me at all if I couldn't sell my new investment for many years if there was the potential for unusually good performance.
6. Investing in common stocks and common-stock mutual funds does not make me jittery.
7. I am willing to endure a significant decline in my principal over a few years if it will result in higher longer-term returns.
8. I am willing to take on greater risk so that I can obtain a hedge against inflation.
9. I don't need a guaranteed return of my principal if foregoing that will greatly increase the potential longer-term growth rate of my investments.
10. If the prevailing economic and investment sentiment seemed gloomy, I would not switch to safer securities.

Take a cue from Harvey, a businessman. Harvey came to us and announced that he was a changed man. He had renounced his former conservative self, divorced his wife, and acquired a new girlfriend and a high-speed red sportscar. He said he wanted aggressive, risky new investments to fit his new image, but even while he was telling us all this he seemed very nervous. He was annoyed when we refused to plunge in head first and, instead, invested only a modest portion of his money in growth stocks. A few days later, Harvey phoned to apologize. He asked us to sell the growth stocks we had just bought for him. He looked at the newspaper for changes in their price every day, he said, and he couldn't sleep at night.

The Risk Profile Quiz will give you some insight into your own tolerance for risk. A score of 40 or higher on the test suggests that you are conservative—a risk avoider—while a score of 20 or less indicates that you are a risk taker. Scores between 20 and 40 place you somewhere in the middle of the spectrum.

Another thing to think about is whether you have enough assets and income to support the level of risk you are comfortable with. The amount you need will depend on your age and goals. Unless you like to play financial Russian roulette, moderate your level of risk, especially if you are substantially behind where you would like to be financially at your age. Look for other means, such as increased savings, to help you catch up.

Congratulations! You have completed your basic training in investments. If you can't remember all the information, don't worry. The only way to get it down pat is to keep using it. Like learning to use a computer, learning to invest may seem hard at first, but you can become used to its benefits very quickly.

APPENDIX 3-1 How to Use Modern Investment Theory to Select Assets and Measure Their Investment Performance

Computer-generated measures of risk built upon modern investment theory concepts allow you to select assets and measure their performance more accurately and by doing so help improve it over time. We will mention just the key measures. If they sound like Greek to you, don't be concerned, they are; they are known by their Greek letters. You don't have to know how to calculate these measures, or even understand them fully, as long as you learn to apply them in your situation properly.

Beta Coefficient. This measurement of risk should be used principally for common stocks. It indicates the percentage change in an individual stock, portfolio of stocks, or equity mutual fund relative to the average stock. It is calculated by comparing the past fluctuation of that asset with a market index, usually the broader and more accurate Standard & Poor's 500 than the Dow Jones Industrial Average. The theory says the risk of any one stock is made up of market-related forces—such as overall business conditions—and forces relating to the individual company, such as how good a product they make. By diversifying, the individual factors balance themselves out. What you are left with is market-related risk as measured by the beta.

A beta of 1 indicates the same risk as the overall market, below 1 shows below-average risk, and above 1 indicates you're taking more risk than average. By examining the beta for your equity investments you can select assets that meet your desired preferences for risk. For example, if you are somewhat conservative in your makeup, selecting a mutual fund with a beta of 0.8 indicates you can expect, on average, that when the market drops you will have a decline of only 80 percent of that for the overall market.

Standard Deviation. We can use this measurement of risk for all types of assets. It is particularly helpful for bonds. The standard deviation ignores market averages in its calculation and measures the sharpness of fluctuations for an asset around its own average price level. The wider the fluctuation, the larger the standard deviation, the greater the risk. For example, when market interest rates rise, a bond fund with a standard deviation of 3.0 is likely to drop by a much greater amount than one with a standard deviation of 1.5. The standard deviation allows you to compare the risk of many different assets with realistic public markets such as stocks, bonds, and commodities on an apples-to-apples basis.

Correlation Coefficient. This is a measurement of the degree to which two assets move together. It can range between –1 and +1. Generally, the individual investment or asset category is compared to an index of the overall market. The most commonly used index is the Standard & Poor's Index of 500 large common stocks. The goal of portfolio diversification is to reduce fluctuations in total portfolio value by selecting assets whose movements differ so that when one category (for example, stocks) drops sharply, another category (for example, bonds) can partly or fully cushion the former's losses by contributing better performance. A correlation coefficient of +1.0 indicates that the two assets act exactly the same, while one of –1.0 indicates they perform exactly opposite to one another. Most assets have no correlation or some positive correlation with one another, which places them in the 0 to 95 percent category. For example, short-term Treasury bills have a correlation coefficient of –0.1 percent with common stocks of large U.S. companies, which can make them a worthwhile addition to your investment mix. The leading performance services often provide R2, which is the coefficient of correlation times itself. This has the effect of eliminating the negative sign.

Alpha Coefficient. This is a measure of risk-adjusted performance for stocks. It is obtained from the same market formula that calculates the beta coefficient. Most people look at raw overall performance. You should look at the risk they took to receive that performance. In fact, the industry body for investment managers is planning to require its members to put risk in addition to return in their performance figures. For example, an investment in a small motion picture company that returned 8 percent a year when certificates of deposit returned 7 percent a year over the same period was probably a poor investment after adjustment for risk. Even though the return is higher, it wasn't worth the extra risk since the company's films could have fallen flat, leaving you with a large loss.

Strong positive alphas over long periods of time indicate good risk-adjusted performance. Negative alphas over extended time frames indicate less favorable risk-adjusted performance. By comparing the alphas for different portfolios, you can gauge how well they do relative to each other.

Sharpe Ratio. This is a measure of risk-adjusted performance for bonds and other assets. It is obtained simply by dividing the return for an asset by its risk as measured by its standard deviation. The higher the Sharpe ratio, the greater the risk-adjusted performance.

You have just read through some of the practical applications of modern investment theory that have perplexed many investment professionals and noninvestment people alike. You can only acquire a working knowledge of this information by using it over time. You won't be the only one trying. Given recent changes in legal interpretations of the law, it is likely that all people involved with handling money for others, including business executives who select and monitor pension fund managers and lawyers who supervise trust funds, will want to do so as well. Modern portfolio concepts may not be simple at first, but they can have positive effects on your decision making and therefore on your performance.

4

Handling Your Investments: The Right Mix

Now that you have the basics of investments down, you are ready to invest. Right? For many of you, the answer may be, "Not yet." You still need to develop your investment approach and learn how to think about more than one investment at a time.

Charles, a retired millionaire, owned shares in just one company. Many years earlier he had been an aggressive investor. He had borrowed against his holdings. During a decline in the market, his assets had been repossessed—all but this one technology stock that was at the time worth relatively little. That stock arose from the ashes and appreciated over a hundred times from under $0.40 per share to over $40. Charles wanted to know what we thought of the company.

We did some investigating and told him Wall Street was uniformly positive on that stock; one analyst said he couldn't think of any potential negatives in the outlook. However, as value-oriented advisors who are highly wary of going along with the crowd, we cautioned Charles against the optimism that had brought the price to unrealistic levels, mentioned a potential threat from a rival company in Japan, and advised him to sell.

Charles was reluctant. He talked about the high taxes he would have to pay. "Isn't there a chance that my shares could go even higher?" he asked. Well, since anything's possible—in seventeenth-century Holland, tulips once reached levels that put them in the precious jewelry category—we agreed that there was a chance the stock might go up. But we suggested that since he wouldn't part with all his holdings, he should consider selling half his shares and putting the money into different investments. Charles promised to sell if the stock rose an additional $10.

As it turned out, the stock did reach this $50 target, but Charles didn't keep his word. We thought about him often as the shares dropped sharply and finally reached the worthless category. We later learned that he unfortunately never did sell.

In case you're wondering, we started the chapter with this sad story to warn you of what can happen if you become too attached to one type of investment, no matter how good it looks. The right way to invest is to take different kinds of stocks, bonds, and in some cases real estate, and put some of your money in each of them.

In other words, you need to diversify. When you own different types of investments, a sharp drop in any one area won't be a total disaster. It will have only a minimal effect on your total worth. Building on the basics of Chapter 3, we will show you how to develop an attractive investment mix—one that targets both higher investment performance and a reduction in investment risk.

Am I invested properly?

This is one of the first questions new clients ask us. We tell them that there is no one mix of assets that is right for all people in all circumstances. There are, however, good and bad investment habits. For example, notice we said *mix* of assets.

Together, your investments make up your portfolio. Your portfolio can be relatively small, say under $10,000. In fact, you can begin to build your portfolio with just a few hundred dollars. No matter the size, a portfolio should have a balance in the same way that your diet should. Just as you choose foods to achieve an attractive mix of taste and nutrition, diversify your money to assure a healthy investment blend.

Making up a gourmet portfolio takes some effort. Look for real nourishing substance rather than fancy packaging. And remember that concentrating on just one investment, however appealing it may be, is the equivalent of living exclusively on a diet of fatty steak; too often, it can lead to serious health problems.

Along with diversification, consider your goals when you are choosing investments for your portfolio. If you are saving for a down payment on a home that you plan to buy next year, choose short-term investments, including money-market accounts. If you are saving for retirement many years from now, you can select from the entire range of securities, even those you believe may not perform well for some time. We recommend more conservative investments when you are saving for nearer-term events such as college, particularly as the date draws closer.

What is a portfolio?

Your individual investments combine to form your portfolio. You should think of your portfolio as an integrated whole—an investment blend—whenever you do your investing. You can't create an effective portfolio simply by scrambling unrelated investments together. You should plan your investment portfolio overall so that the separate elements perform well as a team. We call that a blended investment mix.

If you were a basketball coach forming a team, your first inclination might be to choose all-star players exclusively. But wouldn't you be better off with at least one player who couldn't necessarily score well but who had no ego to support and was adept at passing the ball to the others? If you were conducting a choir, wouldn't you choose a voice that was not particularly outstanding by itself but blended well with the others?

Similarly, you may want to place investments in your portfolio that do not have high-growth or low-risk factors by themselves but contribute by performing well when the other parts of the portfolio do not. Money-market accounts, real estate, international bonds and—to some extent—international stocks, and gold funds have performed that function in the past. In that way, your portfolio will have lower fluctuations overall. We will say more about that when answering the next question.

Why should I use asset allocation?

Asset allocation involves diversification among different markets. We call it "real diversification." The idea has become so important that we believe it is likely that in the near future corporate pension fund trustees, attorneys in charge of trusts, and other people responsible for supervising monies may find themselves being sued if they don't invest in accordance with these principles.

Asset allocation is more than just buying several different stocks and bonds and saying, "Okay, I'm diversified." You have to be careful not to buy securities that all respond to the same factors in the economy. For example, investing in domestic automobile and air-conditioning stocks isn't true diversification because both products are expensive, consumer-oriented items, which you can postpone purchasing in hard times. Both are probably manufactured by large companies. The stocks are likely to move up or down at the same time.

For true asset allocation, you should choose different types of financial instruments—for example, stocks and bonds. You should also choose investments from different sectors of the economy, different sized companies, and different geographic regions.

You'll find asset allocation easier if you invest in mutual funds. They will enable you to buy small quantities of stocks and bonds in many areas. You can choose from money-market, limited-maturity and long-term bond funds, GNMAs, large-capitalization and small-company growth funds, real estate funds, gold funds, utilities, international stock or bond funds, and others, with a minimum investment as low as $500.

Remember, your goal is to buy investments that don't move up and down together. Equity (stock) funds that invest in blue-chip companies can behave very differently from funds that invest in smaller companies. While prices for the Dow Jones Industrial Average—consisting of larger companies—remained flat, the average small-company stock more than doubled during the five-year period from mid-1976 to mid-1981. Long-term bonds and large-company stocks don't move together well either, which makes having investments in both a worthwhile strategy. For further diversification, consider international mutual funds, including international bond funds. International stocks did extremely well in the 1980s, outperforming domestic ones.

Even if you restrict yourself to domestic bonds, buy a variety. Money-market and short-term bond funds generally do best when interest rates rise sharply, while longer-term bond funds do best when rates decline. Intermediate bond funds are somewhere in the middle. In the past, they have provided almost as good returns as long-term bonds with much less risk.

Consider adding real estate to your portfolio because real estate stocks have only a moderate relationship to other stocks, and real estate properties have no relationship at all. You might even choose to diversify by buying a home!

How can I reduce my investment risk?

There are several ways to reduce the risk in investing. Here are some strategies we use.

Buy More Conservative Securities. Substitute quality bonds for stocks—for example, government bonds for high-yield stocks. Replace long-term bonds with short-term bonds. Both shifts can reduce your risk.

Diversify. We've said it before and we'll say it again: reduce your risks by apportioning your assets among several types of securities in different markets.

Buy for Longer-Term Investment. Investments, particularly stocks, are less risky when you hold them for longer periods of time. If you compare stock returns over different time spans from 1926 to 1991, you will see that in any 1 year stocks provided positive returns 70 percent of the time; in any 5-year period, 89 percent of the time; in any 10-year period, 96 percent of the time; and in any 20-year period, 100 percent of the time.

The moral is, forget about short-term fluctuation in prices and investor sentiment. If you are like most people, your temptation will be to sell at the worst possible time, when sentiment is most negative—possibly just before the reversal in that investment's fortunes. Focusing on a finish gate well in the future will help you reign in your emotions.

Stay Away from Current Fashions. Today's fashions in investments sound good—that's why they're in fashion. But just like the pet rock and the Cabbage Patch Doll—remember them?—a short while later they can be as obsolete as yesterday's newspaper. While prices fall to more realistic levels, or even below that, you can be left holding last year's star pick.

Never Buy on Tips. Don't waste your hard-earned money on an investment because of someone else's tip. It's been our experience that for every tip that *does* outperform the market, 10 others *don't*. If the tip is good, it is usually based on inside information, which makes it illegal. In most instances, though, there's no big secret—the fundamentals underlying the stock are poor, and you are the five-hundredth person to hear the tip, which means it is already up sharply. The risk is that you may be the last one holding on when the music stops.

The poor quality of these tips is underscored by Frank's story. Frank asked us to look into a stock he heard was going to rise sharply. But he couldn't remember whether his friend had told him to buy GM or MG!

Never Buy What You Don't Understand. You'd be shocked at how many people are very careful when they are shopping for homes, cars, and appliances—even clothes—yet throw caution to the winds when they make purchases that don't even deserve the name "investments." Rose came in to ask us to modify the asset allocation that we had prepared for her because she had bought an investment from a "perfectly nice gentleman" who called from Denver. He told her about a private partnership in a metal that had and would continue to appreciate 60 percent a year. It was called zirconium. Zirconium?

Never invest in something that hinges on sweet talk instead of hard facts. If something sounds too good to be true, it probably is. Many private partnerships and new issues have prospectuses; reading them will often disclose the risks. Always ask what could go wrong and investigate the background of the individual and firm selling you the product. In the last analysis, pass on all investments that can't be easily explained, backed up, and believed in.

Consider the "Enough Principle." You wouldn't believe the risks some people take to maximize their investment returns. Yet they have no apparent reason for needing extra money. Risks assumed should be related to goals. If you can achieve your goals with less risk, consider what one of our colleagues calls the "enough principle," and shift to more conservative investments.

Do I have to be in the stock market to keep pace with inflation?

We have to tell you about a very disturbing risk. It is called purchasing-power risk. Even if you own the most conservative investments in the world and are confident that your money will not fluctuate in value, you can lose out anyway because the money you receive when you cash in the investment will buy fewer things. Think of it as the ever-shrinking dollar. The villain is inflation. If you buy a $10,000 five-year certificate of deposit and spend the interest income, and if inflation runs 5 percent per year, you will get your $10,000 back, but it will buy only $7800 worth of goods or services.

Even when you reinvest the interest, you may come out behind. Assuming the same 5 percent annual increase in inflation and a 6 percent return on a taxable money-market account, if you are in the 28 percent bracket you will actually lose almost 1 percent in real value each year, even if the income is reinvested.

Investing entirely in debt obligations such as bonds exposes you to this purchasing-power risk. For example, if you retire with total expenses of $28,000 a year and annual income of $30,000 and the cash you receive (aside from social security) is made up of government bonds, certificates of deposit, and money-market interest, in three years you probably will be dipping into your capital. That is because if interest rates don't change, your income from investments will remain flat but your cost of living will climb. That's why, in purchasing-power terms, debt obligations may not be conservative investments after all.

What you need is a component of your portfolio that keeps pace with inflation. Most common stocks do, except in the early stages of unexpectedly high inflation, because the managements of the corporations are able to raise prices to maintain their companies' returns on investment. As profits grow, so do dividends to stockholders and common-share prices. The growth in total return (dividend payout plus increases in stock price) for common stocks has made common stocks a much better longer-term hedge against inflation than bonds. Over all 20-year periods from 1926 to 1991, U.S. government bonds kept pace with inflation only 28 percent of the time while stocks did 100 percent of the time. If income tax payments were taken into account as well, you would have been an even bigger loser with bonds. The percentage of the time stocks and government bonds outperformed the inflation rate is given in Figure 4-1.

In some respects, real estate is an even better hedge against inflation than stocks. You can often pass inflationary rises in operating costs along to tenants. And many investors buy real estate when they expect inflation to rise, which can create a self-fulfilling prophecy. If you are willing to take on the added responsibility of managing a property or are confident in allowing someone else to handle your real estate investment properly, you need not buy equity securities. As best as we can determine, the longer-term returns on rental real estate are approximately equivalent to those for stocks.

There are other so-called inflation hedges. Commodities are chief among these. However, we have yet to find a commodity investment that combines reasonable safety and low investment expenses. Instead, we have seen commodity partnerships that exploit the term "inflation hedge" with cost structures that can drive an investor to the poorhouse. Gold is often thought of as an inflation hedge, which is partly true, but its movement is a reflection of many factors.

No, you don't have to be in the market to keep pace with inflation, but you will most likely need to invest in something other than

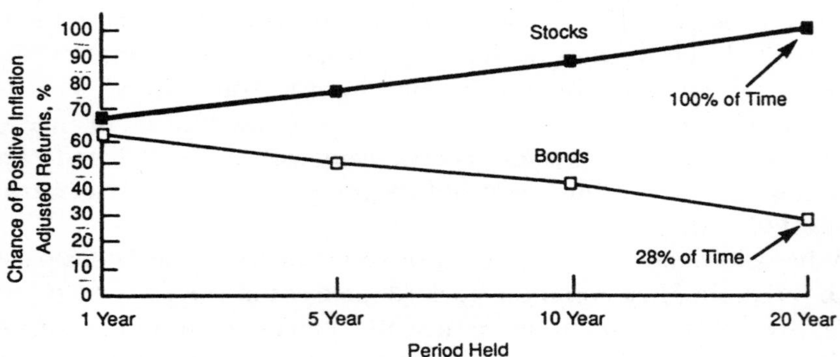

Figure 4-1. Stocks versus Bonds. Percentage of time each outperformed the inflation rate—all periods from 1926 to 1991.

bonds. Common stocks and stock funds can be the most convenient and efficient way to stay ahead.

Should I buy individual stocks or mutual funds?

Individual stocks give you a sense of affiliation with a company, as well as an emotional and financial high when they work out and a corresponding low when they don't. Mutual funds don't provide this stimulation. Their daily fluctuations are much smaller.

What mutual funds do give you is more important. They pool your money with that of other investors so that the shares you buy enable you to purchase professional management and a portfolio consisting of dozens of securities at a relatively modest yearly expense. That expense is moderated by the ability of the fund to make transactions at a much lower cost than the average investor can, and by the expertise of professional portfolio managers. Most funds also provide you with good records of your buy-and-sell transactions.

We don't recommend investing in individual stocks unless you supervise your account on a regular basis or have someone who is capable and willing to act in your best interests for you. Lack of supervision turns your investments into unguided missiles. Some will soar into the stratosphere, but too many will crash land.

No stock should be held indefinitely without supervision. Western Union was once a blue-chip stock, which at its heyday declined to buy out AT&T. Long Island Lighting was the bluest blue-chip utility before its Shoreham nuclear power plant turned the company into a rank speculation for a time and left investors without any dividends at all for a long period.

Bob brought in a portfolio of securities that originally cost him a total of $600,000. However, when we looked over the portfolio and priced it, we found it had a current worth of less than $200,000. His portfolio had obviously performed miserably—something that in true academic theory should not have happened. Why? Bob had succumbed to the fads of the day (in this case, gold mining and other speculative shares), listened to the promise of untold wealth, and then had let his investments fester without supervision.

Bob and other people who won't do their homework—and that includes the vast majority of investors—belong in mutual funds.

There is no promise of open-ended glory there, but then again there should be no reality of bruising losses and damaged egos either. Mutual funds simply provide hard-nosed investment management by professionals.

Our own work and studies by others tend to confirm that over time, excluding any commissions you may pay to whoever recommends the fund, the average stock mutual fund tends to cover its costs. That means you may be getting the professional management and convenience features for free. Moreover, mutual funds are ideal ways to diversify your assets; even relatively small investments will go a long way. After using mutual funds instead of individual stocks in many client accounts that we have managed professionally over the past 10 years, we feel that the case for equity mutual funds is simple, direct, and compelling; they work.

If you are still interested in including individual stocks, a trip to the library or a direct subscription to the Value Line Investment Survey (800-833-0046) plus a lively interest in business conditions will go a long way. Ask the investor relations department to send you information on the company you are interested in and don't be afraid to follow up with questions. However, if neither you nor anyone you trust is supervising your account, we strongly recommend a switch to equity mutual funds.

Are bond funds a good idea for me?

Stock fund portfolio managers and their staffs have many opportunities to differentiate their results from average performance. The companies that issue common stocks have individual tangible and intangible factors—such as investors' hopes and expectations for earnings—that can make them perform differently from the stock market as a whole. In contrast, bonds tend to be more influenced by one basic factor—interest rates. We do not believe anyone can consistently predict the course of interest rates. My published study on the performance of individual bond funds—which was highlighted in the financial press—confirms this belief and indicates that, unlike stock funds, bond fund returns do not cover their overhead expenses.

What does all this mean to you? It means that if you buy individual bonds you have the potential for getting higher returns than if you buy shares in a bond fund. Also consider that individual bonds can be held to maturity, which is reassuring when your bonds have temporarily declined in value, while bond funds, which continue to buy and sell different issues, have no maturity dates at all. However, unless the investment portfolio manager is particularly feeble or interest rates move up permanently, the advantage of holding bonds to maturity is more psychological than real.

Bond funds offer you the opportunity to buy small amounts and perhaps accumulate more over time, while the minimum efficient individual investment size for bonds that may not be held to maturity is generally $10,000 to $25,000, particularly if you don't buy them at an initial offering. If you plan to hold your bonds for a relatively short period of time, or if you will have to cash them in if there is an emergency, bond funds are the answer.

The overhead cost for bond funds has recently declined. Now some funds have total yearly costs competitive with the commissions small investors pay to purchase bonds in the marketplace (after the issuing date). Funds have the advantage of convenience, and you can easily switch between them to accomplish your asset allocation targets.

On balance, we recommend bond funds for accounts of less than $100,000 to $200,000 and often use them in accounts that are even larger.

What are the different types of stock and bond mutual funds?

There is a whole host of funds. In order to determine which ones are best for you, relate your investment mix to your goals and tolerance for risk. There are funds that will help to meet each of your needs. The stock funds below are presented in increasing order of risk.

1. *Income funds.* High current income is a key feature of these funds. Utilities, bonds that can be switched into stocks (convertible bonds), and funds that mix bonds and stocks (balanced

accounts) are three popular income vehicles. Although the exact mix may vary by fund, since a substantial portion of your return comes from cash payments, the risk for these funds is relatively low compared to the overall stock market. The price of the assets themselves increases less than in other stock funds, so you get a lower return than with other stock funds.

2. *Growth and income funds.* Growth in principal, intended to keep up with or ahead of inflation, is the primary goal. Income produced is greater than stock market averages and is an important secondary goal. Often the fund will have a large portion of its holdings in larger, more mature corporations. The income you receive tends to reduce the effects of stock market fluctuations on your portfolio.
3. *Growth funds.* The principal objective is growth of capital. Holdings often are concentrated in companies that are growing at a faster-than-average rate. Risk tends to be about in line with stock market averages.
4. *Aggressive growth funds.* Here the portfolio manager seeks to get above-average returns and takes above-average risk to get it. Some holdings may be fast-growing, more speculative companies but it's hard to say for certain without seeing the portfolio.
5. *Small capitalization funds.* These funds, often referred to as "small caps," invest mostly or exclusively in smaller companies that are more flexible and have the potential to grow faster than many of the larger, more mature corporations. Stock market performance for 1926 to 1991 for these funds has been much better than overall averages, even after adjustment for market risk.
6. *International funds.* These funds invest in firms in foreign countries, many of which recently have had faster growth rates than U.S. companies. The exact risk will depend on the country, its political and economic stability, fund holdings, and foreign currency fluctuations. Investments in these funds tend to support your overall diversification efforts. One variation, global funds, uses U.S. securities as well as foreign ones.

Bond funds also offer choices. They are similar to the applicable individual bonds described in the previous chapter. You might want to refer back to it. The bond fund investments described below are listed in order of risk.

1. *Money-market funds.* These are the lowest risk and most liquid investments of all mutual funds. They invest in debt obligations that mature in four months or less.
2. *Short-term bond funds.* These funds generally offer a modestly higher yield than money markets. Principal fluctuates but generally at relatively low levels. Maturities often run one to five years.
3. *Intermediate-term bond funds.* Also called limited-maturity bond funds, these funds should be compared with general, longer-maturity bond funds. Past tests have shown that intermediate bond funds have provided most of the returns of long-term bond funds and are less affected when market interest rates change. Bond maturities tend to average around 6 to 15 years.
4. *GNMA funds.* Holdings consist of mortgages often with longer-term maturities. Risk is limited by the fact that a U.S. government agency guarantees the funds, and principal and income is paid quarterly.
5. *General bond funds.* Holdings in this category often consist of bonds with longer-term maturities that can range up to 20 years or more. They tend to carry the highest risk and highest return potential of all investment quality bond funds.
6. *Municipal bond funds.* These tax-advantaged bond funds involve the same categories of investments, ranging by maturity from money-market to general, longer-term municipal bond funds, as the first four entries in this list. Municipal returns tend to be most competitive with taxable yield funds with longer maturities. Consequently, the general longer-term and intermediate bond funds tend to have the greatest appeal.
7. *Unit investment trusts.* These are not bond mutual funds at all, but investors sometimes view them that way. Unit investment trusts are groupings of bonds of various types that are offered with a load (sales commission) attached—often 4 percent—but with no one supervising the portfolio thereafter. Therefore, generally there will not be any purchases or sales made on your behalf after your initial purchase of the trust. Since you will own fractions of a share of each security, it will be difficult to sell individual issues should you want to. Instead, you will have to sell part or all of the entire portfolio. The lack of professional supervision, a possible high commission on sale and, in some cases a portfolio geared to

look attractive instead of to perform well, all lead us to prefer mutual funds.

8. *High-yield bond funds.* These funds, also known as junk-bond funds, invest in bonds that are below investment quality. This means that there is no assurance of repayment at maturity; in fact, many are likely to default. The funds resemble common-stock funds more than they do bond funds.

What is the difference between load and no-load funds?

Basically, there is no difference among the funds except for cost. Load mutual funds are offered by brokerage firms, banks, insurance companies, and financial planners who receive commissions. The "load" is the commission they get for selling a particular fund. Contrast this with true no-load funds that bypass the commission agent and are offered by mutual fund management companies directly to you, the consumer.

As a rule of thumb, any recommendation from someone in the financial business—such as a member of a brokerage firm—that comes without fee for the service has a sales load attached (except possibly for a money-market fund). Why else would he or she give you the advice? Whether the person merits the commission depends on the quality of the advice you receive and on the value you place on the convenience of having him or her handle the transaction for you.

To help you determine whether you are receiving your money's worth, it is legitimate to ask how much the commission is. Commissions on load funds (front-end loads) tend to range from 4 percent to 8.5 percent, or $400 to $850 for a $10,000 investment, with the lower figure more likely for bonds and the higher end more likely for stocks.

Some brokerage firms claim to have no-load funds. What they usually mean is that there isn't any initial sales fee, but they take out a sales commission called a 12-b1 fee *each year* in addition to the normal fees for operating a fund. This sales load is often a hefty 1 percent per year. And most funds of this type have a redemption fee called a back-end load. If you sell a fund that has a back-end load before a fixed period, often five to seven years, you get hit with a redemption charge of as much as 5 or 6 percent that declines over that same period. The prospectus should disclose redemption fees. Holding the fund for five or six years doesn't help much because you pay the 1 percent per year while waiting anyway. Clearly, that 1 percent annual commission can amount to even more than the up-front load if you stay in the fund for many years.

As a second rule of thumb, only a financial advisor who gets all his or her revenues from fees from clients (a fee-only advisor), will provide you with true no-load mutual fund investments.

Our own analysis of load and no-load fund results and other studies have shown that there is no difference in overall performance between load and no-load funds except for the commission costs. Some representatives claim that ongoing costs, such as marketing costs, are lowered by purchasing a load fund. In fact, the lowest overhead cost of any major fund family comes from a no-load fund complex.

Obviously then, when you take commission costs into account, you're better off with a no-load fund. In fact, given the wide variety of no-load mutual funds, many of which have relatively low operating costs and highly competent investment managers supervising them, we give them our value-oriented money planning award.

Consider choosing mutual funds yourself using the methods given in this chapter, and be assured that no-load fund representatives on toll-free lines are willing to supply you with information and applications through the mail.

Should I invest in index funds?

Index funds are mutual funds that try to duplicate the performance of market indexes—market measures of average performance. The Standard & Poor's 500, an index of 500 large quality stocks, is probably the most popular benchmark used by index funds. There are other indexes used for stocks, bonds, and other securities that share similar characteristics.

The index fund approach is based on the belief that no one can predict investment performance successfully. Many business school professors believe in the index concept, and a small percentage of advisors use index funds exclusively. They point to the fact that the majority of professional money managers do not achieve even average performance. Indexers therefore attempt to minimize expenses and match, not beat, average performance.

There are negatives associated with the index approach. Buying and selling costs from robotlike cloning of indexes can reduce your overall results significantly. (Exceptions are indexes based on large liquid stocks listed on the New York Stock Exchange and those involving U.S. government securities.) Moreover, indexes are hard to use in matching your investments to your tolerance for risk. Also, as indexing has moved into favor, in our opinion it has carried securities in these indexes to higher valuations than they should have relative to nonindex securities. We believe there will be a readjustment day in which, ironically, stocks in indexes such as the Standard & Poor's 500 will substantially underperform.

Index believers are right on target when they say that short-term trading for investment gain is only going to hurt your overall results, and that evidence in the bond fund area doesn't indicate value added by investment managers. However, there are many instances of equity managers who outperform the market.

But the biggest reason we find not to use an index fund approach is that it consigns you to mediocre results—actually below-market performance when expenses are factored in. Consequently, we prefer a more active style of investing.

Can I choose the best mutual fund by myself?

There is no such thing as the "best" mutual fund. We have seen funds perform well under certain economic and stock market conditions and poorly under others. Again, diversification in attractive funds is the key, as long as you keep it consistent with your goals. And don't worry—if you follow the advice in this chapter, you should be able to choose your funds yourself.

That reminds us of a story. Rosalind and Dan, both musicians, came in with a portfolio of mutual funds and a mid-life crisis. After years of investing for themselves they were suddenly frozen in their tracks, wondering whether they were making the right moves.

This wasn't the first time we'd been consulted about mutual funds. We track over 2000 mutual funds by computer, closely monitor about 200, and pride ourselves on our procedures, investment management record, and ability to put little-noticed fund gems in our clients' portfolios.

When we looked over Rosalind and Dan's portfolio, we found many familiar faces—funds that we recommended and used ourselves. In fact, we didn't take issue with any of the funds they had. They had achieved a very impressive investment record despite the fact that they had no formal training in investments. We listened to their many concerns as a psychologist would, asking questions and nodding at appropriate times, but offered no help other than reassurance that their investment track was not only appropriate, but commendable. The moral of the story is plain: you can do it yourself.

Think of the selection process as taking four steps: matching mutual fund categories with your needs, choosing funds within the categories that are right for you, getting more information, and evaluating positive and negative factors.

Step 1. Choose from among the mutual fund categories listed under the question "What are the different types of stock and bond mutual funds?" in this chapter. Always keep in mind that diversification is a big plus. The idea is to average out the risks of individual investments and arrive at a risk tolerance that fits you. For example, if you are a moderate risk taker and feel comfortable with growth and income funds, you can also place some money in riskier, smaller capitalization funds and balance that with a similar amount invested in money-market funds. Some sample portfolios are given in Tables 4-1 and 4-2.

Step 2. Next, within each category that is appropriate for you, select some candidate funds. There is no shortage of fund alternatives. They are listed in magazines such as *Barron's, Business Week, Forbes, Kiplingers, Money,* and *Worth* as well as in a host of newsletters. Our own preference for fund information is *Morningstar Mutual Funds* published by Morningstar, Inc. (800-876-5005). Each fund is reviewed a few times per year in a one-page, clearly written document; it is the most comprehensive source of fund information we've found. A sample three-month subscription will cost you $55. A less expensive alternative that has many of the same attributes is *The*

Individual Investor's Guide to No-Load Mutual Funds, published by the American Association of Individual Investors, Chicago.

Step 3. Request that the management companies send you a prospectus, annual report, and the latest performance statement for the funds you are interested in. These days, prospectuses are much easier to read and you will be able to collect information from them about the funds' investment strategies and other relevant factors.

Read the annual report to get a feel for portfolio makeup. Look for longer-term performance figures and expense ratios. Use the prospectus to identify the goals of the fund (growth, income, and so on) and the types of investments that are used. Check the most recent performance to get a reading on the fund manager's current feelings and results. If you subscribe to a service such as Morningstar, the published management company data can serve as a check on the service's statistics.

Separate the funds you are examining into stocks and bonds. Bond funds are easy. Once you know in which categories (short-term bond, long-term bond, GNMA, and so on) you want to place the money, look for the funds with the lowest expense ratios. We don't believe fund managers can predict interest rates, but we have found a relationship between expenses and returns: the higher the expense, the lower the performance. Expense ratios for bond funds range from ¼ percent to 2 percent and average about ¾ of 1 percent annually. Narrow your list to those that are at or below the cost averages.

For each of the finalists compare the returns and quality of the holdings (average credit ratings) as given to you by the funds or by Morningstar. Use the exact same time periods for analyzing each fund's return. When returns are about the same, select the bond funds that have the highest-quality holdings. If returns differ, select the ones with highest returns unless the higher return came about through more aggressive kinds of holdings. If a reduction in quality is the reason for the greater return, but the average portfolio credit rating for the fund is still A or above, blend the higher- and somewhat lower-quality finalists according to your tolerance for risk.

Equity mutual funds are a different story. Here, a fund manager's performance can have a greater impact on the fund's value. We have found that there are a number of funds that have significantly outperformed the stock market over extended periods of time, even after adjustment for risk. Confine your selections to those funds whose five-year records place them in the top quarter of funds in their category. Detailed performance figures are readily available through Morningstar, Inc. (see Figure 4-2). Notice we put our emphasis on performance in relation to other similar funds in a category, not in relation to the stock market. Focusing on performance within a fund category can help adjust for under- or overperformance by one fund category over another. By comparing funds that are somewhat similar to each other, you are also providing a rough adjustment for risk.

Dennis owned a growth fund that he thought was attractive when he bought it. Later, however, when he compared it to the overall market, he was disappointed; he found it had underperformed. He telephoned from Los Angeles, asked us to perform a comprehensive investment review of his assets—in this case, in preparation for our managing his account—and sent along a copy of his holdings. We told Dennis that the whole category of growth stocks had been out of favor for a while.

When we compared Dennis' fund to other growth funds we found the relative performance excellent. We told Dennis that on a longer-term risk-adjusted basis, the fund had a leading record. While we recommended many shifts in his holdings we counseled staying with that one. When the growth category moved back into favor, Dennis' fund was an outstanding performer.

Alternatively, you can select equity funds whose performance is above that for other funds in their group by at least 1 percent annually or those rated highest for performance by reputable financial magazines or other publications. *Barron's* publishes performance results quarterly for individual mutual funds and overall fund categories. Use their cumulative five-year performance figures and select those that are at least 5 percent above category averages. Just remember that longer-term—not quarterly—performance is the key. (For more precise measures of risk and risk-adjusted returns for stock and bond funds, see Appendix 3-1 and consult Morningstar for the calculations.)

Step 4. You should now be down to the finals and ready to pick your ultimate selections based on the following factors:

Positive Factors

1. The fund's investment style is value-oriented.
2. The fund's representatives give you the information you want.

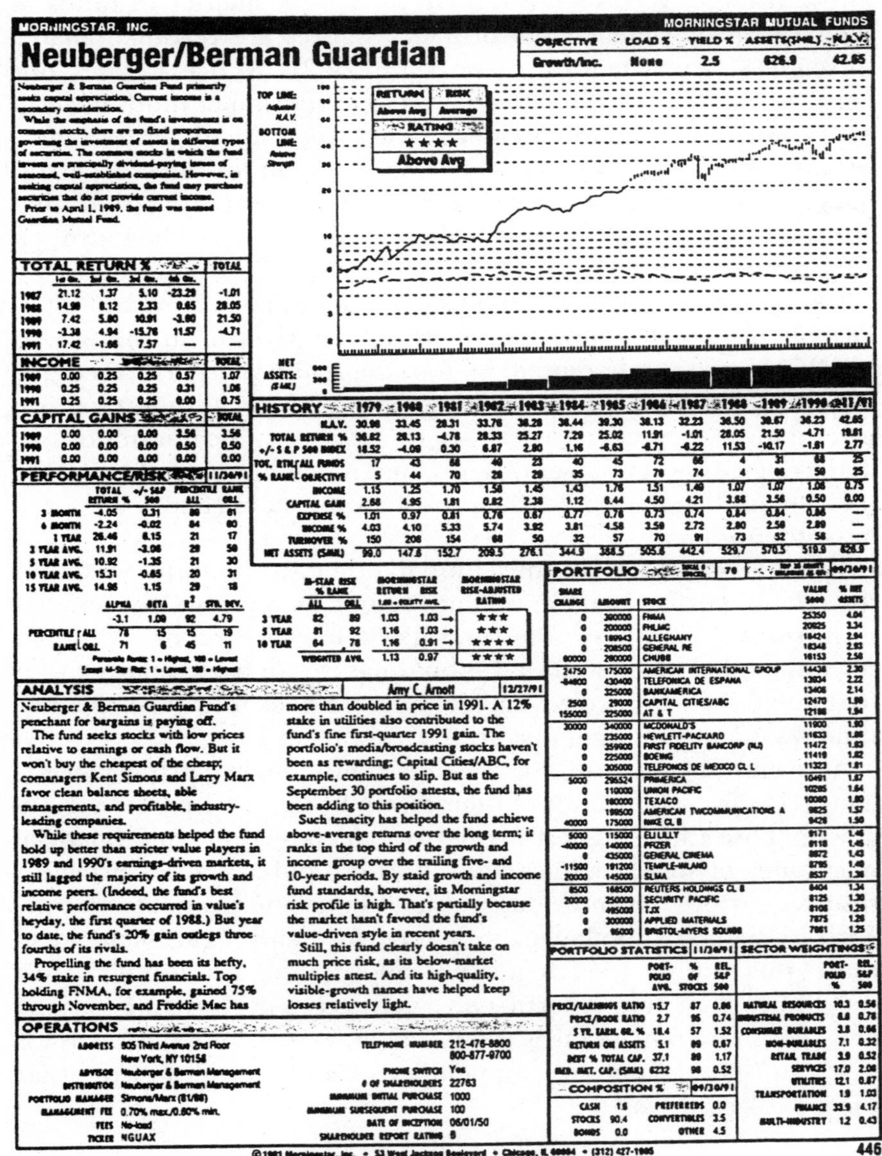

MORNINGSTAR, INC. — MORNINGSTAR MUTUAL FUNDS

Neuberger/Berman Guardian

OBJECTIVE	LOAD %	YIELD %	ASSETS($MIL)	N.A.V.
Growth/Inc.	None	2.5	626.9	42.65

Neuberger & Berman Guardian Fund primarily seeks capital appreciation. Current income is a secondary consideration.

While the emphasis of the fund's investments is on common stocks, there are no fixed proportions governing the investment of assets in different types of securities. The common stocks in which the fund invests are principally dividend-paying issues of seasoned, well-established companies. However, in seeking capital appreciation, the fund may purchase securities that do not provide current income.

Prior to April 1, 1989, the fund was named Guardian Mutual Fund.

TOTAL RETURN %

	1st Qtr.	2nd Qtr.	3rd Qtr.	4th Qtr.	TOTAL
1987	21.12	1.37	5.10	-23.29	-1.01
1988	14.98	8.12	2.33	0.65	28.05
1989	7.42	5.80	10.91	-3.80	21.50
1990	-3.38	4.94	-15.78	11.57	-4.71
1991	17.42	-1.86	7.57	—	—

INCOME

					TOTAL
1989	0.00	0.25	0.25	0.57	1.07
1990	0.25	0.25	0.25	0.31	1.06
1991	0.25	0.25	0.25	0.00	0.75

CAPITAL GAINS

					TOTAL
1989	0.00	0.00	0.00	3.56	3.56
1990	0.00	0.00	0.00	0.50	0.50
1991	0.00	0.00	0.00	0.00	0.00

PERFORMANCE/RISK 11/30/91

	TOTAL RETURN %	+/- S&P 500	PERCENTILE RANK ALL	PERCENTILE RANK OBJ.
3 MONTH	-4.05	0.31	88	81
6 MONTH	-2.24	-0.02	84	80
1 YEAR	28.46	8.15	21	17
3 YEAR AVG.	11.91	-3.06	29	58
5 YEAR AVG.	10.92	-1.35	21	30
10 YEAR AVG.	15.31	-0.85	20	31
15 YEAR AVG.	14.96	1.15	29	18

	ALPHA	BETA	R^2	STD. DEV.
	-3.1	1.09	92	4.79
PERCENTILE RANK ALL	78	15	15	19
PERCENTILE RANK OBJ.	71	6	45	11

Percentile Ranks: 1 = Highest, 100 = Lowest
Except M-Star Risk: 1 = Lowest, 100 = Highest

HISTORY

	1979	1980	1981	1982	1983	1984	1985	1986	1987	1988	1989	1990	11/91
N.A.V.	30.98	33.45	28.31	33.76	38.28	36.44	39.30	38.13	32.23	36.50	38.67	36.23	42.65
TOTAL RETURN %	36.82	28.13	-4.78	28.33	25.27	7.29	25.02	11.91	-1.01	28.05	21.50	-4.71	19.81
+/- S&P 500 INDEX	18.52	-4.09	0.30	6.87	2.80	1.16	-6.63	-6.71	-4.22	11.53	-10.17	-1.81	2.77
TOT. RTN. % RANK ALL FUNDS	17	43	68	40	23	40	45	72	66	4	31	68	25
TOT. RTN. % RANK OBJECTIVE	5	44	70	28	29	35	73	78	74	4	66	50	25
INCOME	1.15	1.25	1.70	1.58	1.45	1.43	1.76	1.51	1.49	1.07	1.07	1.06	0.75
CAPITAL GAIN	2.68	4.95	1.81	0.82	2.38	1.12	6.44	4.50	4.21	3.68	3.56	0.50	0.00
EXPENSE %	1.01	0.97	0.81	0.76	0.67	0.77	0.78	0.73	0.74	0.84	0.84	0.86	—
INCOME %	4.03	4.10	5.33	5.74	3.92	3.81	4.58	3.59	2.72	2.80	2.59	2.89	—
TURNOVER %	150	208	154	68	50	32	57	70	91	73	52	58	—
NET ASSETS ($MIL)	99.0	147.8	152.7	209.5	276.1	344.9	388.5	505.8	442.4	529.7	570.5	519.9	626.9

	M-STAR RISK % RANK ALL	M-STAR RISK % RANK OBJ.	MORNINGSTAR RETURN (1.00 = EQUITY AVG.)	MORNINGSTAR RISK (1.00 = EQUITY AVG.)	MORNINGSTAR RISK-ADJUSTED RATING
3 YEAR	82	89	1.03	1.03 →	★★★
5 YEAR	81	92	1.16	1.03 →	★★★
10 YEAR	64	78	1.16	0.91 →	★★★★
WEIGHTED AVG.			1.13	0.97	★★★★

PORTFOLIO — TOTAL # STOCKS: 70 — TOP 25 EQUITY HOLDINGS AS OF: 09/30/91

SHARE CHANGE	AMOUNT	STOCK	VALUE $000	% NET ASSETS
0	380000	FNMA	25350	4.04
0	200000	FHLMC	20925	3.34
0	189943	ALLEGHANY	18424	2.94
0	208500	GENERAL RE	18348	2.93
60000	280000	CHUBB	16153	2.58
24750	175000	AMERICAN INTERNATIONAL GROUP	14438	2.30
-84800	430400	TELEFONICA DE ESPANA	13934	2.22
0	325000	BANKAMERICA	13406	2.14
2500	29000	CAPITAL CITIES/ABC	12470	1.99
155000	325000	AT & T	12188	1.94
30000	340000	MCDONALD'S	11900	1.90
0	235000	HEWLETT-PACKARD	11633	1.86
0	359900	FIRST FIDELITY BANCORP (NJ)	11472	1.83
0	225000	BOEING	11419	1.82
0	305000	TELEFONOS DE MEXICO CL L	11323	1.81
5000	296524	PRIMERICA	10491	1.67
0	110000	UNION PACIFIC	10285	1.64
0	180000	TEXACO	10080	1.60
0	199500	AMERICAN TV/COMMUNICATIONS A	9825	1.57
40000	175000	NIKE CL B	9428	1.50
5000	115000	ELI LILLY	9171	1.46
-40000	140000	PFIZER	9118	1.45
0	435000	GENERAL CINEMA	8972	1.43
-11500	191200	TEMPLE-INLAND	8795	1.40
20000	145000	SLMA	8537	1.36
8500	168500	REUTERS HOLDINGS CL B	8404	1.34
20000	250000	SECURITY PACIFIC	8125	1.30
0	495000	TJX	8108	1.29
0	300000	APPLIED MATERIALS	7875	1.26
0	95000	BRISTOL-MYERS SQUIBB	7881	1.25

ANALYSIS — Amy C. Arnott — 12/27/91

Neuberger & Berman Guardian Fund's penchant for bargains is paying off.

The fund seeks stocks with low prices relative to earnings or cash flow. But it won't buy the cheapest of the cheap; comanagers Kent Simons and Larry Marx favor clean balance sheets, able managements, and profitable, industry-leading companies.

While these requirements helped the fund hold up better than stricter value players in 1989 and 1990's earnings-driven markets, it still lagged the majority of its growth and income peers. (Indeed, the fund's best relative performance occurred in value's heyday, the first quarter of 1988.) But year to date, the fund's 20% gain outlegs three fourths of its rivals.

Propelling the fund has been its hefty, 34% stake in resurgent financials. Top holding FNMA, for example, gained 75% through November, and Freddie Mac has more than doubled in price in 1991. A 12% stake in utilities also contributed to the fund's fine first-quarter 1991 gain. The portfolio's media/broadcasting stocks haven't been as rewarding; Capital Cities/ABC, for example, continues to slip. But as the September 30 portfolio attests, the fund has been adding to this position.

Such tenacity has helped the fund achieve above-average returns over the long term; it ranks in the top third of the growth and income group over the trailing five- and 10-year periods. By staid growth and income fund standards, however, its Morningstar risk profile is high. That's partially because the market hasn't favored the fund's value-driven style in recent years.

Still, this fund clearly doesn't take on much price risk, as its below-market multiples attest. And its high-quality, visible-growth names have helped keep losses relatively light.

PORTFOLIO STATISTICS 11/30/91

	PORTFOLIO AVG.	% OF STOCKS	REL. S&P 500
PRICE/EARNINGS RATIO	15.7	87	0.86
PRICE/BOOK RATIO	2.7	95	0.74
5 YR. EARN. GR. %	18.4	57	1.52
RETURN ON ASSETS	5.1	89	0.67
DEBT % TOTAL CAP.	37.1	80	1.17
MED. MKT. CAP. ($MIL)	6232	98	0.52

SECTOR WEIGHTINGS

	PORTFOLIO %	REL. S&P 500
NATURAL RESOURCES	10.3	0.56
INDUSTRIAL PRODUCTS	8.8	0.78
CONSUMER DURABLES	3.8	0.86
NON-DURABLES	7.1	0.32
RETAIL TRADE	3.9	0.52
SERVICES	17.0	2.08
UTILITIES	12.1	0.87
TRANSPORTATION	1.9	1.03
FINANCE	33.9	4.17
MULTI-INDUSTRY	1.2	0.43

COMPOSITION % 09/30/91

CASH	1.6	PREFERREDS	0.0
STOCKS	90.4	CONVERTIBLES	3.5
BONDS	0.0	OTHER	4.5

OPERATIONS

ADDRESS	505 Third Avenue 2nd Floor, New York, NY 10158	TELEPHONE NUMBER	212-476-8800, 800-877-9700
ADVISOR	Neuberger & Berman Management	PHONE SWITCH	Yes
DISTRIBUTOR	Neuberger & Berman Management	# OF SHAREHOLDERS	22763
PORTFOLIO MANAGER	Simons/Marx (81/88)	MINIMUM INITIAL PURCHASE	1000
MANAGEMENT FEE	0.70% max./0.60% min.	MINIMUM SUBSEQUENT PURCHASE	100
FEES	No-load	DATE OF INCEPTION	06/01/50
TICKER	NGUAX	SHAREHOLDER REPORT RATING	8

446

Figure 4-2. Neuberger/Berman Guardian. (Reprinted by permission, Morningstar, Inc., 53 West Jackson Boulevard, Chicago, IL 60604)

3. The expense ratio is under 1 percent for equity funds and under ¾ percent for bond funds.
4. The fund's performance over the last five years has fairly consistently been better than average for the overall market.
5. You feel comfortable with the management company.
6. Stock funds have less than $500 million in assets. This allows more flexibility in making changes in holdings. Size is less important for bond funds.

Negative Factors

1. The fund has had a new portfolio manager for part of the five-year period. Eliminate the fund entirely if the management is brand new, because there's no track record yet.
2. The expense ratio is above 1.50 percent. This can be an onerous burden for the future.
3. The fund either has over $2 billion in assets or has over $750 million in assets and has more than doubled in size in the past year. In either case, unless the managers use a value-oriented style they may have difficulty finding enough assets to duplicate their performance.
4. The fund's performance has been very bad in certain years; its strong five-year performance came from one excellent year.

What else do I need to know about selecting funds?

Remember, look for consistently good performance relative to other funds of the same type over long periods of time. Leave the fund-of-the-month fad to others. Beware of shifting your asset allocation because of a change of heart. Your emotions are not as good as your intellect at developing a long-term strategy.

Keep your goal of diversification in mind. We suggest that you have at least three or four funds and preferably more than six if your assets are over $25,000. If you are just starting to invest, you can purchase more funds as your savings grow.

If you are really into investing and not intimidated by the use of modern investment theory and value-oriented techniques, you can further improve your performance. You can do this by more precisely measuring fund results and shifting assets based on sectors that are in or out of favor. We recommend a simple value-oriented strategy in the next question.

Avoid the following:

1. New funds with sexy titles, or those linked to people with appealing names, but no measurable performance record.
2. Funds whose attraction is based on their number-one ranking for the current year. Often this year's star is next year's underachiever.
3. Sector funds—funds that invest in one area such as communications, medical companies, or technology. You may be tempted to buy at just the wrong time, after the shares have performed particularly well.
4. Clone funds. If a "Star" fund is great but has now closed to new investors, don't buy the "Son of Star Fund" or "Star Fund II" unless it has the same portfolio manager who was so successful in developing the original. A new manager may not be able to live up to the success of the fund that attracted your attention.

What percentage of my investment money should I spend on each type of investment?

The money that you spend on each type of investment can reflect on your goals and tolerance for risk. We prefer a modified value-oriented strategy that reduces risk by maintaining a steady percentage of your money in each type of investment. That means when one investment category outperforms the others, you should sell part of it and buy more of one that has not performed as well to keep the right balance. For example, suppose you have targeted 45 percent for stocks and because of good results the percentage moves up to 55 percent; suppose also that at the same time the bond percentage targeted at 30 percent declines to 20 percent. You should sell 10 percent to reduce stocks to their original percentage in your portfolio and place the proceeds into bonds.

Tables 4-1 and 4-2 provide a recommended long-term asset allocation at various levels of risk. If you own a home, chances are that your real estate percentage will be much higher, particularly if you are just starting out. Since realistically you can't sell part of your home, ignore real estate in your asset allocation and use Table 4-2. You can also take your target breakdown from Table 4-2 if you will not be using real estate as part of your investment mix.

What is the simplest way to build my investment portfolio?

If you have $200,000 or more in investable assets, you can hire an investment advisor who will manage your assets for a moderate fee. We recommend you select a professional manager who uses modern investment theory concepts, a value-oriented approach, and charges only fees (not commissions) for services. This will eliminate any temptation your advisor may have to buy or sell securities just to earn commissions.

For most of you, though, the best way to build an investment portfolio is to use mutual funds. If you are reluctant to select these funds on your own, use a financial planner or a registered representative to do so. If not, save the commissions or fees by selecting the mutual funds yourself.

Whatever you decide—mutual funds or individual securities—follow the recommendations set forth in this chapter and Chapter 3.

Table 4-1. Target Long-Term Asset Allocation, Including Real Estate, by Type of Individual

	Young, fairly aggressive	Middle-aged, moderate risk	Retired, lower risk
Domestic stocks	45%	35%	25%
International stocks	15	10	5
Domestic bonds and CDs	10	25	45
International bonds	5	5	5
Real estate	20	15	5
Money market	5	10	15
Total	100%	100%	100%

Table 4-2. Target Long-Term Asset Allocation, Excluding Real Estate, by Type of Individual

	Young, fairly aggressive	Middle-aged, moderate risk	Retired, lower risk
Domestic stocks	55%	40%	30%
International stocks	20	15	5
Domestic bonds and CDs	10	25	45
International bonds	10	10	5
Money market	5	10	15
Total	100%	100%	100%

One basic point is to diversify by asset category. In Table 4-3 we have summarized the important investment alternatives we discuss in these and other chapters and given them each a grade. "A," of course, is excellent; we all know what "F" is.

We evaluated each alternative on the basis of the following factors:

1. *Income.* This tells you how high the annual cash payout is, whether in the form of interest or dividends.
2. *Growth.* This projects increases in the value of your investment. It excludes income.
3. *Safety.* This is an overall appraisal of the risk of an asset. It includes the fluctuation in asset price due to movements in the stock market, changes in interest rates, and factors related solely to the individual asset being held such as the possibility of a permanent loss of principal.
4. *Hedge against inflation.* This factor answers the question, "How good is the asset as insurance against getting hurt by a substantial long-term material upturn in the inflation rate?"
5. *Diversification benefit.* This represents how much of a contribution the asset makes to the proper blending of your portfolio. Remember that the goal is not only to get a favorable return but also to reduce risk as well. Risk reduction can often be accomplished by selecting a category that doesn't move well, or correlate, with the rest of your portfolio. We have chosen the Standard & Poor's index of 500 large-company stocks as the standard to measure correlation against.

Table 4-3. Investment Alternatives
(Relative Rankings for Key Characteristics by Type of Investment)

	Income	Growth	Safety	Inflation hedge	Diversification benefit
Stock sector:					
Income	B–	B	B	B	B
Growth and income	C+	B+	B–	B+	C
Growth	C–	B+	C+	B+	C
Aggressive growth	D	B+	C	A–	C+
Small cap	D	A	C	A–	B–
International	D	A	C	A	B
Bond sector*:					
Money market	B–	F	A	C	B
CD	B	F	A	D	B
Short-term bond	B	F	A	D–	B
Intermediate-term bond	B+	F	A–	F	B
Long-term bond	A–	F	B+	F	B
Series EE bond	B	F	A	F	B
GNMA	A	F	B+	F	B
CMO†	A	F	C+	F	B
High-yield bond	A+	F–	D+	F	B–
International bond	A	F	C	C+	A–
Real estate sector:					
REIT	B+	B+	C+	A	A–
Private self-ownership‡	B+	A	C	A	A
Other:					
Gold	F	B	C	B+	A
Life insurance	B–	F	B+	F	B
Fixed annuity	B–	F	B+	F	B
Commodities§	F	B	F	A	A

* Short-, intermediate-, and long-term bonds assumes that there is a mix of high-grade taxable bonds. Municipal bonds would generally have the same grades except that they would rank higher in tax benefits.

† Assumes lowest tranches which are the ones overall having the highest quoted yields.

‡ Assumes that there is moderate debt and management by individuals themselves. Unlike the above marketable securities, real estate has liquidity risk: You could be penalized in the event of forced sale, for this type of asset would be hard to sell over a short period of time.

§ Represents basic raw materials bought on margin (largely financed through debt). See the question "Aside from stocks and bonds, what other types of investment are attractive?" in Chapter 3 for reasons why we don't recommend investing in this area.

6. *Tax benefit.* This reflects the ability of the asset to provide tax relief. It should be of greatest advantage to those in the 28 percent or higher tax bracket.

Since we are the ones giving out the grades, we should mention that they are subjective. But just as the good teachers did in elementary school, we have based the grades in large part on past performance.

Use these categories and grades to form the building blocks for your portfolio. Don't worry if your weighting and selections differ from those of your neighbor. Both of you should value the growth and safety factors strongly, but one of you may place more emphasis on high income and high safety, the other on growth and tax benefits.

You can complete the building of your portfolio by taking the following steps:

1. Decide on the overall breakdown of assets by sector (for example, stocks, bonds, real estate, money market) that you are comfortable with. We have provided some target allocations for overall categories in Table 4-1. Incorporate an honest assessment of your tolerance for risk based on the risk profile score you achieved in the questionnaire provided in Chapter 3.

2. Choose the categories within each sector. Refer as needed to Table 4-3 on investment alternatives and the description of each individual category given in this chapter. As we mentioned before, you can average out to your overall risk tolerance by selecting categories that are above your risk tolerance and balancing them with some that are below your risk tolerance. For example, if you are a conservative investor, you may have selected 30 percent of your total investments from the stock sector. You may want to put 20 percent of that amount in the conservative growth and income category and 5 percent each in the more aggressive small cap and in the more conservative income sectors.

3. Select the individual funds that will be used in each category. Use the techniques given in the question "Can I choose the best mutual fund by myself?" in this chapter. If you have trouble finding out which category your funds fit into, just ask the management company that offers the fund.

When you have completed these steps, pat yourself on the back. You will have used several of the key modern investment theory concepts—overall portfolio selection, asset diversification, and incorporation of risk as well as return. These concepts that recently enabled Markowitz, Sharpe, Modigliani, and Miller to win Nobel prizes in economics can improve your portfolio performance.

How can I implement my new investment strategy?

First, remember that your individual selections should be made after you decide on how much to invest in each category—your asset allocation by sector. You should stay within the category you allocated. Of if you have made selections already, organize them by category. If you decide to use a financial planner or a registered representative, he or she will help you make those decisions. If you want to save their cost in commissions or fees, you basically have three ways to go about it.

The first is to select one fund management company that offers many mutual fund alternatives in both the stock and bond areas. This approach can simplify the order taking. If you select from direct-to-the-consumer no-load companies, aside from a few low-load funds (no-load management companies that charge a modest 1 to 3 percent to purchase the fund), you will pay no commissions. But our analysis of performance suggests that all major management companies have relatively good- and bad-performing funds. Some do better with stocks, others with bonds. Therefore you can't assume the stamp of one fund family's name is automatically an indication of strong overall performance.

Your second alternative is to select from the entire universe of mutual funds available. It is our experience that highly attractive funds are in both large and small management companies. Some management companies develop an expertise in a particular area—for example, international funds. By choosing among all funds you get to select the best of the best. The disadvantage is the mountain of paperwork that you can be subjected to in opening accounts, making purchases, keeping records, and closing your accounts if you diversify across a large number of funds and change selections over time.

The third alternative can be a happy compromise: open an account with a discount broker. These are the only brokers who offer to buy and sell no-load funds at a relatively modest price. You receive one monthly statement that details your holdings in all funds, and can switch from one fund to another within a broad range in a matter of days. The only truly national brokerage firm with offices in most major U.S. cities offering this service is Charles Schwab & Co., Inc. (800-435-4000); we have found their services in this area to be of high quality.

Finally, monitor your individual selections. Don't look in the paper for results too often; you could become nervous over nonessentials. Instead, measure your fund's performance in relation to other funds in the same category once or twice a year.

You can get annual performance figures from *Barron/Lipper Mutual Funds Quarterly* (800-328-6800), Morningstar, Inc.'s *Mutual Fund Survey* (800-876-5005), or other services. If the fund's performance in its category is poor for one year, call them and ask why. Don't be bashful; they are used to handling the most direct questions. If the fund family's service representative isn't particularly helpful, ask to speak to a portfolio management representative. If what he or she says makes sense at all, don't sell—yet. Wait until the end of the second year. If performance is still poor, you can call again. But this time the story will have to be extremely good—or else it is time to switch to another fund in that category with a better long-term record.

Another reason to sell part or all of your holdings in a fund is to maintain a constant percentage in one area. For example, suppose you decide that having 20 percent of your portfolio in growth and income stock funds is best, and because of good performance your percentage is currently 25 percent. Suppose also that utility funds have declined from a targeted 15 percent of your portfolio to 10 percent. Shift 5 percent of your holdings into the utility area that has not performed as well. Deposit new savings into areas with less than your targeted percentages. Naturally, if your goals or resources change appreciably, you should revise your asset allocation.

The pleasant part of this approach is that practically anyone can do it. Mutual funds have professional management, a comforting thought that should help you sleep well at night. They can provide fine performance if you resist the temptation to change strategy because of either near-term positive or negative news.

Reviewing your portfolio can take as little as an hour or two a year. Remember to forget about today's occurrences. Keep whispering to yourself, "These investments are for longer-term performance."

Is my corporate pension plan invested properly?

Ten years ago almost no one asked us this question; today we hear it all the time. This isn't surprising if you stop to think about it. After all, your pension is very often your largest retirement asset, whether it is a traditional one based on your salary, a profit-sharing plan, a simplified employee plan, an optional 401(k) or 403(b) plan, a long-term deferred compensation arrangement, or a combination of these.

First, let's eliminate the situation in which you needn't be concerned. That is when your company makes a commitment to provide you with a fixed sum when you retire based on your salary and years with the firm. In that circumstance, you can be less interested in performance since the sum is guaranteed by your corporation and up to a maximum of $2352.27 per month by the Pension Benefit Guarantee Corporation, an agency of the U.S. government.

More frequently today, corporations give employees choices about where to put their investments, particularly in voluntary contribution plans such as 401(k)s. At a minimum, corporations using these plans should offer you a money-market fund; a long-term, high-quality bond fund, a growth stock fund, and a conservative stock fund. Where mutual funds are used in corporate plans, the proper investment vehicles are true no-load funds, with no sales commission deducted on entry or during your holding of shares and no redemption fee when leaving—even if you withdraw just two days after enrollment.

Use the techniques described in this chapter to review investment alternatives and get an idea of their risk-adjusted performance as compared to other funds. In a corporation plan, your fund choices may be limited; if performance has not been good, we recommend that you choose the most conservative alternative—it will be harder for the fund to do poorly. You can compensate by being more aggressive with your nonpension investments.

In many instances, you won't have any say in the matter. The corporation supervises the investment of your money. How much you will get when you leave or retire will depend on performance. You should analyze the following factors:

1. How has performance been? Look at the past three to five years. Compare performance to aggregate indexes such as the Dow Jones Industrial Average or, better yet, the Standard & Poor's 500, and with mutual funds that have the same type of investment style.
2. Is the account being managed professionally? Is the money invested with an investment advisor who operates on a fee-only basis, as opposed to a registered representative with little portfolio management experience or by the principals themselves?
3. Is the pension diversified? In other words, is it in different types of assets?
4. Is the money being managed on an overall portfolio basis rather than as a cluster of individual assets?
5. Does the pension have a written statement of investment policy, and does your corporation review the investment results at least twice a year?
6. Is the pension measuring risk as well as return?
7. Is the portfolio taking into account inflation risk? Generally this will be indicated by having a portion of its assets in stocks and/or real estate.
8. Are execution costs reasonable? For example, when the pension uses mutual funds are they no-load mutual funds? Are trading costs being discounted?

Be aware that the corporation and its owners and officers have a responsibility to supervise the management of the assets in a careful and skillful way. This responsibility exists whether they manage the assets themselves or delegate the task to an outside investment advisor. Many requirements are stated in the U.S. Department of Labor Standards under ERISA.

And now, under the influential draft of the Third Restatement of the Law: Trusts, your corporation will be legally held to new and higher standards of conduct and performance. For example, placing all the money in "safe" government bonds and certificates of deposit can subject the corporation to litigation based on many grounds, including lack of diversification and nonincorporation of inflation risk.

Most larger corporations have complied with these more specific standards. Many smaller and medium-sized companies have not. However, in the instances when our firm has been called in either as a financial consultant or to become the investment manager for the pensions, we have found that, more often than not, the reason for noncompliance is ignorance about responsibilities in this area. The draft of the Restatement's reference to more-detailed standards, to modern investment theory concepts, and to use of investment advisors should result in greater attention to these areas.

You should treat your pension assets like your other assets. Where you have control over the money, use the concepts listed in Chapters 3 and 4. Even when you have no control, include them as part of your overall asset allocation. Keep in mind that our normal stress on longer-term performance is even more appropriate here.

How should I invest a lump-sum distribution or an inheritance?

A lump-sum distribution is a payment of the savings you have accumulated within a company at the time you leave. Recognize that if this money comes from a qualified pension plan [pension, profit-sharing, SEP, 401(k), 403(b)], it has important tax benefits. In most instances we recommend transferring it to a rollover IRA so that the tax benefits can remain. For more on this topic, see Chapter 9.

From an investment standpoint, the two factors that make this money different are the potential tax benefits and the length of time before you will need the money if you are still years away from retirement. Since the income from this money will not be taxed until you make cash withdrawals, you should place some of the money in higher-yielding quality taxable bonds or bond funds. Also, because you will be investing the money for payoff many years from now, you should feel particularly comfortable placing a good portion of this money in growth vehicles such as stock mutual funds.

Even if you are retiring soon, chances are most of the money won't be used for many years. Follow our overall guidelines for asset allocation given in Tables 4-1 and 4-2 and add your pension and non-pension assets together in doing so.

When you receive a large sum from an inheritance or an insurance settlement the first thing you should do is put the money in a safe place—such as a bank or mutual fund money-market account—temporarily. Then identify what the money will be used for. Will you be using it to buy a new, larger home soon, or will you save it for retirement or other longer-term goals? Your investment strategy for the money will depend on whether it will be needed shortly. If so, it should go into money-markets accounts, certificates of deposit, Treasury bills, or limited-maturity bonds or bond funds (averaging five years in maturity). If your goals are longer-term, then treat the money the same way you would the rest of your assets. As with pension proceeds, join your inheritance and regular savings together for asset allocation purposes. Use Table 4-2 to help you.

If your inheritance is in the tens of thousands of dollars, be sure to figure out whether the interest income will place you in a higher tax bracket, in which case you should consider municipal bonds. And don't forget to save some splurge money for yourself, as we often suggest for clients.

The principal difference between pension and personal assets is that you won't put lower-yielding, tax-free municipal bonds in a tax-advantaged pension because there are no benefits in doing so. Instead, you may want to put disproportionate amounts of more aggressive securities in your pension because of the long period before you will need these assets.

In both situations, lump-sum distributions and inheritances, you should recognize the importance of investing properly, particularly if amounts are greater than a few thousand dollars. This may be the first time that you have invested substantial sums of money. If after reading Chapters 3 and 4 you are unsure of yourself, we recommend hiring a financial planner who can help build your portfolio or just check on what you have set up yourself. Because of the importance of the sums involved it is a possible exception to our feeling that most people can invest by themselves. For more on when and if you should select a financial planner and which type is best, see Chapter 13.

What return should I target for my investments?

Your investment return will depend on a number of factors: risk tolerance, tax rate, investment approach, overhead expenses, and inflation. First, consider your risk tolerance. How conservative are you in selecting your investments? The greater the proportion of more risky growth investments such as stocks, and the smaller the amount of income-type investments such as bonds, certificates of deposit, and money-market funds, the faster your assets will grow.

Next, consider the rate at which your investment earnings are taxed. Returns should always be calculated on an after-tax basis. As we show below, tax-free municipal bonds will look more appealing to you if you do. For example, let us compare a taxable U.S. government bond and a tax-free municipal bond for a person in the 28 percent income tax bracket.

	Taxable U.S. government bond	Tax-free municipal bond
Pretax return	8.0%	7.0%
Tax payment	2.2*	0.0†
After-tax returns	5.8%	7.0%

* Based on assumed tax rate of 28.0%.
† Based on assumed tax rate of 0.0%.

You can see that a municipal bond that is not taxed provides a considerably greater return than the U.S. government bond, even though the pretax rates could fool you into assuming the opposite. Because pension plan–type contributions reduce taxes when contributions are made and postpone the payment of taxes in investment income earned until withdrawals, they can add as much as 1 to 3 percent or more to your yearly growth rate.

Now, think about how sharp you are in selecting your investments. Use of value-oriented investment approach can help raise returns directly while diversification across many types of investments can reduce your overall risk.

A fourth factor is the expense: the lower your overhead expenses, the higher your returns. This argument favors no-load mutual funds over load funds.

Finally, your returns should be adjusted for inflation. it is then called a "real" return. If you earn 6 percent before tax and 4 percent after tax, and if inflation runs 5 percent, you have had a real return of −1 percent. In this case, even though you are investing more money each year, the real value of your assets (that is, its purchasing power) actually declines. Longer-term real returns on investments (after inflation and taxes) can run −2 percent to +5 percent, with taxable money-market funds on the negative end and aggressive value-oriented investing on the positive end. For help in developing your own estimate, see "Determining Your Investment Return" in Appendix A.

Through use of the principles we outlined in this book you should at least have a longer-term real return of 0 percent and just keep pace with inflation. The average investor should aim for a real return of at least 1 percent annually, which at recent rates—before adjustment for inflation and taxes—translates into a yearly total return of about 8 percent.

Use of the techniques explained in this chapter should place you ahead of most people who manage their own investments. It will also leave you plenty of time to do what you like best, whether that is working hard on the job, working hard at play, or just plain taking it easy.

5
Selecting Insurance

Insurance should play a central role in your financial planning. It may be hard for you to deal logically with this topic; that's because people buy insurance for so many different reasons. Your reason may be the most obvious one—to recover money in case of a loss. Or you may feel that insurance is a good investment and that it will take care of people you are concerned about. In addition, it can provide you with forced savings, or supply you with emotional comfort at a trying time. We suggest you think of insurance as part of a broader concern—risk management. That will help you focus on the key issue: the possibility of a loss and its impact on your plans.

What does risk management mean? It means looking at areas in which you could be vulnerable to loss and deciding how to deal with them. The first step is to try to *avoid* risk. If you have a reckless, accident-prone teenager and if adding him or her to your policy as a driver at age 17 would double your insurance rates, you have two good reasons to wait a few years before allowing your child to get a driver's license. Next, try to *reduce* risk. For example, practicing good health habits can reduce medical risks at no extra charge.

Thinking in risk management terms can take much of the emotion out of insurance planning. We had a discussion some time ago with an insurance agent who was trying to sell a disability policy to our client Steve, a 32-year-old executive with a poor long-term benefits package and no disability coverage. We told his agent that we were going to look at other policies and compare their advantages and disadvantages. He said that was a fine approach, but what would happen if Steve became disabled in the meantime? Steve recognized that argument for what it was—an appeal to emotion instead of logic. As it turned out, the agent's policy was so deficient the real risk would have been to buy it.

You shouldn't try to insure against every imaginable loss. Why? Most people can't afford to. And it doesn't represent good financial value. Instead, you should put dollars aside to cover the possibility of those losses that could seriously hurt your future. Then think about assuming some risks by self-insuring, that is, absorbing the loss yourself. This is often cheaper than buying insurance, and we recommend this approach within limits.

Figuring out how much insurance you really need is important; it costs extra to overinsure. Who do you think is getting the best of the deal when your ring is appraised at 25 percent more than it is really worth? On the other hand, risk management is flexible enough to accommodate your own level of tolerance for risk. For instance, if you were very worried about Steve's short-term lack of disability coverage, you probably tend to avoid risks. You even may feel content only when all conceivable risks are covered.

It is very satisfying to be able to say, when something is lost or damaged, "My insurance will cover it." Nevertheless, if you insure against things that are unlikely to happen and would not result in a great loss anyway, you will be taking money away from building assets or improving your standard of living and placing it on a long shot.

As with any other form of financial planning, you should take a logical approach to your insurance needs. In this chapter, we'll help you select the insurance that is right for you.

What types of insurance should I consider?

Your insurance needs can be separated into three categories of risk. The first is personal risk—the risk that something can happen to you or your family. You can cover this risk with life insurance, disability insurance, and health insurance. By far the fastest-growing cost in this area is for health insurance.

The second risk is property damage, which is the risk of losing your house, car, or personal possessions due to such causes as accident, fire, or theft. You can cover this through automobile and homeowners' insurance with an addition, or rider, for expensive individual items.

The third risk is suit for injury or damages. You can protect yourself from this risk by buying liability insurance. The various types include automobile, homeowners', negligence, and malpractice insurance. Malpractice insurance is most often handled by the insured person's employer.

What should I look for in an insurance policy?

When you look for insurance, your task is to understand and compare policies from different insurers. Like everybody who wants to sell you something, insurance companies try to make it seem as if their products are special, to create bells and whistles that may add hype instead of substance. For example, some companies offer a double payout on life insurance policies if you die accidentally, which can have the effect of costing more and preventing you from comparing the price with other policies. Does the cause of death really affect the family's financial needs?

Whenever possible, choose a policy that offers large deductibles (amounts you pay before the insurance company assumes the rest of the loss) of $500 or $1000 or more. Why? The insurance company has to price its services to take into account not only the possibility of a loss but also the cost of servicing your claim. It can cost the insurance company $100 to pay out a $50 claim and that cost, in turn, is built into the price you pay for the policy. The higher the deductible, the lower the cost of the policy. From a financial standpoint, you can probably pay a modest deductible without feeling much of a pinch.

Here are some rules to follow with any policy:

1. *Read the contract.* This may be difficult considering the dense language some policies use, but it is the only way to know to what extent you are truly covered. If you don't understand the policy, call your insurance agent, financial planner, or the firm itself for an interpretation.
2. *Look into group policies first.* Their cost is often lower. Pay careful attention to the coverage, however, before selecting.

3. *Examine the quality of the insurance carrier.* How solid is the company? Read our information on the safety of insurance companies in "How can I judge how safe my insurance company is?" in this chapter.
4. *Always take inflation into account.* Your $50,000 of personal property insurance may be sufficient coverage when you buy it, but it may be wholly inadequate to cover the same items five years later. Try to get policies that automatically adjust for inflation as long as premiums for the policy rise at a reasonable rate compared to inflation.
5. *Think about insuring things you're strongly attached to emotionally.* Getting cash back after a loss won't prevent bad feelings, but it can help to reduce the sting.

How much life insurance is enough?

This question is probably the one we are most frequently asked about insurance. The answer depends on many factors.

You must recognize that life insurance in its purest sense is insurance against premature death. It is insurance that benefits your loved ones, not you. Your dependents must be the first consideration in your planning. If you are single and don't have dependents, you don't need any life insurance—unless you plan to get married and worry that you might be uninsurable at that time or if you are using insurance to reduce taxes on a large estate. (See Chapter 10 for more on this topic.)

That reminds us of Susan, who started her own business when she was in her late sixties. When we met Susan, she was in her seventies, had a large free cashflow, and had a pension plan to reduce taxes and provide life insurance. Since she didn't have any children and her husband was financially self-sufficient, we asked her why she had the insurance. She said that it automatically came as part of the pension and that her insurance agent said it wouldn't hurt and couldn't be taken out. This virtually useless investment was costing Susan $3000 a year. We promptly terminated the arrangement and transferred her pension plan elsewhere.

Next, think carefully about the amount of income that you might need to replace. Are you the sole breadwinner? Are you assuming that your spouse will not work after your death? Why not? Providing for someone's financial independence can be very expensive.

Keep in mind that having enough assets to be independent of the need to work is very rare; many people achieve it only late in life, others never do. Nonetheless, some people are attracted to the idea of matching the insured person's expected lifetime earnings.

Bert and Rosalie, a young couple of modest means, received an inheritance when Bert's parents died. Both were employed. They planned to have children soon, but Rosalie wanted to get her M.B.A. first. She refused to use the inheritance, which she felt was exclusively her husband's, for her education and planned instead to borrow money for graduate school. Bert took us aside and asked how much insurance he would need to provide for his wife and two children (who had not been born yet, remember) for their entire lives. We explained what a burden that could be, but Bert wanted to go forward. We projected that $1.5 million would be necessary, and under current investment assumptions Bert would have to spend $7000 a year to provide that amount of coverage. Since a sum like Bert's is clearly beyond the resources of most couples, when you're considering life insurance coverage we urge you to forget the ideal amount and think about what is appropriate for you.

Deciding not to completely cover the surviving family members' cost of living can reduce your insurance needs. Do you and your spouse both feel it is necessary to maintain the same living standards if the main breadwinner dies prematurely, or could the remaining family members live more frugally? Could the surviving spouse go to work if he or she is not already working? Even though you may not want to deal with this now, it pays to remember that many widows and widowers remarry and share their expenses with their new family.

Also consider the amount of your assets. Most people's assets climb as they grow older; life insurance needs decline correspondingly. In Figure 5-1 we show the decline and eventual elimination of the need for insurance for one of our clients.

Other factors to think about include inflation rates and investment returns. If the surviving spouse has a higher risk tolerance, he or she could potentially earn greater returns with a competent investment program. The higher the return, the lower the amount of insurance that will be necessary. For example, if the survivor invests part of the insurance proceeds in stocks, instead of investing

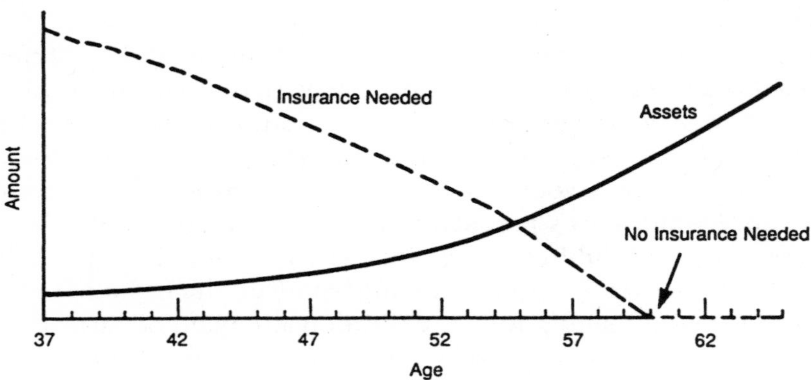

Figure 5-1. Insurance Needed Until Retirement.

100 percent in certificates of deposit, he or she should need less insurance money. If you use inflation hedge investments such as real estate or common stocks, you won't have to worry as much about the future inflation rate. If, on the other hand, you are unwilling to make such investments, you may need to purchase extra insurance to guard against a rise in inflation.

As a rule of thumb, you have enough coverage when your insurance is equal to four times each individual's yearly salary. Add double your salary for each child that needs to be raised and educated. Then subtract the amount of your current investable and pension assets. For example, a couple making $30,000 each with two children and $50,000 in investable and pension assets would each need eight times salary, or $240,000 (four times for each spouse plus twice for each of the two children), less the $50,000 they've already saved, or $190,000 in insurance. You can get a more accurate calculation by using the Insurance Worksheet in Appendix B.

How can I judge how safe my insurance company is?

There is no foolproof method of determining how safe your insurance company is. In the past people often made the mistake of assuming that insurance companies were safe because they were large, had been around a long time, and offered seemingly safe products.

With a few exceptions, insurance companies are like other service-oriented business corporations. They offer their services for a fee, which, in most cases, is an agreement to take future risk off your hands for a current payment or a series of payments (premiums). Then they invest the money they receive for their services and keep it invested until they have to pay it out. Figuring out how much to pay out and when these payments will be made is an inexact science. Miscalculations can lead to earnings problems and instability.

The main difficulty that insurance companies have had lately is in the investment area. Many invested in lower-grade junk bonds that paid higher-than-average yields, but a substantial number of the corporations issuing these bonds have run into financial troubles. Many insurance companies also lent money on real estate property that turned out to be a poor investment and were left with bad loans. As a result, certain insurance companies are now on shaky ground. To assess how safe insurance companies are, you must look into how they invest their money.

In general, select companies with the following characteristics:

1. Junk bonds are no more than 4 percent of investable assets.
2. Real estate loans are no more than 40 percent of total loans outstanding.
3. The insurance company has been in business for at least 25 years and has at least $1 billion in insurance outstanding.
4. The company's product line is licensed in New York State. That state has the tightest requirements of any in the country, and only a minority of firms qualify to operate there.

There are several independent firms that rate insurance companies. We prefer Standard & Poor's, Moody's, or Duff and Phelps. The investment grade ratings range from AAA (the highest) to BBB (the lowest). We recommend that the insurance company you select be rated AA or better. The agencies charge a fee to the company for rating it, and companies that refuse to pay may not be rated. Question any large company that isn't rated by at least one of the three agencies.

No rating agencies can guarantee that an insurance company is financially healthy because they don't have the ability to independently evaluate all the assets the company holds. They are likely to readjust their ratings in response to new developments in an individual company's circumstances and in overall business conditions.

Because of policyholders' current concern about insurers' finances, any change in circumstances could have a self-fulfilling aspect; that is, negative news about a company or the economy could cause panicky policyholders to make sudden withdrawals from their accounts, causing a cash stampede and putting a company in trouble even when the anxiety isn't merited.

Fortunately, many states' insurance regulatory agencies have funds set aside to help when companies get into trouble. They also use their influence to guide healthy insurers to take over sick insurers' activities one way or another. However, a state fund does not guarantee that your claim will be honored. Even if a company survives, it is likely that sickly companies will provide lower returns on the money that is invested with them.

The dynamics of buying insurance have changed. Searching for the cheapest price is no longer enough. By keeping to the suggestions we have just given you—especially choosing a company with an AA or higher rating—you can greatly reduce the chance of a financial surprise, and you may even lower your longer-term costs.

How can I get short-term coverage?

You may find yourself temporarily without adequate insurance coverage when you change jobs. If it is at all possible, negotiate with your new employer to begin your new insurance coverage immediately. Jim, a highly paid television executive, called in a panic when he changed jobs and was told he would have to work at his new position for three months before he could enroll in the company's insurance program. We spoke to an agent about arranging temporary insurance but, when we called Jim back a day later, he had favorably renegotiated the issue with his new employer. Under Federal "COBRA" guidelines, your old employer is required to provide you with continuation of your coverage for a period of 18 to 36 months.

Interim insurance is available but at a high cost. It is wise to protect yourself from needing it. It's better to have your old and new coverage overlap for a short period of time, that is have two policies in effect for a few weeks, than to be without coverage. If you do need such temporary insurance, call an agent you trust and explain your situation.

One short-term insurance policy that is quite popular is flight insurance. This is insurance that you buy, often at an airport, before taking a trip. The insurance is usually in effect for that one flight only. This is not a cost-effective measure. Statistically, it is not a good investment because the odds of a plane crash are very slight. Besides, some credit card companies are now providing flight insurance automatically when you buy your airline tickets with their cards. Still, you'd be surprised at how many people are dismayed when we advise them to give up this type of insurance. They seem to think that buying it prevents the plane from crashing.

Should I buy life or term insurance?

This question is likely to ignite a flame in any social gathering. Before we answer it, let's go over the characteristics of term and whole life insurance.

Term insurance is pure coverage for the risk of death. So as you get older, your mortality risk goes up, and so do your yearly term insurance premiums. By age 60 or 65, the cost of term insurance may be prohibitive. In contrast, whole life insurance payments are level over your entire life. In early years you pay more, as compared to term, but in late years you pay less.

The low initial cost of term insurance enables you to fully insure yourself at a young age when you are probably earning less. The cost of the policy cannot be increased over that projected without raising the rates for the whole class of policyholders. Since term insurance is simple to understand, it is easy to compare one company with another and, as a result, policy prices are highly competitive. Commissions for term insurance are much lower than those for whole life insurance, which can create more incentive for an agent to recommend whole life insurance; profits on whole life insurance policies are generally larger as well.

Whole life insurance is often sold as an investment product. A portion of the payment made on whole life insurance is put in a separate account called a reserve account and earns a rate of return. Over time it builds up a cash value which will be returned to you if you decide to cancel the policy. Depending on the amount you pay into the policy and the yearly return on the reserve account, you might receive good dividends, which you can withdraw or use to buy additional insurance.

Whole life insurance provides a one-step method of combining insurance and savings. It is a form of forced savings, beneficial if you have trouble saving on your own. Because the cash value you build up is not taxed unless you withdraw it and withdrawals exceed premium payments, life insurance is considered by some to be a tax shelter. We don't like to categorize whole life insurance as an investment vehicle because the cash value built up through yearly investing is not paid out at death—only the face amount of insurance in force upon the insured's death goes to the beneficiary. Any loans of cash value are deducted from the death proceeds.

Life insurance policies come with a variety of features that make it difficult to compare the cost of one policy with another. Often the projections of returns on cash values are virtually useless, since they are too optimistic to be used as a guide.

Most insurance agents strongly prefer whole life over term insurance. They call term insurance "baby insurance" (or temporary insurance), suggesting that when you are all grown up and can afford it you will move up to whole life insurance. Many agents tell horror stories of the cost of term insurance at older ages. They neglect to mention that if you invest the difference between the cost of life and term insurance at a younger age, you won't need as much insurance later on.

In fact, if you follow the principles of this book and become financially self-sufficient, you may not need any life insurance at all.

Overall, term insurance can be the least expensive form of insurance for you. Whole life insurance will cost less for you if the money saved by purchasing term insurance would be invested only in relatively low-yield investments such as high-quality bonds with shorter maturities, money-market funds, or certificates of deposit. Even then, you would be better off with term insurance if you will give up your policy within the first 10 years. It takes about that long to achieve the normal rate of return on whole life policies.

You might think people wouldn't give up their policies within 10 years. However, for reasons such as spending the money on their current lifestyle or switching to a different policy, a significant percentage of policyholders terminate their policies within the first few years. Anyone who cancels a life insurance policy within the first 3 to 4 years will receive little or no money back. Your initial payments will go mainly to pay the sales agent's commission. And the profit difficulties that many insurance companies are having today are likely to result in lower yearly returns over the next several years.

To sum up, term insurance is the best buy financially. We give it our value-oriented money planning award in the insurance area. It enables you to compare policies very easily and gives you more flexibility to shift or to vary amounts of coverage. We recommend it over whole life insurance for the majority of our clients.

But we must say that whole life insurance is more popular. People like the level payment and not worrying about the increased cost of coverage at age 60 or 65, when term costs become prohibitive. Since comfort is an important factor in insurance decision making, perhaps we will give well-researched whole life insurance the runner-up award.

How do I select the best term insurance product?

Now that you have decided whether to choose term insurance or a whole life product, how do you determine which individual contract is the best? One overall factor that you must take into account is the financial health of the insurer. A guarantee is not really a guarantee if the insurer goes out of business. A company that is in financial difficulty may be forced to raise rates or reduce returns. That is why we view high quality as a requirement and have shifted in our practice from recommending companies with a minimum rating of A to recommending those with a minimum rating of AA.

Choosing a term insurance policy is fairly easy. The things to look for in the contract are a guaranteed renewable clause and provisions preventing its cancelation. A guaranteed renewable policy provides that as you age, your rates cannot be raised beyond those indicated in the contract without the rates being raised for the whole class of policyholders.

Noncancelable policies contain a provision that the insurance company has to continue to insure you until a certain age, normally 65 or 70, provided you pay the premiums as specified in the policy. Be careful that the guarantee is unqualified—not, for example, subject to your having a medical examination every few years in order to keep getting the company's lowest rate.

Robert bragged that he had the lowest cost term policy in existence. When we looked, we found out why. While his policy couldn't be canceled, Robert's rates could rise dramatically if he didn't pass a physical exam every five years. We recommended that he transfer to a new policy, but he continued to focus on the low rate. The next year we were notified that Robert had been ruled ineligible for the company's lowest rate because of his elevated cholesterol. His insurance rates doubled, but his situation could actually have been worse. He could have had a serious illness that rendered him uninsurable by any other carrier, and his rates could have soared astronomically; or, if he didn't have a noncancelable policy, he might have been dropped altogether.

Stay away from other features such as decreasing term insurance taken out to ensure the repayment of your mortgage over time. Such features hamper your ability to compare policies, and you end up paying more for the feature than it's worth. One exception is term insurance that is convertible into an attractive whole life policy—a particularly worthwhile feature if you bought term because you couldn't afford comparable whole life coverage and you would like to switch to whole life insurance later. If you seriously want to convert your policy to whole life, consider the characteristics in the next question.

Once you have investigated the details of the policy, you can make an "apples-to-apples" comparison based on price. Don't choose a policy because its cost for the first year or two is the lowest. Some companies reduce their rates in early years and charge much more than their competitors over the rest of the policy's life.

The precise way to measure cost is through the interest-adjusted net payment cost index. This figure discounts your payments over a long period, commonly 10 or 20 years, to the present day, which allows you to identify the lowest cost policy. You can and should request these figures from those companies from whom you are considering buying insurance.

If the policies don't differ much in their payment structure in the early years, you can get a rough estimate of relative costs just by adding up the first 10 or 20 years of payments for each and comparing them.

You can get quotes on term insurance from your local insurance agents. Be careful to impress on them your financial requirements and interest in the lowest rates possible. Many agents who can offer policies for several companies favor one or two because of their higher commissions, affiliations, or lighter paperwork. On the other hand, a good agent—one who is licensed and held to proper duty and care—will respond to your needs and put your interests first.

You may also want to investigate low-load insurance policies in which you deal directly with the company and save on agents' commissions. Some companies that offer low-load insurance are USAA Life (800-531-8000), Ameritas Life Insurance Company (800-255-9678), and Lincoln Benefit Life (800-525-9287). Be sure to assess their current financial condition.

You will find that life insurance from a savings bank is often reasonably priced. A company, fraternity, or other organization to which you belong may also be a good source of low-cost insurance. Finally, there are a number of nationwide organizations that will screen policies offered in your area for the lowest cost. Take into account the fact that some of these firms may not be impartial but in fact are looking for business themselves.

If you do your homework, you can often save a great deal of money. As we mentioned before, we have seen policies that provide the same amount of coverage with the only real difference being that one company charges double the other's price. By doing your own investigation and being open only to logical information, sometimes you will find that your preferred insurance agent can provide coverage with a less expensive policy.

How do I select the best type of whole life insurance product?

In this section we'll tell you which type of whole life insurance product to buy. The next question shows you how to choose individual policies.

Selecting a whole life insurance policy is much more complicated than choosing a term policy. First you have to choose your insurance company. There are two types of life insurance companies: mutual and stockholder. Most life insurance companies are mutual companies, owned by the policyholders. They pay dividends based on their profits. The dividends can be used to reduce your annual insurance payments, increase the cash-surrender value of your policy, or buy more insurance—or you can take the dividends in cash.

Stockholder-owned life insurance companies, on the other hand, may be participating or nonparticipating—that is, they may provide yearly dividends, or they may offer insurance coverage for a fixed annual fee that is not offset by dividends.

As you might suspect, the differences between the two kinds of companies are reflected in their rates. Mutual companies tend to have higher initial rates but if you include the payment of dividends, the rates may turn out to be lower. Stockholder-owned companies have an advantage: their fixed-fee policies offer guaranteed rates that aren't subject to the profits or losses of insurance company investments.

Next, you have to decide which type of policy is best for you. There are three basic types of whole life policies.

1. *Traditional whole life.* Traditional whole life provides a fixed amount of coverage for a fixed annual payment that can be reduced by dividends. Therein lies the problem. You have little control over the return you will receive. The insurance company assigns you a rate based on its own investment experience and other factors. When interest rates rise sharply, it is likely that your assigned returns will fall behind market rates.

2. *Universal life.* Universal life offers an alternative to the rigidities of ordinary life. Its rates, however, are usually closer to short-term money-market rates. Therefore, its rates are more likely than traditional whole life to reflect current returns. In addition, universal life has a great deal more flexibility in payment terms and in varying the amount of coverage outstanding.

The disadvantage with universal life is that with all this flexibility in payment, if you are not careful and ignore insurance company mailings, you can slip behind in required contributions and unintentionally lose coverage or even have your policy dropped over time.

3. *Variable life.* Variable life insurance offers more types of investments than universal life. You can select from mutual funds of stocks, bonds, and money-market instruments, and the returns are credited to you. In this way, you can get a rate of return before overhead charges are deducted that is equal to what you would get on the market; if you choose equities, your portfolio has the potential to grow rapidly.

The major disadvantage is that your investments can go down as well as up, and if you don't put in more money to offset your losses, your insurance coverage can decline. Some policies do guarantee minimum death benefits. A second disadvantage is that you can't choose who your money manager will be; if you are dissatisfied with your portfolio manager, the only thing you can do is transfer to another type of investment or to another life insurance product with another sales commission. Finally, if you invest through variable insurance companies, you have higher administrative costs deducted from your performance than if you invest with an efficiently managed independent fund company.

Why not take the policy with the lowest-cost, interest-adjusted net payment cost index? Because, unlike term insurance, the figure can be highly suspect. As we have pointed out, life insurance agents and sometimes insurance companies themselves base their estimates on returns that are highly favorable for comparative purposes but, in our opinion, are unlikely to be reached. If the agents could actually achieve the rates they dangle in front of a prospect, even independent investment managers might recommend life insurance over the funds they themselves handle.

Often, insurance companies project that the cash value of your policy will build up so quickly that after 10 years it will be fully paid up. They suggest that the dividends you earn on the cash value of the policy will be enough to cover future annual payments. This policy is officially called a "limited pay" policy, but the agent may give it special fairyland status by calling it a "vanishing premium" policy. Who wouldn't think it was great if their insurance premiums vanished? In reality, the policy's actual returns are often considerably less than you were told. Instead of vanishing in the time period indicated, it could take several years or longer to pay up the policy. The extra annual premiums can remain a nagging reminder of how you fell prey to exaggerations or unethical sales conduct.

In sum, variable life may sometimes have an advantage of higher returns that you can use to buy additional insurance. However, we don't like the higher costs, volatility, and your inability to choose the investment manager. We generally don't recommend variable life. Traditional whole life has a minimum guaranteed payout. We recommend the stockholder nonparticipating policy for you only if you are very conservative and worried about the future stability of the entire insurance industry. These policies are likely to cost you more money over the longer term. We prefer universal life policies for all others who, like us, would rather have their investment returns more likely to be influenced by independent performance measures instead of solely based on what the insurance company chooses to give you. This is even more important now when insurance companies may be more concerned with building up their own financial health than offering high returns to their policyholders.

How can I compare individual life insurance policies?

You may have trouble comparing different life insurance products because policies can vary greatly. Most companies offer special features such as a waiver of premiums if you become disabled, and double indemnity, which pays twice as much if you die accidentally. Some companies show the policies paid up in 10 years, others in 12 years, while still others show payments for the rest of your life. Some companies are more aggressive in projecting returns than others. To choose among them, think about which features are most important to you and use the following steps in your decision-making process:

1. Before you begin to compare policies, decide whether whole life, universal life, or variable life is best for you. The previous question can help. You will be in a better position to choose the best policy if you know which one you want before you look around.

2. Try to compare policies of the same type with the same features. Let us tell you how we decide which policy to buy. We ask the agents for various policies to calculate interest-adjusted cost indexes (the correct measure of performance—the cost to you after the company pays you interest) three ways. First, we have them run the

index based on their projected rate of return. (Be careful, though. This approach can reward those companies that exaggerate their projections.) Second, we have them drop the projections for the average company by 1 or 2 percent and then give us their calculated index. We call this our modified insurance company projections. We don't believe in projected rates that come out greatly above the rate of return on 10-year U.S. Treasury bonds. Third, we give each agent a rate of return and ask them to run the interest-adjusted net payment cost indexes on that basis. We use the same rate of 1 percent below the current rate on 5-year U.S. Treasury bonds or longer-term certificates of deposit for each policy. This approach disregards cloudy projections of investment returns and rewards those that run a tight ship. Unless we believe the individual company's projections to be realistic—in which case, we use the first approach—we then just take an average of the interest-adjusted net payment cost indexes under the second and third approaches. Using this average, we can clearly compare what we believe are more accurate representations of the true cost of various policies.

3. Compare quotations on agent proposals, using the methods outlined above, with those for low-load companies (see the question "How do I select the best term insurance product?" in this chapter) that deal directly with policyholders and for organizations with which you're affiliated. Your company's policy can often save you a significant amount of money because your company buys large amounts of insurance coverage and sometimes will pay part of the cost for employees. Low-load companies that do not charge commissions generally offer higher cash values earlier, which can benefit you greatly if you cancel your policy within the first 5 to 10 years.

4. It is a good idea to ask your insurance agent to provide you with the insurance companies' 10-year, historical, actual growth versus past projections of growth in dividends from A. M. Best, a company that analyzes the insurance industry in detail, to see how mutual companies have performed in the past. This will allow you to check on future promises versus past delivery.

Ted decided that he wanted universal life insurance. He had six proposals from six different insurance agents. He thought they all sounded good, and wondered how he should arrive at a decision. After discussing it with us, Ted narrowed his list to those companies with ratings of AA and above. He then got the agents who originally made proposals to send us their past dividend history and to calculate interest-adjusted net payment cost indexes for each policy: first, based on a rate that was 2 percent below their projected figures, and second, based on a uniform return for all companies of 7 percent. He made sure that each quotation was based on the same no-frills coverage.

After examining the results under both approaches, two policies came out as clearly best. Ted put 50 percent of his insurance money into each policy. This solved Ted's dilemma and had the further advantage of diversifying his insurance needs.

If you prefer a simpler approach, you have two choices. The first is to pick an insurance company with a very strong financial rating, a favorable record of dividend growth, and recent large inflows of cash from policyholders who are looking for quality insurers. That recent increase in cashflow should enable the insurance company to raise profits and provide a more secure level of dividends for participating policies.

There is considerable trust involved in choosing an insurance carrier. There is also little opportunity to leave your insurer if its investment performance is poor because you will be faced with surrender charges on the old policy and a new sales commission from your next insurer. If you are having trouble making a decision, your second choice is to reconsider the simpler alternative—a basic term insurance policy.

When should I change my life insurance policies?

The answer depends on the type of life insurance you have. For term insurance, since no cash value builds up, the quick reply is whenever you find a cheaper policy with the same terms. That is, of course, if the saving merits the extra paperwork and another physical examination. Another good time to change is when you believe the insurance company is in financial difficulty. Be sure to pass your physical examination before you cancel your old policy. Incidentally, it is not smart to shift from company to company simply to take advantage of the come-on rates for the first year or two. You may be denied coverage later by a company that sees the pattern of behavior or you could get sick and be forced to stay with a high-cost policy.

For whole life insurance, comparisons of a new policy with an old one are difficult because you have to add in the commission cost you will pay for the new policy. To compare, first be sure that the two policies are structured the same way and that the new policy has a reasonable projected investment return. Then take the difference in yearly payments between the two and compare that with their projected cash surrender values in 10 or 20 years.

Keep in mind that even if the new policy comes out better, you will be hurt significantly if you cash it in prematurely. We recommend that you use our rule of thumb: any whole life policy that you have had for more than four to five years will probably not be worth cashing in unless its issuer is in financial difficulty.

Is disability insurance necessary?

You'd be astonished at the number of people we see who have life insurance but no disability insurance, or only minimal disability insurance through their employer. Yet a disability policy could be far more important to them. In fact, a better name for this insurance is "living insurance," because it provides benefits to you when you are alive but unable to work. As one financial planner said, "It is the rose you can smell," meaning that this insurance is for you and not for your heirs—although it benefits your family too, relieving them of the financial burden if you are disabled.

How likely is it that you will be seriously disabled? More than one-third of all Americans suffer a disability that prevents them from working for at least 90 days. Disability payments through social security can provide some help, but it's difficult to meet its qualifications. A large number of businesses provide disability coverage, but when you examine the policies closely you can see that in many cases this is for only a limited time and may be terminated if you qualify to do any kind of work whatsoever—as would social security.

Warren, a middle manager with a major corporation, felt certain that his disability needs had been met by his company's group insurance coverage. We examined his policy and found that if he were disabled and could no longer function as an executive but was well enough to do a simpler job, such as answer phones or work in the mailroom, he would not be eligible for insurance payments. We advised Warren to take out a personal disability policy that would cover him if he could no longer perform his own occupation. If you are earning a good income because you have developed an important specialty, unless you are willing to downgrade your career and income considerably, we advise you to look for a policy with "own occupation" as the criterion for receiving disability payments.

How much disability coverage should you have? That depends on the same factors given earlier for life insurance. See Schedule B-3 in Appendix B to determine your disability needs. If you are in the middle-income category, 60 to 70 percent of your current salary is an appropriate amount of disability coverage. Anyway, that might be the most you can get. If you are the one who pays the premiums, the disability cash you receive is nontaxable, so you don't need 100 percent income replacement to receive the same after-tax cashflow that you earn at present.

When we perform a disability analysis, we look at projected needs over a number of years, not just the current year. Needs change over time. If you are young and your income is rising, look for policies that allow you to buy more insurance—without a medical exam—as your income goes up. If you are middle-aged, saving regularly, and already have some disability insurance, you may not need additional coverage because the growth of your assets may take care of inflationary increases in your cost of living. If you are at, or are nearing, financial independence because you have accumulated a large amount of assets, you may need little or no disability insurance at all.

Disability policies have improved significantly over the years and are now an integral part of risk management programs. We recommend them for many of our clients, and we believe that if you can afford it, you should consider this type of insurance too.

What should I look for in selecting a disability policy?

Disability policies are highly complex contracts in which the way the company phrases a sentence can decide whether or not you will receive thousands of dollars in benefits. The situation can be aggravated if the information the sales agent gives you is not accurate.

We were searching for the best disability policy for one client and wading through the mysterious language in the contracts. Each insurance company provided a computerized printout comparing its contract with others in the field. Naturally, each emphasized the benefits of its own policy. In the process of getting information on key differences, we called each company's sales representative. In many instances, the answers to our questions conflicted.

We decided to invite representatives of the best companies to come in to our offices at the same time to present a clear picture of the essential differences among their policies. Each sales agent arrived with an expert from his or her firm. We were worried that our meeting would turn into a shouting match. Instead, each firm's arguments were quietly ruled on by the other members of our panel of experts. By the end of the afternoon, believe it or not, all panelists agreed on which company had the best disability policy! In fact, the others mentioned that their companies planned to meet the benefits provided by the winner.

Here are the requirements of a good policy:

1. It provides for long-term disability, with payments to the insured through age 65 or 70.
2. It is guaranteed renewable and noncancelable, meaning payments remain level throughout the contract's life and the insurance company must continue the policy until a specified time (usually age 65).
3. It provides residual benefits; partial payments continue when you go back to work part-time or if, as a businessperson, you are suffering a partial loss of income.
4. There is an inflation rider. After you are disabled, payments go up by some inflation benchmark rate. Otherwise, the purchasing power value of your payments will go down over time.
5. It provides for guaranteed insurability. You can buy additional coverage over time without passing another medical exam. Make sure that you can buy additional coverage at least every other year. This can prevent your coverage from decreasing in inflation-adjusted terms before you are disabled.
6. It contains an "own occupation" clause that ensures payments will be made if your disability prevents you from continuing in your

own occupation. Beware of policies that will not pay if you can do any work whatsoever.

Choose the three or four companies that offer policies with these features, meet the financial safety criteria we mentioned in the question "How can I judge how safe my insurance company is?" in this chapter, and are thought to be major in the disability field by size and reputation. The leading companies are more likely to introduce improvements in their new contracts and, believe it or not, sometimes provide them to existing clients at no extra charge.

Compare the policies' costs, using the same factors for all companies. Stay away from additional features that only cloud the issue and give you the headache we had when we tried to evaluate them before the disability summit in our office.

Judge these private policies against group insurance coverage available through your employer or other organizations you belong to. The latter may be cheaper, but make sure they have the essential features we just listed. See if you can transfer them if you leave the company or organization. Consider getting a policy that supplements your company policy and provides portability should you change jobs.

Consistent with our feelings about large deductibles—we're for them, remember?—we recommend at least a 90-day waiting period before disability payments start. The company you work for may continue to pay your salary during this period; but even if it doesn't and you have to dip into savings to cover your expenses, unless you are hard pressed for cash it is well worth the savings you'll reap from buying a lower-priced policy.

The right policy represents a blending of benefits and costs. Because of the technicalities involved in a contract, we tend to emphasize higher-quality companies unless the cost differences are particularly great. Luckily, even leading companies often have significant differences in costs.

Is the health insurance provided by my job enough?

The answer depends on the quality and extent of the coverage. Some employers provide very liberal coverage and even extend care to employees' families; others expect employees to share in the costs.

The cost of medical insurance has risen astronomically in the past few years. One of our clients actually turned down a job because the new company had an inferior medical policy that could have cost her and her family thousands more in insurance expenses.

The only way to determine if your company policy provides enough coverage is to examine it carefully and compare it with other policies that are available to you. Look at the following provisions:

1. *Deductible.* Are you expected to pay the first few hundred dollars of medical bills before your coverage begins? We often recommend policies with large deductibles if you can afford it, because they are less expensive to you in the long run. In fact, our figures indicate that you may often be better off financially taking a policy with thousands of dollars in yearly deductibles and using the policy only for serious and costly illnesses.
2. *Hospital coverage.* What does your policy cover in the event of a hospital stay? How much of the room is paid for? Are expenses such as tests, drugs, X rays, laboratories, and operating room covered?
3. *Surgical services.* Are these provisions the same as those for a hospital stay? Are the surgeon's fees paid by the insurer? Is elective surgery covered in whole or in part? What is your policy's definition of "elective surgery"?
4. *Long-term illness.* What is the benefit limit for a serious accident or a long-term illness?
5. *Doctors.* Are you expected to go to a doctor from a list that your company gives you or to a particular clinic, or can you see the doctor of your choice? Are all visits to the doctor covered?
6. *Family.* Is your family provided for? If not, can you supplement your coverage for a small fee and include your family on your policy? Does your family need coverage, or are they covered under another policy, perhaps one your spouse has?
7. *Maternity.* What hospital charges and doctors' fees are covered for a maternity stay?
8. *Mental health services.* Are visits to a psychiatrist, a psychologist, or another mental-health-care professional covered, at least in part?

9. *Dental insurance.* Are dental fees covered? Many medical policies do not deal with dental surgery or regular dental care, but sometimes for a small monthly charge you can arrange for such coverage.
10. *Contributions.* Are you expected to contribute to the cost of the policy? If so, how much? How does that charge compare with the cost of a policy you can get on your own or through an organization you belong to?

If you haven't reached middle age and are in good health, this is one case in which a medical policy provided by a large employer or through a professional or fraternal organization may not cost less than one you can arrange on your own. That is because these group policies have to accept those people who have high medical costs because of poor health. In addition, in some instances the policies have been formulated to have the young overpay in order to keep annual medical insurance costs for older people down. We recently reviewed a client's policy from his professional association. We found that at his age (34) he could do better with an independent policy for which he would pay thousands less per year.

If you find that your company's health insurance is not enough, you may want to broaden your coverage by adding a major medical policy that will give you extra protection in the areas of doctors' fees, surgical costs, hospital stays, prescribed drugs, and nursing care related to an illness. We recommend having at least $1 million of coverage per person over his or her lifetime and, given inflationary increases in medical costs, we prefer policies that have unlimited lifetime coverage where available. Remember, one long-term or serious illness can be very costly. Make sure you and your family are adequately protected.

What do I have to know about home insurance?

There are two kinds of protection you should be concerned about for your home: liability coverage, which will protect you if someone suffers an injury in your home or on your property, and property coverage, which will insure against loss or damage to your real property (your home) or your personal property (usually the contents of your home). Homeowners' insurance can protect you against both kinds of loss.

Basic liability coverage (which protects you both inside and outside your home) on a homeowner's policy is $100,000. You may want to consider extending this coverage further. For a little higher cost, you can get triple the basic coverage or more and protect yourself against injuries to your guests. Remember, most accidents occur in the home, and if the home is yours, you may regret saving a little now and not having adequate protection when you need it.

In many instances, it is enough to insure your house against loss for 80 percent of its replacement value. However, if your house burns to the ground, you will need 100 percent replacement cost to avoid suffering a financial loss. If you want total coverage, make sure your policy covers the foundation of the house and the land. Guaranteed replacement value is not the cost at the time you purchased it, nor the resale value of the house today, but the amount it would take to replace the house if it were destroyed by fire.

There are many different types of homeowners' policies available. The basic homeowner's policy, HO-1, protects you against fire, lightning, vandalism, theft, glass breakage, explosions, and malicious mischief. The "broad form" policy (HO-2) protects you against those basic hazards, as well as frozen pipes, faulty electrical wiring, and building collapse. The "all risks" policy (HO-3) covers all risks on real property except those that are particularly excluded, such as flood, earthquake, or war. The HO-5 policy similarly covers you in the event of all risks both on real and personal property except those particularly excluded. Also, the HO-7 policy covers all risks except those excluded and the replacement costs of both real and personal property. Finally, if you have home insurance and still feel insecure, consider taking out a personal umbrella liability policy that will give you excess personal and automobile coverage of at least $1 million above the basic policies.

If you are a renter and want tenant's liability and personal property coverage that will also include improvements you have made, ask for an HO-4 policy. If you own a cooperative apartment or condominium and worry that you might be charged a share of the damage to common property, check with your building to see if you are assessable; then, if applicable, ask for special policies that cover that situation.

To decide how much insurance you need, start by taking inventory of personal items in your house, including furniture, electrical appliances, clothing, and other personal property. List the cost and replacement value for each item, total it up, and add a small amount for miscellaneous items. If possible, attach your receipts from the purchase of the articles, so you will have them handy in case you do make a claim.

Many policies replace only the depreciated property. For example, the insurer may decide that a recently stolen stereo system which cost $1000 five years ago was only worth $500 when it was taken, figuring 10 percent yearly depreciation over a five-year period. In that case, they would only award you $500 even though it might cost $1250 to replace it. If you find that you have unusually expensive amounts of personal property in your home, and you would like to be able to replace your possessions without personal financial strain, make sure your policy allows for more than the standard replacement value after depreciation. You can buy a policy that offers full replacement coverage for an extra cost. Replacing an appliance today will often cost more than buying the original some years ago. Furthermore, many people decide to upgrade their appliances when they are forced to replace them. Don't expect your insurer to assume these extra costs unless you have an inflation endorsement that increases the real value of your policy.

Any valuable collections that are not likely to be included in standard homeowners' insurance policies should be separately insured. You can get these items appraised and list them in a personal property floater (an attachment to your standard homeowner's policy). Consider insuring art, stamp, or coin collections, jewelry, rare books, furs, silverware, and antiques. Be prepared to supply cost figures, current value, and a complete description of each item. In addition to the original receipts, it is a good idea to keep photographs or a videotape of these objects in your own files. Some high-end insurance companies will come to your house and help you set up a record of your belongings. Keep a set of these records in a safe place outside your home, such as a safe-deposit box, so that if there is a fire or other damage, your list will be intact. If you want to avoid conflict with your insurer as to how much they will pay you in the event of a loss, ask about insuring your valuable items for a fixed amount.

Shop around, and compare costs on policies. Check on the financial soundness of the insurer, find out from your state insurance commissioner's office about the company's record in satisfying policyholders' claims, and make sure you understand the terms of the policy before you buy the insurance.

How do I select an automobile policy?

To some extent your policy may be determined for you, depending on who owns your car. If the car is registered to a business, even if you are the owner of that business, you will not be eligible for a personal automobile policy, but you may be eligible for personal policy rates. For most people, though, the personal automobile policy will provide the most appropriate protection for themselves and any family member when driving their own or any other car.

Although the provisions of an automobile policy do not vary, costs may differ from one company to another. Once you have decided on the amount of coverage you need, comparison shop to keep your costs down. You can save from 30 to 50 percent on insurance costs by comparing costs on the same amounts of coverage.

Costs are typically based on the following factors: age of the operators of the vehicle, driving records of the operators of the vehicle, place where the car is kept, and the frequency and purpose of the car's use. Your home state, your driving record (which indicates how likely you are to have an accident), and even your sex all play a role in your automobile insurance costs. Automobile insurance is more expensive for young drivers, and especially young male drivers, because statistically they have more accidents than older drivers. We recently heard of one company that won't insure young, single women because it has had bad experiences with women who let their boyfriends drive (and supposedly damage) their cars.

One family we know had their teenaged daughter Heather insured under their policy. When Heather lent her new sports car to a friend who didn't have a driver's license, he drove the car into a ditch. Heather's family chose to pay the $600 it cost to repair the car themselves rather than to report what had happened to their insurance company, even though according to their policy they were supposed to report all accidents. They feared that Heather's poor judgment and her friend's poor driving skills would have led to a great increase in their insurance rates. Heather's friend is still working at a restaurant after school to repay the $600.

Other factors that affect the cost of your premiums are the age and the value of your car. As your car ages and its value decreases, your premiums should cost less, but because of offsetting annual increases you will rarely see a decrease in your payments.

One way to decrease the cost of your automobile insurance is to accept higher deductibles. We also suggest thinking about eliminating collision insurance when your car ages. Ask yourself whether the car would be worth repairing. Compare the collision insurance expense against the cost and likelihood of an accident. You may decide to leave this provision out of your automobile insurance policy. However, note that if you drop your collision coverage, you will have a rise in your costs for fire, theft, and vandalism coverage so that you will save some, but not all, of the costs for collision insurance.

What should my automobile insurance policy include?

Considering the possibilities for damage to your car and other vehicles, and for personal injury, reasonable amounts of automobile insurance are essential. Although automobile insurance is mandatory in most states today, not all drivers have it, and amounts of coverage vary according to the policy.

Make sure that your policy provides insurance for the following areas:

1. *Liability.* You should be covered for physical injuries to others and expenses arising out of such injuries, such as compensation for absence from work. Your policy should also protect you from costs for damage to another's property.
2. *Medical.* You need protection from medical costs for injuries incurred by occupants of your vehicle, including you.
3. *Uninsured or underinsured motorist.* If you are in an accident with a vehicle whose owner has no or insufficient insurance, your policy should assume the expenses involved.

4. *Comprehensive and collision.* Your policy should pay for collision and other damages to your car, such as fire and theft. There frequently is a deductible that you pay before your insurance company assumes the cost for the rest of the damage.

Automobile policies are written to express the total amounts of bodily injury, liability, and property damage coverage. A policy of $25/$50/$20 indicates that you have $25,000 coverage for an individual injured in a single accident, $50,000 for all persons injured in that accident, and coverage for property damage of $20,000 for one accident. Each state has its own minimum requirements for the coverage you need. In most instances your coverage should be well in excess of this minimum.

How much protection you choose should depend on several factors, including your state's requirements, the replacement cost of your car, and medical coverage you already have under other policies (the more medical insurance you have, the less you might need through your automobile insurance).

If you are willing to attend annual safe driving classes, some companies will reduce your costs. Look around. Include in your analysis well-established insurers that do business through the mail. Doing so can "drive" your automobile insurance costs down.

6 College Financing

Maybe you've never thought of a college education as a financial investment, but it is a very important one. Although we have all heard of people who are successful without a college degree, statistics show that on the average, lifetime earnings for college graduates are hundreds of thousands of dollars higher than for high school graduates. Education can help your children achieve the American dream—whether it is to maintain or improve on the lifestyle of their parents or to become financially independent at a relatively young age.

Like all investments, a college education involves costs. After four years of sacrificing their job-related income and spending your money on tuition and other expenses, your children can receive a very attractive return not only in current and future dollars but in self-esteem as well.

If your children have not yet started college, you probably are concerned about educating them and wondering how you will be able to afford it. We tell our clients not to despair. We believe that it is possible for a student from any financial background to attend most colleges in this country regardless of cost, provided that he or she meets the admission criteria.

How? We will explain.

How much will my children's college education cost?

The cost of a college education will vary with the type of school your child attends. The average private college in 1992 cost about $13,000 a year for tuition, fees, and room and board, while the average public university cost less than half that at about $6000 a year. Including books and personal expenses, some private colleges cost over $25,000 a year today. A public university that is close enough for your child to live at home can cost less than $10,000 a year.

Notice that we said *today*. College costs have been climbing faster than inflation. Over the 1982–1991 period, private college costs increased at an average rate of 7.6 percent per year, public colleges increased 6.4 percent per year, while consumer prices overall increased only 3.6 percent per year. In Table 6-1 we show the average cost to attend college and how it has increased over time.

The largest factors in rising college costs are faculty and support-staff salaries, and we assume that in the future college employees will continue to want salary and benefit increases that exceed the infla-

Table 6-1. Total College Costs*

	Private four-year college	Public four-year college
Academic year ending:		
1982	$ 5,947	$2,704
1983	6,646	3,032
1984	7,244	3,285
1985	7,849	3,518
1986	8,551	3,637
1987	9,276	3,891
1988	9,854	4,250
1989	10,620	4,525
1990	11,423	4,757
1991	12,320	5,013
Ten-year growth rate	7.6%	6.4%
Inflation rate	3.6%	3.6%

*Figures include tuition, fees, and room and board. Inflation rates based on academic (not calendar) years.

SOURCE: The College Board

tion rate, although they may not get them. In addition, many schools are having financial problems because of a decline in enrollments, which are not projected to rise again for several more years. Finally, the U.S. government and many states concerned about balancing budgets and holding down tax increases will continue to decrease their support for public and private colleges. That's why the bad news is that costs directly related to college are likely to continue to grow at an above-average rate.

The good news (and this is as good as it gets) is that the rate of increase may be moderately less than before—say, 2 percent above inflation. While in the past public college expenses rose at a slower pace than private college expenses, future increases may be more in line with those of private colleges and universities because of current state fiscal difficulties.

When should I start saving for my children's education?

Greg and Clarisse set aside money to pay for educating their three children. Two of the children would attend college for seven years and earn law degrees, and the third would go for eight years and earn a medical degree. Greg and Clarisse conceived this detailed plan despite the fact that their children hadn't been born yet!

There is no magic date when you should begin saving for your children's education. The sooner you begin, however, the lower the effect your savings will have on your yearly cashflow. The amounts you need to save depend on when you start saving. For example, imagine saving $1000 each year beginning when your child is born. To achieve the same results you would have to save about $3000 each year if you begin to save eight years before your child begins college, or over $7000 per year—seven times as much—if you begin to save when your child enters high school.

Where your savings will be invested will affect the rate of return on your money. Be sure to deduct income taxes when you estimate your investment return. Table 6-2 and Schedule B-4, "College Planning Needs," in Appendix B will enable you to calculate your own needs.

Table 6-2. Beginning Annual Savings Required to Fund College Income

Number of years until college begins	Annual costs today			
	$5,000	$10,000	$15,000	$25,000
18	1,356	2,711	4,067	6,778
17	1,411	2,822	4,233	7,055
16	1,473	2,947	4,420	7,367
15	1,544	3,087	4,631	7,718
14	1,624	3,247	4,871	8,118
13	1,715	3,431	5,146	8,577
12	1,822	3,643	5,465	9,108
11	1,946	3,892	5,838	9,729
10	2,093	4,186	6,280	10,466
9	2,270	4,541	6,811	11,352
8	2,487	4,975	7,462	12,437
7	2,759	5,518	8,278	13,796
6	3,109	6,219	9,328	15,547
5	3,577	7,154	10,731	17,884
4	4,232	8,464	12,697	21,161
3	5,216	10,432	15,649	26,081
2	6,858	13,715	20,573	34,288
1	10,142	20,284	30,427	50,711
0	20,000	40,000	60,000	100,000

Note: Select the *one* beginning figure that applies to your situation. Thereafter, increase your savings by 5 percent annually.

Note that the table assumes a 5 percent increase in the amount put away each year. This allows you to start saving a lesser amount than you would if you use a flat annual contribution; at the same time, the contribution need only increase a modest 5 percent annually, which may be about in line with your yearly growth in income.

The figures in Table 6-2 represent a starting sum for savings which will increase annually by an assumed 5 percent rate of inflation. By building in a modest 5 percent increase in the amount saved each year instead of a level sum, you can start with a smaller amount and have your savings build as your income grows.

While it would be nice to think that most people start saving for college when their children are young, the only money saved often seems to be gifts from Grandma and Grandpa. We strongly recommend a systematic savings program that begins at least eight years before your first child goes off to college.

What if my child is in high school and I have no savings?

You don't have to feel guilty if you haven't saved and your child is well into high school. Many families don't think about funding educational costs until two or three years before college; some do not begin to save until the college bills come due.

What can you do about it now? You may decide to begin a crash program in savings when high school begins. However, unless your family has an income high enough to meet college tuition and expenses as well as your usual monthly expenses, your last-minute effort is likely to fall short. Another alternative is to take an additional part-time or full-time job to raise money, but keep in mind that it can reduce or eliminate the amount of student aid for which you would otherwise qualify. Your last option might be to borrow part or all of the money, either through student loans (see the question "What kinds of college aid are available?" in this chapter) or from some other source.

If you decide to assume the tuition obligation yourself—rather than giving your child the obligation of paying back student loans—the best source of funds is often a home equity loan. You can get a tax deduction for the first $100,000 in excess of your current mortgage and can repay the loan over a longer period of time than student loans.

If a home equity loan is not available to you, consider personal loans, sales of assets, or borrowing or making withdrawals from your 401(k) plan. None of these options has a tax deduction feature. Compared to these alternatives, we prefer student loans, which at least have a subsidized interest rate.

What kinds of college aid are available?

Aid comes in three forms: grants, work-study, and loans. Grants are preferable, because they are a gift to your child. They do not have to be repaid. Grants are given by the federal government, state governments, colleges, alumni, and organizations to help meet the student's "need" as defined by various criteria or to honor students with certain talents, and by groups that want to promote education for particular classes of students. Recently, some inner-city schools have had "angels"—in the form of successful businesspeople—adopt whole classes of students and offer to pay college tuition for those who stay in school.

Work-study is a federally funded program that is based on your family's need. The college determines which students are eligible for this form of aid. Your child works several hours a week, for example in the college library, dining hall, or offices, and is paid in part (70 percent) by the federal government and in part (30 percent) by the employer. Federally funded work-study income will not affect your child's federally determined need.

If your child is not fortunate enough to receive a grant but you need financial aid, you can look into various borrowing alternatives. One of the most common ways to borrow money for college is through Stafford loans (formerly known as guaranteed student loans). The federal government regulates the program, subsidizes the interest on these loans, and guarantees that the loans will be repaid. State and private nonprofit guarantee agencies insure the loans and are reimbursed by the federal government for the insurance claims they pay the lenders. Local lenders provide the principal loan funds and administer the loans. The college determines and certifies the student's eligibility for the loan based on criteria established by the federal government, the guarantee agency, and, in some cases, the college itself.

The loans sometimes have a rate lower than market interest. However, the interest you pay is not deductible. Payments begin six months after graduation (or when the student drops below half-time enrollment) unless your child attends graduate school, and he or she is expected to be all paid up 5 to 10 years after graduation.

The student is legally obligated to repay the loans. In the past, it was not uncommon for people to think of the loans as a kind of governmental gift. They repaid their loans when and if they wanted to. But recently the government has gotten tougher. Stephanie was surprised when her company began to deduct 10 percent of her salary a month for outstanding college loans. The payroll officer told her that the company had received a court order to send this part of her salary to a U.S. marshall each payroll period because Stephanie had defaulted on her loans. We spoke to Stephanie's company, an attorney, and the marshall, but there was no way she could avoid these deductions.

Under certain circumstances some government loans can be deferred, and Perkins loans—federal low-interest-rate loans—can be reduced or may not have to be repaid at all. For instance, if your child is willing to donate several years of his or her time to helping others, he or she can have the Perkins loan reduced or even forgiven by joining the Peace Corps, VISTA, or the Public Health Service; becoming a teacher in a low-income school; or enlisting in the armed forces.

There are many types of loans and grants that you can look into:

- Pell grants are a type of federal aid. These grants are based on need as assessed by standardized measures. You can read more about this in the next question.
- Perkins loans are low-interest-rate loans provided by the federal government and administered by the college. Your college will let you know if your family's income is low enough to quality for this loan. Perkins loans are available only to low-income families.
- As we've pointed out, Stafford loans, also based on financial need, are low-interest-rate loans given by banks, savings and loans, credit unions, and other agencies. The federal government picks up the interest on these loans while your child is in college. He or she can borrow up to $17,250 as an undergraduate student. After graduating or leaving school, your child begins to repay the loan.
- Parent loans to undergraduate students (PLUS) and supplemental loans for students (SLS) are federally regulated and guaranteed loans made by local lending institutions to families who don't qualify for other loans. Parents of dependent students can borrow up to $4000 per year from the PLUS loan, or a maximum of $20,000 per student; independent students can borrow up to $4000 per year with a maximum of $20,000 from the SLS loan. Repayment is expected to begin within 60 days of getting the loan, but this can be deferred while the student is enrolled full-time. A review of the borrower's credit history may be required. Ask your college aid office where you can get one of these, or call 800-333-4636.
- For further information about whether your child qualifies for federal government aid, call 800-4-FED AID; to find out the status of your child's application, call 301-722-9200.
- Check with your state education department to see what aid your state supplies. Some states base their aid solely on need, while oth-

ers have an achievement requirement. Most states help only state residents who enroll in a college in that state.

- Ask your employer about aid programs. Many employers subsidize job-related education and training for their employees; some also extend at least partial benefits to their employees' families.
- Private scholarships are available for students in various categories, such as those who have certain talents, or belong to various ethnic groups. It is mainly left up to you to discover and apply for suitable scholarships. For sources of grants, see "Further Reading."
- Colleges and universities themselves provide financial aid in the forms of athletic and academic scholarships, need-based grants, loans, and work-study programs. College aid packages usually incorporate work-study assistance—that is, the student is paid for doing some work on campus, for example in the library or cafeteria. The student is expected to contribute a stated amount of the fees from his or her earnings. Many jobs on campus are made available only to students on assistance. The financial aid office of each college can give you specific information about its programs.
- Military scholarships are offered without regard to financial need. In exchange for duty in the Reserves or the National Guard, or for enlistment in the service, you can receive help with college costs. The type of aid ranges from reduced fees at state universities, enrollment at the noted military academies, or ROTC scholarships that cover 80 percent of tuition, books, fees, and a $100 monthly allowance. For scholarship information apply to the branch of the service that interests you.

Consider how much of the financial burden you will assume, and how much your child will accept. This will depend on your particular circumstances and attitudes. One family asked us to arbitrate their difficulties. The son, Paul, wanted to go to an expensive private school out of town. Paul's parents had undergone some financial reverses, had no savings, and did not qualify for meaningful financial aid. The parents were well into their fifties and were late in planning for retirement. They were concerned about mortgaging their future with loans. Instead, they wanted Paul to apply for student loans. Paul calculated the debt he would assume after graduation and was shocked by the amounts that he would have to repay.

Both Paul and his parents felt guilty about bringing these points up and did not want the college payment issue to affect their relationship. We recommended using an objective source to obtain an appropriate parental contribution. They looked up that figure in the College Scholarship Service's "Meeting College Costs" (which they found in their high school guidance counselor's office), and came up with an amount based on their assets, income, and family size.

Paul's mother decided to go back to work full-time even though that resulted in eligibility for less aid; she made enough "extra" to cover the parents' college contribution and had some left over to make retirement contributions as well. Paul attended the college of his choice and contributed by working part-time and summers. He is now living at home, working, and repaying his debt quickly.

How do I know if my family qualifies for financial aid?

To determine how much aid, if any, a family should receive, colleges throughout the country use the "congressional methodology"—that is, Congress has mandated that they apply the same standards of need to determine most federal aid awards. Most colleges use this methodology to award their own funds. The two main firms that administer this evaluation process are the same ones that do the college entrance exams—The College Board's College Scholarship Service, which is responsible for the Scholastic Aptitude Test (SAT), at P.O. Box 6344, Princeton, NJ 08541, telephone 800-772-3537; and the American College Testing Program (ACT) Student Need Analysis Service at Box 1002, 2255 North Dubucque Road, Iowa City, Iowa 52243, (319) 337-1000.

The services use identical criteria that meet federal government guidelines for deriving the family contribution, and each charges a fee for its analysis. The student should complete the forms required by the schools he or she is interested in attending. The College Scholarship Service uses the Financial Aid Form (FAF). The American College Testing Program's form is the Family Financial Statement (FFS). Note that most colleges also ask for your family's income tax returns, including any filed by your child. When determining aid, colleges use the previous year's tax return. For example, if you apply for aid for 1992–1993, your 1991 tax return will be closely scrutinized.

The size of the aid package is based on your income, family size, certain expenses such as how many family members are attending college, and your assets. The assets and income figures for parents and dependent children are treated separately and differently.

How much will our family be expected to contribute to college costs?

Even if you do receive some form of financial aid, you will probably have to cover a portion of the costs yourself. How much will depend on your income, certain expenses, and net assets after liabilities. The aid your child will receive is reduced by a maximum of 12 percent of your defined assets depending on your age and marital status, and 35 percent of the dependent child's assets. For example, $10,000 in a college-aged dependent child's account will reduce aid by $3500 annually. In addition, your child's aid will be reduced by your income earned. Your adjusted gross income, taxable income before other deductions, and exemptions lowers your child's aid package by a minimum of 22 percent of its amount.

Your child's income reduces aid by a whopping 70 percent of the amount your child earns after taxes. The federal government assumes that your child will work during summer vacations and will be able to contribute at least $700 toward his or her first year of college, and at least $900 every year thereafter, whether the student actually works or not.

You can send for the forms your child needs to apply for aid by writing to The College Board's College Scholarship Service or the American College Testing Program Service; or get them from the financial aid office at the college your child is applying to or from his or her high school guidance counselor.

A point to remember is that your child must reapply for aid, and his or her needs will be reevaluated each year. If you don't feel you got enough aid in any one year, you can request more the next time. You may receive it if you can provide evidence that your need has increased. On the other hand, if your income has increased, you are likely to be offered less.

How can my child receive the maximum college aid package?

The methods listed in this section should help you increase your aid packages. Warning: A massive shift of assets just to gain more aid dollars is regarded unfavorably by aid agencies and colleges. Some of the strategies listed here can skirt the intent of the system, which is to distribute scarce aid dollars fairly. But we'll list them and leave it up to you to decide if you are comfortable with them.

1. *Minimize children's assets.* Assets held in children's names are assessed at a steep 35 percent. Those same assets in parent's names would be assessed at a maximum 12 percent. Therefore, keep assets in your own names; transfer gifts made to your children to your own accounts when possible.

2. *Reduce assessable assets.* Cash and marketable stocks are included as assessable items, while personal possessions that aren't investment-related—such as a car, television, or furniture—are not. By buying such things for cash earlier than you might have otherwise, you are reducing assessable assets.

When you calculate the fair market value of major assessable assets, keep in mind that housing prices are currently depressed in many sectors of the market. It isn't in your best interest to overvalue your home when you apply for college aid. But you should know that the aid system checks when the current value of a home doesn't exceed its cost plus a 3 percent compounded annual growth factor and a housing index multiplier available from the U.S. Department of Commerce, Bureau of Economic Analysis. In view of the weakness in real estate in many markets in the United States, many colleges are just using the 3 percent cumulative growth factor.

The uniform aid forms don't ask for information about pension plan investments, insurance policies, or tax-deferred annuities, but some individual colleges want to know about these assets; they adjust their aid packages accordingly.

3. *Increase liabilities that offset your assets.* A mortgage or a home equity loan is an assessable liability because it reduces the realizable value of your home. Any other outstanding debt that doesn't pertain to business or investments doesn't count in the appraisal. By replacing your personal credit line, automobile loan, or credit card debt

with a home equity loan you will not only reduce your after-tax interest expense, you will also reduce your net appraisable assets.

4. *Swap taxable bonds for municipal bonds or tax-deferred annuities.* Interest from municipal bonds in the state you live in is tax-free, and deferred annuities are tax-deferred. Both can serve to reduce your reported income for aid purposes when you have a significant amount of taxable interest income. Remember, though, tax-deferred annuities are not easy to access until you reach age 59½.

5. *Sell investments you are losing money on.* The first $3000 of long-term losses will reduce your current income, and the rest will be deferred for future years. Each will reduce your expected contribution over the normal four-year college period.

6. *Prepay insurance policies.* By paying more for your insurance policy than is currently due, you can prepay future years and add to its cash value. The effect can be to reduce your assessable assets. As we've said earlier, some colleges do ask about this asset.

7. *Use a 401(k) or other pension plan.* If you will be age 59½ when your child attends college, you will have access to this money without penalty. You are not denied aid because of money in your pension account. By saving money here for at least 8 to 10 years, you may get an extra deduction that can even merit a 10 percent early withdrawal penalty. On the other hand, be aware that taking money from a pension type account can jeopardize your savings for retirement needs.

8. *Apply for federal and state aid and scholarships.* The principal vehicles for federal aid are Pell grants. However, your need has to be determined by a formula to qualify, and the total amount granted for 1992 will not exceed $2400 per year. State aid varies considerably; in many states it is being cut back. Non-income-related scholarships are available and are awarded on the basis of high academic ability, major area of study, parents, business or fraternal organizations, minority aid, or other reasons.

9. *Become an independent student.* You are automatically considered independent if you are at least 24 years old by December 31 of the year you seek aid, are a veteran of the armed forces, have no living parents or are a ward of the court, or if you have legal dependents other than a spouse. Also, students who have set up their own households, had resources of at least $4000 for two previous years

(including income, student aid, personal educational loans, gifts, and support received from sources other than parents), and have not been taken as an exemption on their parents' last two tax returns are considered independent. Furthermore, married, graduate, or professional students who are not claimed as exemptions on their parents' current returns are independent students too.

Usually independent students' aid packages are based on their and any spouse's assets and income without regard to their parents' finances, although some colleges may require parental information if the student's income is very low or if the student resides with relatives. Consequently, their aid package can be the largest of all, even though most of it may be in the form of loans. On the other hand, students who are independent and earn enough to support themselves may find that they no longer qualify for aid.

10. *List special needs.* Don't forget to include special hardship situations on your child's statement of financial need. Detailing your particular problems won't hurt and may even get your case personal attention.

11. *Get to know the college financial aid officers.* Financial aid officers have considerable discretion in deciding how much aid your child will receive and in what form—outright grants, work, loans or, more often, a mixture of the three. They can take special circumstances not covered in the standardized form into account.

College financial aid officers can also decide to match aid packages given to your child by other colleges. Engaging in a little friendly competition if handled properly can raise your child's aid at the college of your choice. Erica, a single mother whose daughter had good but not outstanding grades and SAT scores, was able to raise her daughter's outright aid package by over $5000 a year by explaining her fluctuating income as a commissioned salesperson and by initiating a well-handled bidding contest between two universities that had both accepted her daughter.

Don't be afraid to explain your particular problems. Many aid officers are sympathetic to genuine instances of individual need. If you don't explain your special circumstances, they can't know what your needs are. It is likely that all personal and financial matters you disclose to the aid officer will be treated with confidentiality, but check with the aid office if you're concerned about this. And, be careful not to burn any bridges in the process of negotiating for a better aid package.

One last thing. Most schools offer aid packages that, with loans and a part-time job, will enable any student who meets the academic criteria to attend. Moreover, the financial aid office can offer an aid package rich in outright grants. *The amount you are expected to pay should stay about the same regardless of the costs of a particular college.* In other words, you may be able to send your child to an expensive private school for the same price as a less expensive public university.

Marion wanted to go to a private college in Ohio; her parents were determined to send her to their state university. The Ohio college's financial officer put together a package that brought the private college's costs to par with those of the state university (not all colleges can do this), and tried to convince Marion's parents that they could now afford the private school. Although Marion's parents agreed to send her to the private college, it took two semesters of statements from the bursar's office before they really believed they were not going to pay more than they had been prepared to spend at the state school.

Don't feel awkward about accepting aid and sending your child to a more expensive school. You will probably find that a large portion of the student body is receiving some form of financial aid and that no stigma exists against students who are attending on this basis. For those whose sights are set on education at a private college, we give this strategy of moving from a public college to a private school at no extra cost to you—particularly when it is accompanied by an increase in the quality of education—our value-oriented money planning award.

Should I put assets targeted for college in my child's name?

Not if you will be seeking college financial aid. Your aid package will be reduced because your asset evaluation will be at least three times greater if the assets are in your child's name than if they are in your own possession.

The answer is not as clear when you are planning to finance college costs yourself. You see, until your child is 14 years old, the first $550 of non-job-related income is nontaxable and the following $550 is taxed at the child's own tax rate. Since your child's rate is probably lower than yours, this can be a tax shelter for you. The amount you should deposit to your child's account will depend on the interest rate earned. For example, if the interest rate is 8 percent, placing $13,750 in the child's name will use up the first $1100 of tax benefits.

Until the age of 14, any income over $1100 is taxed at the parents' rate. After the fourteenth birthday, your child's entire unearned income over $550 will be taxed at the child's rate. At this point, you might want to transfer more assets to your child. You can gift $10,000 per parent or $20,000 per couple annually without paying gift taxes. Taking the assumed $12,500 (from the previous paragraph) plus two years at $20,000 per year, your child will have $52,500 plus interest earned in his or her account. How much will you save in income taxes? The tax savings for the year using your child's 15 percent bracket, versus leaving the entire sum in your name taxed at 28 percent, at an 8 percent return, will be over $600. Additional monies deposited in future years would increase the benefit.

If you, like many other families, don't have that much money to transfer, do as much as you can. This strategy works for smaller sums as well.

The negative side to all this is loss of control. If you place the money in your children's names, there is no assurance that they will use it for college. Mark's son, Brian, lived with him after a messy divorce. The boy, although quiet, seemed well-adjusted. Mark put funds in the bank under Brian's name, intending to use them for college expenses. Two days after Brian—who was then 18 and no longer a minor—graduated from high school, he took the funds and left town, turning up penniless a year and a half later.

Another teenager, Daniel, inherited some money and wanted to use most of it to buy a foreign sports car. His parents wanted him to use it for education and living expenses. Since the money was in Daniel's name, they could do nothing except plead with their son to think about his future. We acted as mediators to the family and suggested that Daniel take a small amount of money to buy a sporty but not very expensive car, and use the rest for his education.

Most families will not have such unpredictable children, but do you want to bet your money on it? Furthermore, any monies you give to your children cannot legally be taken back in an emergency, but can only be used for extraordinary expenses related to the children. Therefore, we recommend that the money be left in your name unless the sum involved is over $50,000 and you are sure you won't need it. In that event, you can set up a trust that requires the money to be used for college only. If your child does not complete college, or if there is money left after college, give any money that remains in the trust to your children when they reach an age of reputedly greater wisdom—say, 25, 30, or even older.

How should my college savings be invested?

Investing for college savings is not that different from your overall investment strategy. In general, you should be investing in securities that can provide a good return relative to your tolerance for risk.

Almost equal amounts of college savings are needed at precise times over a four-year period. That's why we recommend that you treat your college savings more conservatively than other types of investments. In fact, if the investment will be held for less than two years, we recommend that you place the money only in bonds.

Here are our comments on investment vehicles that are often considered most appropriate for college savings. Read more about investments in Chapters 3 and 4.

Series EE Bonds. These bonds, which should be held in parents' names, provide the highest safety. When they are held five years or more, the return is 15 percent below that for five-year U.S. Treasury bonds. In the bond area, Series EE securities—which are indexed for inflation after 1990—are most attractive if you expect to earn less than $60,000. Taxes that are normally deferred until amounts are withdrawn are eliminated entirely if you have an adjusted gross income of under $60,000 and use the proceeds for payment of tuition, fees, and books. To qualify for the elimination of income tax, the bonds have to have been purchased after January 1, 1990.

U.S. Government Bonds. These are the highest quality, and offer competitive returns; the income they generate is free of state and local income taxes.

With zero-coupon government bonds, interest payments and the amount of the bonds can be timed to fall due when you need them to finance a college payment. But the value of these bonds changes, and therefore they become a risky investment if you have to sell them before their maturity date. Most important, the interest you earn annually will be subject to federal taxes despite the fact that you don't receive cash until the bonds mature.

Regular Certificates of Deposit. These are high quality and convenient for depositors, but returns are fully taxed. Recently the returns have often been lower on an after-tax basis than government bonds.

College Paying Certificates of Deposit. The yields on these CDs are based on college inflation rates. Unfortunately, the returns have been below those for other certificates of deposit and, as with other CDs, the returns are fully taxed. In our opinion, you are paying much too much in the form of lower yield for a partial insurance against sharply higher college inflation, which may never occur. This product plays on a basic emotion: fear. Avoid it.

Zero-Coupon Municipal Bonds. Where available, these can be a simple, attractive tool when the bonds fall due around the date you will need the money.

Municipal Bonds. Higher-rated municipals provide high-quality, tax-free returns that are highly competitive after adjustment for their tax benefits. These are most suitable for people in tax brackets of 28 percent or greater.

Conservative Stocks. There are no "whisper in the ear" stock tips here. You may use conservative (that is, blue-chip) stocks if you promise to have the portfolio supervised properly, either by you or by a professional investment manager.

Mutual Funds. They possess similar qualities to the above-mentioned stocks and bonds but grant more latitude on the types of stocks and bonds used in the portfolio. When you buy these funds, you will have professional managers in charge of your investment.

Deferred Annuities. Fixed annuities are lower-risk investments that don't fluctuate in value; variable annuities are like mutual funds. The principal advantages of both fixed and variable annuities—deferral of taxes until withdrawals with "borrowing" of money for college payments—are attractive. However, high administrative costs can eliminate the tax benefit. In addition, the benefit could be taken away by Congress if it decides that "borrowings" should be taxed as actual withdrawals.

Pension Plans. These plans include qualified pension plans, IRAs, and 401(k)s. You might not think of them as education savings vehicles. But the tax shelter received from deductions on contributions and tax deferral until cash is withdrawn can more than offset the penalty on withdrawals before age 59½ if you have kept the money in the account for about eight years or longer.

In our practice we often recommend a combination of equity mutual funds and bond or bond mutual funds for college savings. Municipal bonds are best if you are in a higher tax bracket. U.S. Treasuries form an alternative that makes most sense when your child is 14 or older and the money is placed in his or her name and subject to the low 15 percent tax. If you use municipals or Treasuries, try to time maturity dates to the periods when you will need the money.

As we explain more fully in Chapter 4, bond mutual funds with low costs provide an attractive alternative and often a preferable approach to individual stock and bond investing.

Should I use a prepaid college education plan?

There are two types of college prepayment plans. The first type, which was initiated some years ago, enables you to lock in current college costs if you promise in advance to send your children to a particular college or to college in a particular state when they graduate from high school, assuming they meet minimum enrollment standards. You must prepay one to four years of tuition and other costs.

This is a real gamble. Will your child want to attend that particular college (possibly your alma mater or your local college)? Will the college have the programs that mirror your child's skills and interests? Will prepaying the college tuition and other expenses years before they are required offer protection against rising costs? Or conversely, will it be a poor way to invest your funds over a period of many years?

Prepaying for college can seem attractive, and it has the advantage of freeing you from decision making later on. There are too many variables, though, including the fact that the college you choose may not be there when you need it or may have changed substantially.

Some of the colleges that were at the forefront of this type of prepayment plan are no longer offering it. Apparently it was too difficult for them to invest the deposits conservatively enough to guarantee preservation of principal and, at the same time, aggressively enough to provide for the substantial annual increase in college costs.

Let your sons and daughters choose the colleges they will attend. If you don't, you may have unhappy children. You may even have to ask for a refund and lose the return on your investment.

The second type of prepayment makes more sense. Some colleges offer students who are college age and have already been accepted the opportunity to prepay all four years when they enroll. In this way, the costs for tuition and room and board for each of the four years will remain stable instead of rising with increasing college costs. Some colleges will lend you the money to prepay, and others will help you get a bank loan to meet the prepayment.

At least in this arrangement your child has chosen to attend a particular school. But what if he or she has a change of heart before the four years are up? Before you prepay, inquire about your rights to a refund.

As with any other loan, check the terms before deciding whether this is appropriate for you. If you prepay the entire four years, think about what else you could be doing with your money over that time period.

7
Considering Real Estate

Real estate can and should be part of your investment thinking. This is true even if the only real estate you own is your home. You may think of your home in nonfinancial terms—a haven from the daily grind, a spot to put your feet up and let your hair down, or a meeting place for your friends and family. But it can also be one of your best investments. This chapter will show you how to approach financial issues concerning your home.

In addition, you may want to consider investments in income-producing real estate. They can extend from marketable securities—such as mutual funds or investment trusts—to a nearby property that you purchase by yourself or with friends. Why? Often real estate will give you tax advantages, a good cash payout, and reasonable growth prospects. And it is a particularly good investment in periods of high inflation. You can begin investing in real estate with just a little money—say, a few thousand dollars.

Our value-oriented approach to money planning can work very well in this area. Not long ago we were cautioning against your buying real estate that was "hot." We believed that you could get burned from the heat. For example, one of our best value-oriented real estate investment decisions was to encourage our clients to stay out of all Northeast real estate when it was popular and as much as 50 percent higher than it is now.

Today in many markets, depressed prices and frigid forecasts for properties prevail. In fact, housing costs as a percentage of the average person's income is at the lowest point in about 20 years. While there is no guarantee that prices won't decline further, we believe that well-thought-out real estate, whether in the form of a home or outside investments, will present an unusually attractive opportunity throughout the nineties. We will demonstrate how you can take advantage of it.

Let's start with some basic questions about what is likely to be your first real estate purchase: your own home.

What kind of home would suit my needs?

A home is much more than an investment. The bricks and mortar represent many things—peace, security, comfort, privacy, family unity, and so on. More than any other material possession, your home can bring a sense of pride in achievement.

A typical pattern is for you to rent an apartment until you can afford a "starter house" and then trade up as you become more affluent. When your children are grown you might consider selling, but you may never do so because of the emotional attachment you have to your home.

On the other hand, you may like city life and prefer the hassle-free advantages of renting or owning an apartment. It's very much a matter of lifestyle.

What is a physically attractive home? That is a personal decision. One of our clients, Greg, was drawn to a charming old wooden farmhouse that somehow has remained standing in the midst of a big city. The only trouble was its size. Greg's family was growing, and the rooms were so small Tom Thumb would have had problems living there.

Another client, Gwendolyn, lives all by herself in the suburbs in a house with a great many rooms. She told us she thought buying the biggest house she could afford was a good investment, but we believe that the main attraction was the pride Gwendolyn felt in owning this large chunk of real estate. Because the purchase had already been made when we met Gwendolyn and she had no intention of moving, we didn't tell her that the high upkeep made the house a relatively poor net investment.

Big-city dwellers crowd themselves into small apartments with incredibly high purchase prices and expensive upkeeps just so they can be where the action is. One cartoon expressed these living conditions best. It showed two convicts in a jail cell saying, "I like the open airy feeling here—it beats the Manhattan studio a friend and I converted out of a walk-in closet!"

As you can see, financial advisors have to tread lightly in this area. Because beauty is in the eye of the beholder, we confine our recommendations to financial factors.

How good an investment is a house?

Most of our clients want their home to be a good investment. And as we mentioned, it can be. In spite of the early 1990s experience of weaker house prices, for many Americans, the home is their most valuable asset. Over the 20-year period from 1971 to 1991, average home prices increased by 6.6 percent a year, during a period when the overall inflation rate was 6.1 percent a year. As shown in Table 7-1, home prices did better than inflation in the mid- to late seventies but have lagged behind in recent years. Notice also that prices tend to do better in good economic times and less well in weaker economic periods. This moderate overall price appreciation by itself doesn't make a home a particularly attractive investment.

Your home also represents a form of forced savings—you must keep up with the mortgage payments or risk losing your asset. If you have trouble putting money away, this forced saving can be a positive factor. You are putting away money that you can recapture later when you sell the house.

If you follow the usual pattern, you are probably financing a large part of your home (especially if it's your first home) through a long-term mortgage. This allows you to buy a bigger house (that is, have a larger investment) than you could otherwise afford. As long as you can cover the first year's mortgage payment, you will probably be all right, because in subsequent years your income is likely to rise while, on average, your mortgage payments will not.

Sometimes the forced-saving feature can be taken to extreme. One family we know, the Caseys, recently bought a condominium in

Table 7-1. The Home as an Inflation Hedge (Yearly Increases in Prices)

	Single-family home	Inflation
1991	0.9%	3.1%
1990	1.4	6.1
1989	3.8	4.7
1988	3.6	4.4
1987	5.9	4.4
1986	4.8	1.1
1985	2.0	3.8
1984	4.4	4.0
1983	2.5	3.8
1982	2.5	3.8
1981	8.0	8.9
1980	10.4	12.5
1979	15.0	13.3
1978	14.1	9.0
1977	11.2	6.7
1976	7.7	4.9
1975	10.2	6.9
1974	9.6	12.3
1973	8.5	8.7
1972	6.8	3.4
1971	6.2	3.3
1971–1991	6.6%	6.1%

Home prices based on U.S. Department of Commerce figures. Inflation statistics based on the Consumer Price Index.

town as a compromise between renting an apartment and buying a house. They financed the purchase largely through a mortgage for an amount appropriate to their income, yet they constantly complained of being cash poor. We thought they must be exaggerating because we knew that Mrs. Casey had just received an important promotion, and together the couple earned a lot of money. Yet, when we visited them, their house was virtually bare. Nor did the Caseys take any vacations, eat out, or indulge in any of the other minor extravagances of life. Hiding our personal curiosity in professional terms, we asked how this could be. Mrs. Casey said that she didn't have any idea, but things should improve after they finished paying off their five-year mortgage!

In this case, financial realities and the quality of life that the Caseys wanted indicated that a longer-term mortgage with lower monthly payments would make more sense.

The final characteristic you should consider is your home as tax shelter. The government blesses home ownership with certain tax benefits. The sale of one home will not trigger income taxes if you buy another home of the same or higher value within two years. And the interest on the mortgage is tax-deductible if the mortgage financing the original purchase is $1 million or less. The good news is that the tax deductibility feature means that if you are in the 28 percent federal tax bracket, for every $100 in interest you pay, Uncle Sam contributes $28 in the form of lower taxes. If you are 55 or older, the first $125,000 gain on the sale of your home is free of taxes.

When basic appreciation in the value of your home is added to its tax shelter benefits and its forced-saving component, the home takes on its legendary investment characteristics. If your home is purchased entirely by cash, it may provide a humdrum 5 percent a year as its return. However, if that same home is mostly financed through a 15-year mortgage, with monthly payments counted as a tax-deductible expense and disregarded for purposes of calculating investment returns (most of our clients regard the entire amount as an expense, like rent), then it results in a large asset owned over time. As we show in Table 7-2, at the end of the 15-year period your home will be fully paid up and worth more than twice its original cost and more than 10 times your original cash investment.

Table 7-2. Investment Value of a Home

Assumed yearly inflation rate	5%
Projected yearly growth in value of home	5%
Number of years until loan paid off	15 years
Period home owned	15 years
Original cost of home	$150,000
Down payment	$30,000
Bank debt	$120,000
Amount owed at end of 15 years	0
Projected value of home at end of 15 years	$312,000
Change in value of home	2.1×
Change in value of original cash investment	10.4×

Should I buy or should I rent?

The question of whether to buy or rent comes up most often when house prices are weak. It is also common if you are not sure you want the responsibility of owning your own property. In that case, you are really asking for proof of a financial benefit that will persuade you to change—or not to change—your current lifestyle.

You can compare financial costs and benefits between buying and renting fairly quickly. Contrast the place you are currently renting or one that you are considering moving into with a house, condominium, or cooperative apartment that is comparable in size, quality, and location. Don't include costs that you would have in both your current home and the one you are considering. Keep in mind that homeowners' interest costs and real estate tax costs are both deductible for income tax purposes.

Don't forget to include the amount you could have earned on the down payment if you had invested your money elsewhere. For example, if you rent instead of buy, the down payment could be invested in securities. Use the long-term after-tax rate on investments you are attracted to today—a 6 percent approximation may be appropriate.

Be aware of the difference between interest and principal payments. Principal payments reduce the amount you owe, thereby increasing the value of your investment after debt is deducted. Interest costs compensate the institution that loaned you the money. If you have a 20-year or longer mortgage, principal payments during the first few years of the mortgage are relatively small and don't have to be considered.

The most important factor in this whole comparison is likely to be the growth in the market price of your home. Don't be put off by weak prices or gloom-and-doom forecasts. We believe good real estate that is properly cared for will increase in value over the longer term, as it has in the past. As we mentioned before, when the housing market is weak, it is actually a good time to buy.

In any event, you should attach a growth rate to the value of your home. Given the close longer-term relationship between property prices and inflation, we tend to use the projected long-term inflation rate as an approximation of the growth in price for well-located property. Currently, we are assuming a 5 percent inflation rate per year. If you have trouble placing any growth rate at all on your property, it could mean that you should rethink the value of that property.

There are some other factors besides costs to consider. If you don't expect to live in a property for at least three years, from an investment standpoint we would recommend that you rent. It is difficult to predict how real estate prices will progress over shorter periods of time. Prices can be unstable and the house could be temporarily illiquid (you would be unable to sell it at anywhere near its value). Therefore, under severe circumstances, you could find yourself with a substantial loss. Possibly you would not even receive enough to cover your mortgage repayment if you sold too soon after buying.

Martin and Susan bought a large house at a seemingly attractive price when they moved to Connecticut. They knew that their company would be transferring them to another state in 18 months. When we mentioned the risks of short-term home ownership they shrugged and said, "Home prices will continue to rise in the Connecticut market." Unfortunately, it took them almost two years to sell their Connecticut home after they were transferred. They lost more than $40,000 in the process.

Recognize that even though your house increases in value, you won't see any of that profit until you sell. Therefore, your profit won't be available to subsidize the cash you need for the upkeep of your property. If you are never going to sell your property, the fact that it has increased in value isn't going to ever help you—although it will help your heirs. Because you need to sell in order to personally realize the benefits, we have had to grit our financial teeth and agree with some elderly clients that they should not buy property they intend to live in for the rest of their lives even if it was offered to them at bargain prices.

We have found that the cost of owning a property is generally more than the cost of renting before considering tax deductions and projected increases in the value of the home. After adjusting for tax deductions, yearly cash costs are much closer for people in a 28 percent or higher tax bracket, but are still greater than renting.

However, when you take the potential increases in the value of your home into account, owning a home generally comes out well ahead. It is for that reason that we almost always tell our clients to buy instead of rent.

How much can I spend on a house?

There are two methods we recommend to determine how much you should spend on your home. First, you can estimate spending as a certain percentage of your take-home pay. According to this method, your home-related costs, including maintenance, principal, mortgage interest, real estate taxes, and insurance, should amount to 30 percent or less of your gross pay.

This percentage is sometimes hard to apply in high-cost areas where real estate is expensive. Instead, we recommend a looser approach in which you essentially pay the most you can afford in the first two years. You might think it odd for financial advisors to recommend such a strategy, but we believe some flexibility is called for because homes properly bought make excellent investments. While you may feel pinched at the beginning, the upkeep will become easier over time. That is because your mortgage payments will remain the same under a fixed-rate mortgage (where interest rates remain level throughout the mortgage period) and—unless rates change dramatically—be approximately flat in an adjustable rate mortgage (where interest payments vary depending on current rates). At the same time, your income should increase each year at least by the rate of inflation. Because a sharp increase in interest rates could throw off your planning, we recommend you use either a fixed-rate mortgage or a variable rate mortgage that has limitations on interest rate increases over the first three years. For fuller information on mortgages, see Chapter 2.

You can use the cashflow schedule in Chapter 1 to help figure out how much you can afford to spend. It is a good idea to have a reserve fund of at least three months expenses set aside in liquid funds or an assured source of borrowing in case of emergency.

How can I get a good deal when shopping for a house?

A home combines personal and investment characteristics. Many people we know pay little attention to investment merits and select a home because they "fall in love" with it. Love in this case is the enemy of finance since it can convince the lover to make irrational decisions, such as paying higher-than-market prices for a particular property. From an investment standpoint, you should forget love.

Choose a home in an established quality neighborhood or in one that is up and coming. Try to stay away from houses in areas with long-term unemployment problems because it can be difficult to have your property value grow steadily in a neighborhood suffering from economic difficulties and population outflows. Remember to have the soundness of the home's structure certified by an engineer, and factor in the expense of any necessary prepurchase repairs as part of the home's cost.

Select a home that is typical for its neighborhood, not one that is the most expensive house on a not-so-good block. For value purposes it is often best to select the least expensive house on a good block. Before you buy, get a sense of values in the neighborhood by canvassing the area, and asking for the prices of homes for sale and those recently sold. It helps to try to familiarize yourself with the overall real estate climate—for example, whether homes are in great demand and turning over fast, or if the market is sluggish.

Armed with this information, you are ready for our "love them and leave them" strategy. Restrict your search to those homes that attracted you, but don't fall in love with just one. Select a half dozen properties and place bids on each at 20 percent *under* recent sales prices in that neighborhood. Adjust the figure for your own temperament and raise or lower it based on whether the climate is strong or weak.

Be very polite to the existing owners. Do not worry about insulting people with too low an offer, but do not affront the owners by insulting the house. On the other hand, no matter how much you love the house, calmly point out certain features that you find pleasing and, at the same time, tactfully cite some shortcomings. Mention that if they become interested at some point, they can contact you, and you will be ready to close at your offering price.

What might happen is that one owner has to sell now or panics—or that there is an estate sale, in which case prices may be more reasonable. If an owner contacts you but is not quite ready to accept your offer, you can compromise and close, at a more moderate discount than 20 percent. If after three to six months, or longer if you are not in a hurry, you have no luck, modify your stance by raising your bids slightly.

One woman we know offers low bids for real estate, criticizes the property she wishes to buy, incurs the annoyance of 9 out of 10 homeowners she approaches, and closes on 1 out of 20 properties she bids on. She isn't as polite as we recommend, but she has been very successful in buying real estate properties at prices significantly below their true value, fixing them up when necessary, and reselling them at great profits.

Don't expect much help with this strategy from real estate brokers. Because of their interest in quick turnover, they are more likely to warn you of the risks of waiting. They would probably prefer you to focus on just one property; they might tell you how comfortable and attractive that house is at its regular asking price. Insist on seeing many properties, not just one. You can sometimes get an even better deal by checking newspaper advertisements and dealing directly with the seller. If you resist all the pressures to buy but wait until the real estate market in the area you like is soft—that is, many houses are for sale at prices at least 10 percent below what they were a year ago—and then practice our love-them-and-leave-them strategy, we will give you our value-oriented real estate trophy.

You may be surprised at how often the love-them-and-leave-them approach has worked for our clients. Allen and Brenda, a just-married couple clearly preoccupied with all that was required to set up their own household, asked us what we thought of a house they were about to buy for the asking price, which in a weak market was 10 percent lower than the original price. We explained our strategy and the risk that any of the properties they looked at might be snapped up by other suitors. Nonetheless, Allen and Brenda took our advice, went through our recommended love-them-and-leave-them process, and received interested replies from two property owners at their lower bids. They actually closed on the house that they originally wanted at about a 20 percent drop from the price they would have paid before coming to see us.

There is one last thing. Hire an attorney who is familiar with real estate transactions as your representative in negotiating and signing the contract. Tell him or her to put in as many options to get out of the contracts in writing as possible. For example, make the final closing subject to satisfactory financing, satisfactory appraisal, a satisfactory engineer's report, and a satisfactory environmental report (that is, no radon, storage tank, or septic problems). That will give you an "out" in case unexpected problems turn up.

How much should I place as a down payment on a home?

If you want to trade up to the highest-priced house you can buy, or if you are just starting out, you should pay as little as you can. In other words, take the most that the bank will lend you assuming you have the cashflow to support it. In the days of the swinging eighties, in some circumstances almost nothing was required as a down payment. In the current environment, lending institutions generally require a 20 to 25 percent down payment.

If you have enough cash savings to afford a smaller mortgage, the amount of the down payment will depend largely on what you can earn by investing the money elsewhere. Compare the cost of the mortgage with the expected annual return on the investment. If the investment is taxable, don't forget to consider this factor. For example, if your mortgage is at a 10 percent pretax rate, it should take more than a 10 percent rate of return on an investment to persuade you to finance a larger mortgage. Try to look at all investments on an after-tax basis. Then, for example, you may find that the after-tax return on a tax-free municipal bond may exceed the after-tax cost of the mortgage.

Take into account other considerations as well, such as a reduction in flexibility when a large portion of your investable funds are given to a down payment; by making yourself less liquid, you can be squeezed in an emergency or when an unusually attractive investment is presented to you. Finally, some people feel less well off when they have less in investment assets.

In general, you should try to focus on the big picture. Barbara and Neil, both doctors with a strong yearly savings rate, decided to move back to the United States after living abroad for several years. They asked us whether they should place a mortgage on the $1 million home they wanted to buy. They had $1 million in cash in a bank account in a foreign country. Our first concern was the risk of their entire life savings sitting in one account that was dependent on the financial health of one bank with no FDIC insurance. And Barbara had told us that they were extremely conservative! (Certificates of deposit and Treasury bonds were as high a risk as they were willing to go.)

Our second thought was, what a field day a commission-oriented advisor who had no feeling of responsibility for the best interests of their clients could have! Given a 20 percent down payment for the home, a recommendation of investment products for the $800,000 balance could result in $30,000 to $100,000 in commissions for the advisor.

Considering Barbara and Neil's very conservative risk tolerance and the likelihood of a strong monthly future cashflow to replenish their liquid funds, we recommended no mortgage at all, the entire $1 million going to purchase the house. But first, as calmly as a doctor might have explained the need for emergency surgery to a patient, we had them wire their money to a secure place in the United States.

Should I take out a second mortgage on my home?

Your home is one of the best sources for obtaining capital. You can borrow at relatively low rates on a pretax basis, and the interest you pay on the first $100,000 you borrow for non-home-related uses is tax-deductible. If you are considering taking out a loan to buy an investment, follow the procedure outlined in the previous answer to find out whether the investment is worth it.

If you are taking a loan to obtain monies for noninvestment purposes, be careful. As financial advisors, we caution against using second mortgages, home equity loans, and lines of credit as seemingly open-ended checking accounts. It is too simple to take out these loans and, particularly with lines of credit, you can lose the discipline of a regular repayment schedule. It may be easy for you to pay off the interest, especially when—if you run short—you just borrow more. But what happens when you reach the borrowing limit? If you are caught short, you can lose your principal asset—your home.

Limit this type of mortgage borrowing to carefully planned investment programs, major outlays such as college education, or remodeling, not to frivolous expenditures. Stick to the repayment schedule with the goal of repaying the entire sum no later than on your retirement.

Should I take out a home equity loan or refinance my mortgage?

At this point you have probably gotten the message that we like home-related loans. We don't want to overemphasize them, though, so that we can't be accused of tempting you to buy a home just to take out a low-cost loan, as one client suggested. However, if you need additional funds and are deciding between a home equity loan or complete refinancing, consider the following factors.

A home equity loan will generally cost you 1 to 2 percent more than a new mortgage because the lender considers it riskier to have the second mortgage on a property instead of the first. On the other hand, in certain instances home equity loans are currently offered without points, the substantial administrative charges which virtually all first mortgages have. And if you have an existing first mortgage with a lower-than-market interest rate, which has a substantial amount still outstanding, a full refinancing will cause you to lose that interest benefit.

Ask yourself why you need this new financing. If it is for remodeling your home, particularly in ways that will enhance the value that you hope to realize one day, then a full refinancing may be most economical if your existing mortgage is no great interest bargain. Similarly, a full refinancing for well-thought-out long-term business or investment purposes can also make sense.

On the other hand, refinancing because you have piled on significant credit card or other debt doesn't make sense. If the answer to your reasons for new financing is that you are living beyond your current income or taking the loan to meet shorter-term needs such as buying a car, taking a vacation, or financing your child's college education, you need to repay the amount over a few years, not over 15 to 30 years. In that circumstance a home equity loan, along with the discipline to repay the amounts on time, is your preferred alternative. Don't make the home equity line of credit an ever-larger amount that would, at a minimum, interfere with your retirement plans.

Should I select a house, a condominium, or a cooperative apartment?

If you live in a major metropolitan area, your choice can be between a cooperative apartment (a "co-op") or condominium (a "condo") in the downtown area or a house in the suburbs. The downtown area offers more excitement and an easier commute; the suburbs are more peaceful and generally less expensive. If you are starting a family, by the time the second child arrives the economics often decisively shift to the suburbs.

Let's assume locations are the same among the three alternatives and discuss other characteristics. Co-ops and condos can allow you to skip many of the hassles of home ownership because maintenance operations are done by management. A cooperative apartment is like a mutual fund in that you own shares in an enterprise—the building you live in. The building itself may have debt.

An advantage of co-ops is that the shareholders have some control over who is allowed to own an apartment in the building. A disadvantage is that the shareholders have some control over who is allowed to own an apartment in the building. Let me explain. I served as unpaid president of the board of a co-op in which a clean-cut dentist applied to buy an apartment. We all felt he would be a fine neighbor until he happened to mention he had a brother who was a saxophone player in a rock band, practiced often, and would live with him when the musician was in town—about 50 percent of the time. And other members of the band would visit from time to time. The dentist was turned down. That sort of thing may be great when you live in the building, but if you are trying to sell your apartment and the dentist offers you 10 percent more than the next highest bidder, you might feel resentful about the board's action. Some people we know have paraded a great number of prospective buyers before their boards only to be turned down each time. Furthermore, if you wish to rent your apartment or refinance your mortgage, you will also need board approval.

A condo doesn't have that problem. You own your apartment and can sell it to whomever you want. This does have a downside: so can your neighbor. Do you really want the saxophone player practicing next door to you? Financially, the condo may be safer than the co-op since you often have no overall building debt to be concerned about. Moreover, with a co-op you are obligated for the debts of other shareholders. For instance, some of our New York City co-op dwelling friends have been forced to pick up more of the building's maintenance costs when their neighbors defaulted on their share of the expenses.

The house owner has maximum freedom of choice in decisions—generally no one can say how you should handle the exterior or the interior of your home. The living space is often larger; but the maintenance cost is higher, and real estate taxes per family may be higher as well.

Generally, the most important factor in choosing the best investment will be location. If locations are comparable, we usually recommend a house. Even though it needs the most ongoing care, we believe a house provides the best form of investment over the longer term. As sole owners, you have full control and can decide which improvements will most raise the resale price. When you are ready to sell, you may find that most buyers prefer to invest in their own private home rather than share the responsibilities of a condo or co-op.

What should I know about selling my home?

Your goals in selling your home are usually to get the highest possible price in the shortest amount of time. Your strategy will differ a little, depending on whether you must move soon or you have some time. In either case, you should find out what comparable homes in your neighborhood have recently sold for.

Place your house for sale at about 20 percent above the going level. That high a price will give you a feel for the current market, since you can solicit bids below that point, and leave yourself room to negotiate down. Some clients of ours put their apartment up for sale and on the very first day with the very first buyer their asking price was met. While they were happy, we realized they had failed to take into account a surge in buying interest in the past few weeks and received less that they might have.

You might want to try to sell the property yourself and pocket the selling agent's commission of about 6 percent. Tell your friends of your interest in selling. They might know someone who is a potential buyer. This works particularly well in condos or co-ops in which buying into "community friendships" is sometimes important.

Establish whether your house is one that will appeal to many people or is a "special situation" whose style or location need the "right" buyer. Special situations will usually take longer to sell.

If you have plenty of time, use it to establish a price that a truly interested buyer will bring. Don't be discouraged by people who bid substantially under what you think is the going price. They are either not serious or are looking for a bargain. They may be trying out our value-oriented love-them-and-leave-them buying techniques.

If you find that your price is higher than the market will support, bring your price down to meet the bid. We recommend you don't get caught up in emotional haggling over a few thousand dollars. It isn't meaningful compared to the price of the house and could have you lose your buyer.

If the country is in a recession and the resale market is severely depressed, consider waiting. However, sellers who have to move do not have the luxury of time. Establish a higher-than-market asking price, but bring it down more quickly. Your negotiating position will be weakened considerably if you have moved and the buyer sees that the house is empty.

Keep in mind that if you use an agent, he or she can give you lots of useful information but, as we mentioned before, is most interested in closing. Therefore he or she might persuade you that the last bid price is the best you can get. Don't panic. Keep perspective, and weigh the possible additional revenues from waiting for a higher price, say for one year, against the upkeep of the empty home. If it doesn't clearly come out in favor of waiting, and you have a solid offer, try to get it raised somewhat but move to close.

Our recommendation is not to buy a new home until you have sold the old one. Too many times we have found people faced with the upkeep on two homes under emotional stress for a considerable period of time. We make exceptions only when the new one is truly a bargain.

Can I afford a second home?

Do you view a second home as a form of paradise, a blissful escape from the normal day-to-day rat race? Or do you think of it as a bother to get to and to maintain? If you plan to buy one, it's a good idea to rent in the area you are interested in first. Not only will this give you a better feel for costs and investment values before you make a commitment, but it can help you find out if a second home becomes less attractive over time.

If you are still interested, we advise you to consider the following factors. Take a look at the home on a current cashflow basis. Use the same approach as you would for a first home, working out cash inflows and outflows. Interest costs and real estate taxes are once again deductible.

Try to increase your emergency fund by one year's worth of cash that you might have to lay out for this home. In that way, you can guard against the panicky feeling of having to sell should your income decline temporarily, which usually occurs at the wrong time, when the economy is in a recession and home prices are depressed.

Next, think about whether the home is a good investment. A key to determining whether you can afford it is the price at which you could sell it at retirement. Consider both the condition of the home and the quality of the community before you buy. Is the home well built? Is it in an attractive, stable area? Is it today, or will it at some point as the population grows, become a primary home site? Then a growth rate in value of 5 percent or more per year may be called for. Alternatively, is it little more than a shack, inexpensive but with poor future prospects? Perhaps then, despite the effects of inflation, you would be lucky to get your money back.

Richard T. bought a modest vacation home in the now-posh Hamptons on Long Island, New York, 20 years ago. It is worth much more today than his primary home. Syd S. bought a house in upstate New York many years ago and is currently deciding whether to put a substantial sum into upkeep or abandon it as valueless. As you can see, choosing your vacation home carefully can mean the difference between being stuck with an expensive burden or cornering an attractive investment.

Is your vacation home going to be your retirement home? Investment characteristics are somewhat less important if the purchase allows you to liquidate your more valuable primary home when you retire.

When you are trying to decide if you can afford a second home, consider rental income. Can you and are you willing to rent the premises for part of the year? Under those circumstances, you would split your costs between personal and business use.

You should now be ready to put all the costs and projected benefits into your overall financial planning. Unless you have compelling investment reasons, from a strict financial standpoint buying a second home should be a low priority until you have convincing evidence that you have a clear path to such goals as education and retirement planning. But quality-of-life considerations count as well. Why, you can even rationalize that by improving your psychological well-being, the second home makes you more effective in your job and lets you spend more time with your family!

When you have adequate yearly savings and good prospects for income growth, we generally suggest going ahead. Keep in mind, though, that vacation home prices tend to be more changeable than those of first homes. We recommend waiting for a low point in the economic cycle before you buy.

What makes real estate an attractive investment?

We have discussed your home as an investment. Now we are going to tell you how to find value in other types of real estate.

There are three fundamental reasons that income-producing real estate—real estate that produces yearly cashflow—may be an attractive investment: the income it produces, tax benefits, and growth in investment value. Real estate is the prototypical hard asset. By that we mean that unlike a common stock, you can touch a building and, if it is in a good location, it is less subject to becoming obsolete with changing styles and technology. While real estate prices fluctuate, their long-term stability was shown in the bleak days that followed wild investing in private real estate limited partnerships. At that time, people in the business referred to the partnership holdings as "neutron buildings"—after high costs, heavy debt, and possibly misleading information had totally destroyed the promoter, the operating partner, the investor, and sometimes the bank, the buildings remained intact.

Real estate is not without its risks. First, the asset can be difficult to sell should you need cash quickly. Second, a change in the economy or in neighborhood dynamics can substantially shift profitability. However, it is often poor management or large borrowing against the property that create problems. Quality real estate that is watched carefully by its owner can bring you a strong annual cash return. Moreover, this income can grow over time because rents can often be raised to keep pace with inflation.

Another advantage is that income-producing real estate is a tax shelter. A portion of a building's cost can be taken each year as an expense for wear and tear—called "depreciation"—even though you spend no cash for it. (Under the tax act of 1993, the allowed rate of depreciation on nonresidential property was reduced, but not eliminated, while the rate on residential property was kept the same. Sorry, you can't depreciate your own home.) This reduction in taxes is especially appealing because good buildings don't depreciate, they go up in value over time. In some instances, you can find yourself with a tax loss while you actually receive cash income.

You can take advantage of another great tax break. The first $25,000 of tax losses on properties that you have actively participated in managing (not as a passive or silent partner) can be applied against your regular income. This reportable loss can potentially reduce your taxes significantly. The deduction is phased out gradually as your income rises from the $100,000 to the $150,000 level.

Income real estate also has the advantage of increasing the value of your investment. Rental revenues and profits rise over time, boosting the market price of the property. From the mid- to late 1980s to the early 1990s, we have not had the same hike in rental rates; there currently is more than enough real estate available in many cities throughout the United States. But as long as properties are in good locations and the population continues to grow, prices for real estate will tend to increase rapidly after years of underperformance.

Inflation can add to the market value of real estate because it is usually fairly easy to pass along cost increases. Also consider that the market value of older buildings tends to be influenced by the current cost of constructing new buildings (replacement value), which rises with inflation.

How can I buy income-producing real estate?

Basically you should know about three alternatives—publicly traded real estate securities, limited partnerships, and purchase of your own real estate.

Real Estate Investment Trusts. Publicly traded real estate often comes in the form of real estate investment trusts (REITs). REITs somewhat resemble mutual funds but hold groupings of individual properties instead of common stock from individual corporations.

REITs may concentrate on actively managing their own properties, having part ownership, making loans to other owners of real estate, or a mixture of all three. They may invest in specific property types such as apartments, offices, shopping centers, hotels, or hospitals, or they may combine many different types. Sometimes they concentrate all their properties in a specific geographic area.

REITs earnings are free from corporate taxes. Aside from that, unlike the case with other privately held real estate, there are no tax benefits. You generally pay taxes on the entire dividend you receive.

In evaluating REITs, you should value the cash they generate today, their current yield provided by their dividend, the prospects for future growth in cashflow, and the confidence you have that the projections will be met. REITs tend to be affected by how the public stock and bond markets are performing as well as pricing in the private real estate markets. Although many buy REITs because of their high current yields, their performance will be influenced by trends in interest rates. However, over very long periods of time REITs tend to perform in line with other equities. They can be rewarding additions to your investment portfolio.

If you are planning to choose your own REITs, stick to companies that principally own real estate rather than owning mortgages on real estate and that have conservative amounts of debt, strong cashflows and dividends, and total values in the stock market of over $100 million. Be careful about investing in hotel or hospital REITs—you are buying day-to-day operating activities as well as real estate. Be sure to diversify your holdings to limit the risk of any one providing disappointing results.

Private real estate requires time and increases your risk. As a holder of REIT shares, you have no management responsibility and your exposure will be limited to your original investment. Moreover, you can make as small an investment as you like.

You can begin your analysis with those REITs that are covered by *Value Line* and send for the annual reports and talk to the investor relations representative of the company directly. A registered representative of a brokerage house can also supply you with information. If you prefer having a full-time investment manager make the selections in this area, there are a few real estate mutual funds that invest in REITs that you can use.

Limited Partnerships. Under this setup, you are a partner in profits, but as a limited partner your losses are restricted to the amount you invested. In the 1970s and early 1980s, limited partnerships were a favorite because of the strong performance of real estate back then and the tax benefits allowed, and because as private investments their price fluctuations generally weren't noticeable as they were for publicly traded securities. That isn't to say that they didn't fluctuate in value, just that some people prefer to think that what they don't see won't hurt them. Unfortunately, the performance of these limited partnerships did hurt; the overwhelming majority of limited partnerships have performed poorly over the past 10 years.

Because of limited regulation by the Securities and Exchange Commission (SEC), we have serious reservations about contributing to a partnership with people you don't know. If you decide to go ahead, look for partnerships in which at least $0.85 and preferably $0.90 of every dollar raised goes into the investment, not into the pockets of the promoters.

There are some currently operating private limited partnerships that the original buyers offer through brokerage firms at a sharp discount from their true value. However, the average investor should stay away. In a secondary partnership, it is difficult to differentiate between a panicky original investor selling out at any price and a crafty pro who knows that the private deal is one step away from bankruptcy. And the overwhelming majority of the partnerships have either no or poor liquidity. It may be impossible to sell your limited partnership.

Purchasing Your Own Real Estate. Owning your own income-producing property can be the most productive area of real estate investment. We give it our value-oriented money planning award in the real estate area. Unless you are a sophisticated real estate investor, restrict yourself to markets and types of real estate you know. Pick a time when people are negative about real estate and prices have declined. For example, select the house in your area that is up for sale in a weak market and can be rented out, or a building in a developing part of town. If you cannot afford to buy alone, do it with friends or relatives. The bank can help, but limit yourself to a fairly conservative debt level, about 50 percent. Always make sure you can comfortably cover both operating and financing costs.

Remember, of course, that owning real estate means you are a landlord. You or your agent will have to collect the rent, make repairs, answer questions and complaints, and possibly dispossess people. There is a lot of responsibility attached to the rewards. Also, remember that you will probably be personally liable if you cannot make the bank payments and that real estate can be temporarily illiquid—you may be unable to sell it if you need funds in a hurry. But as you probably have gathered, for those people who are willing to take on the responsibilities, we believe that well-thought-out and well-run real estate can be extremely rewarding.

One couple who came to our office—Nancy was a secretary, Peter a public school teacher—asked whether they should invest their money in bonds or real estate. The real estate they were considering was in their neighborhood in Staten Island, New York, in what they considered an improving area. Peter was handy with tools, and the couple didn't mind managing the property.

Our projection clearly indicated the real estate would do considerably better than the bonds. There were no outside management fees and no commissions involved, Nancy and Peter had tax benefits that allowed them to take initial tax losses on the property against their normal income, and they were putting "sweat equity" into the property that would probably turn out better results, and certainly cheaper ones, than if they had used professional helpers. Besides, they felt they would enjoy the responsibility and feeling that goes with owning another piece of bricks and mortar. We were glad to recommend that they purchase the real estate.

Rebecca, a middle-aged woman who came to see us, had no formal education beyond elementary school. She lived in an inner city in the Midwest and, in contrast to our normal frank relationship with our clients, refused to tell us how much money she was making. Despite her background (or because of it) she had managed to purchase a string of apartment houses. All but the first had been bought by using the cashflow from one building to finance the purchase of the next. She had become rich by buying properties when their prices made sense in relation to the cash they generated, and then—through personal supervision—kept them in good working order. Does that give you any ideas?

What do you think about buying time-shares?

Our advice is to stay away from time-shares. These are part ownerships of properties, often in resort areas. Don't be misled by a hope of saving money and vacationing for free. As absentee part owners, rentals of your property and ultimate resales are often left to a management company and are beyond your immediate control. Often results are disappointing. These are among the most illiquid real estate investments, which means you cannot sell them at any price. The only beneficiary is frequently the person who converted the units to time-shares.

The next time someone invites you to spend an inexpensive or free weekend viewing a time-share, be aware that you will probably pay for your weekend with time spent listening to a highly sophisticated and persistent sales pitch. Tell them "no thanks."

Should I borrow the money to finance my real estate purchase?

We told you earlier to borrow heavily to finance your home purchase. Just be sure you can afford the payment. As we mentioned, we believe that buying a home is a better investment than renting and can provide you with a form of forced savings. For other types of real estate, the factors to consider are different.

You might have read about the no-money-down ways to buy real estate for investment. This could lead you to think that your ability to finance a large percentage of your income-producing real estate through debt—so-called leverage—is an advantage. Over the past 50 years or so, this has usually been true. For most of that period until fairly recently, inflation was higher than expected; holders of hard assets such as real estate were big winners, and owners of bonds were losers.

Over the past 10 years, circumstances have changed. After adjustment for inflation, the banks have raised the cost of borrowing money. At the same time, cashflows from buildings have declined to the point that they cannot support a large amount of debt. Banks, meanwhile, have toughened up credit standards and generally require a personal guarantee before they lend money, thereby preventing people from tossing a plugged investment coin: heads, I win (real estate prices and profits move up); tails, the bank loses (I turn my failed gamble over to the banks at no personal loss to myself).

Now most banks hesitate about lending overall for investment purposes and require a material down payment. Large-scale borrowing works in your favor when your cashflow is secure and is currently higher than your borrowing costs, and when you can improve the earnings of the property or when inflation and real estate prices rise in relation to your fixed-rate interest payment.

If you are willing to take the extra risk, you can borrow to help finance your acquisition. As we mentioned, limit yourself to a conservative ratio of around 50 percent. And don't borrow more than the property can cover from operations. Always have a fund to tap equal to at least three months' interest and principal payments. Conservatism is the key. Otherwise you can find yourself with the same problems some of the real estate moguls have, except that you won't be too big to put into bankruptcy.

As part of our continuing interest in real estate, a few years ago we met separately with two of the leading real estate owners in New York. Each had come from a modest background to control large holdings. Each had used bank financing to create his wealth. Neither was hesitant about saying he was worth over $100 million. Both of their businesses are close to bankrupt today. Contrast that with the value-oriented real estate investor we know who gets no headlines, does not borrow to the hilt, and is currently creating a second fortune by buying up property at a fraction of what it will be worth 10 years from now. Need we say more?

What percentage of my portfolio should be allocated to real estate?

The percentage of your investment portfolio allocated to real estate is often beyond your control. This is true because a home is often by far the largest portion of a person's portfolio. A more relevant question is, should you consider your home as an investment? As a firm, we have wavered in our opinion. Sometimes we have excluded the home, other times we have included it, depending on individual circumstances. We have even split the difference, at times including 50 percent of the value of the house in the portfolio. Basically, your home should be included if you intend to sell it at retirement or some other time and buy a smaller home or move into a rental unit. It should not be included if you don't intend to sell it.

If your home is not included in the figures on asset allocation, we recommend that real estate make up 10 to 20 percent of your investments. You can make an exception if you manage your real estate yourself. In that case it could account for as much as 50 to 75 percent of your portfolio, provided you have a reasonable degree of sophistication in real estate and are aware that you have a heavy concentration of your assets in this one area and have access to funds in case of a reversal in the profitability of your real estate holdings.

Remember that real estate varies in quality. In deciding on the exact percentage of real estate in your portfolio, consider the characteristics that drew you to the investment. Give proper attention to the location, the condition of the property, the costs for upkeep, your relationship with your partners, if any, and the amount of cash you initially have to invest. Think, too, about what else you could do with that money if you weren't tying it up in real estate. How long do you expect to keep the property? Can you wait until the next upswing in prices to sell? You are making a major decision, which can work very well in your favor. Treat it seriously, do your research, follow an informed value-oriented style, and you can come out a winner.

8
Tax Planning

Taxes enter into all phases of your financial and economic life. When taxes rise, you may make some financial decisions based on the tax advantages they provide. These days it is harder to come up with new tax reduction strategies. The Tax Reform Act of 1986 reduced income tax rates sharply, tightened regulations, and also made it harder to find tax loopholes. Then again, it also eliminated many types of investments that were more harmful than helpful to individual taxpayers.

What can we expect over the 1990s? The bad news is that income taxes are likely to increase over the longer term. Not only will they climb at the federal level, but because the federal government has shifted some responsibilities for social services to the states, state and local taxes are likely to rise as well. Increased taxes may be hidden in the form of lower deductions, but they will be there.

All this gives us even more incentive to take another look at our taxes—and not just on April 15. By paying careful attention to tax planning fundamentals throughout the year, you can reduce your tax burden. We will show you how to take charge of your taxes in this chapter.

First, however, we feel we must caution you not to succumb to tax avoidance fever. Practically all the people we meet, from those earning $15,000 to those making more than $150,000 a year, believe they are paying too much in taxes. We respect their concern and strive to help them lower their taxes. Even so, we've noted that when tax avoidance fever strikes, otherwise rational people will do almost anything to reduce their taxes.

Marie came to see us about investing her money in nontaxable municipal bonds with short-term maturities. She was an elderly, retired factory worker on a modest fixed income that placed her within the 15 percent tax bracket. We pointed out that U.S. government bonds or even a money-market fund would pay substantially more than comparable municipal bonds—so much so that even after taxes they would provide a better return than the nontaxable municipal bonds. Marie replied that she understood but, "I am not going to pay the government one red cent more than I have to." This was a clear case of tax avoidance fever.

Stop feeling sorry for Marie, and read on to learn about more constructive techniques for reducing your taxes.

How can I figure out my tax return?

There is nothing mysterious about an income tax return. It is split into three major parts. The first part—gross income—requires you to list all your sources of income: salary, business income, interest, investment income, social security, and any others. The second part arrives at adjusted gross income by deducting for certain outlays such as pension payments. The third part—the computation of taxes—subtracts itemized deductions and exemptions from adjusted gross income to arrive at taxable income.

Itemized deductions is the part that you and/or your accountant focus on. Common allowable deductions include medical expenses, charitable donations, home mortgage interest, state and city income taxes, property taxes, and certain other miscellaneous expenses. If your deductions are not over $3600 for 1992 and you are single, or $6000 and you are filing a joint return, you should choose a standard deduction. You will then be given exemptions based on the size of your family and your income. Your taxable income in conjunction with your marital status (joint, single, or head of household) determines your tax rate.

Should I have my tax returns prepared professionally?

There are basically two reasons to have your tax return prepared professionally. The first is convenience; the second is expertise. If you have trouble organizing records and doing math, you may want to consult a tax specialist. The convenience of having someone else do what you find painful to even think about is tempting. However, even if someone else prepares your tax return, you should examine it carefully since you are liable for its contents. If you have a simple return, however, you can do it yourself. The IRS will answer your questions or even fill out the forms.

If your return is more complex, we recommend that you have it done professionally. Over time, a good tax specialist can more than pay for his or her fee. Since we are frequently asked by clients for referrals in this area, we have developed relationships with specialists we consider particularly good.

Recently we consulted one of them about Gene, who had moved out of a condominium he didn't like and moved into an apartment. Since he couldn't sell his condo, he rented it out. Thereafter, Gene bought a house and moved again. Since he moved and seemed to be renting the condo as a business activity, Gene was prepared to pay a tax on a six-figure gain on its ultimate sale. A quick call to a tax specialist uncovered a ruling that the rental of a property does not have to result in the loss of its designation as a principal residence if there is an inability to sell due to a depressed real estate market. Therefore, the gain on the sale of the condo was deferred by the purchase of Gene's new residence and a large current tax payment was eliminated.

Find a qualified expert by looking for evidence of specialized training, such as a certified public accountant's degree (CPA), an LLB in taxation, or an MBA in taxation. The person you choose should also have several years experience in the field.

How can I reduce my taxes?

There are basically four ways to reduce your tax burden: basic tax reduction, elimination of taxes, postponement of taxes, and income shifting. Basic tax reduction involves finding additional expenditures that are tax-deductible, such as home mortgage interest, state and local income tax payments, and real estate taxes. It is the common search that many of us point to with pride when we find another allowable item. One way to reduce taxes is to cluster expenses that aren't deductible unless the total sum exceeds a certain amount.

The term "elimination of taxes" has a magical ring to it, doesn't it? It sounds like a fantasy. Yet there are perfectly legal ways to eliminate taxes entirely. They include investing in your state's municipal bonds, making fringe benefit arrangements in your job, or donating appreciated stock to charity.

Another approach is to postpone taxes. This strategy allows you to have use of your money for a longer period of time. The effect can be very significant, as in a qualified pension plan where you can postpone taxes for many years. Sometimes you can save so much that it almost doesn't matter what your final tax bite is.

Finally, you can use income shifting, that is, transferring the tax burden from people in high tax brackets (often you and your spouse) to ones in lower brackets (perhaps your children). One way to do this is to gift assets to your child if he or she is over age 14.

We discuss each of these tax reduction techniques in greater detail later in this chapter.

If you are among the minority of people who are subject to the Alternative Minimum Tax (AMT), you will be subject to rules and recommendations substantially different from certain advice we give in this chapter. Included are those who have high itemized deductions in relation to income and/or those who have so-called tax preference items such as certain donations of properties to charities that have grown sharply since purchase. Under the tax act of 1993, the AMT has been raised and many more people will be subject to it. Check with an accountant if you think you might be in this group.

Are tax shelters still available?

We will let you in on a secret. There were never as many good tax shelters as people believed there were. True, there were plenty of tax loopholes. But by the time the average person bought the typical "tax-advantaged investment," the advantages were gone and only the disadvantages remained.

Here's how it worked. At the height of tax shelter mania in the early 1980s, brokerage firms were offering salespeople high commissions (a full 8 to 12 percent of the purchase price) to recommend tax shelter investment deals. The potential income was so high it was difficult for some commission-oriented advisors to remain objective in recommendations to their clients.

Few investors bothered to calculate the figures behind the investments offered as tax shelters. If they had, they would have discovered that often one-third to one-half of the dollars invested were wasted in promotional costs, unusually high administrative costs, and other nonearning assets. There was often no way the investment could stay alive, much less pay an attractive rate of return! However, many investors chose to see only the immediate reduction in their taxes instead of the long-term loss of part or all of their investment.

The moral of this story is that the tax shelter side of an investment is not enough. It needs to be supported by fundamentally sound investment features. One of the things we are proudest of is not falling for tax shelter mania. We kept our clients out of investments marketed as tax shelters—even though we lost some clients because we wouldn't recommend these types of investments for them.

Then there is the biggest tax shelter of all—an underground economy in which people simply don't report their income to the Internal Revenue Service (IRS). One day a middle-aged husband and wife came to see us. They wore old clothes and seemed rather agitated—in fact, the man was sweating profusely. The couple refused to give us their names. The man pulled out a wad of bills—he said it totaled $750,000—which he swore he had earned legitimately. He wanted us to recommend a foreign tax haven.

We assured him that the only outside laundering we did was our shirts, and sent the couple packing. But they did make us wonder if, as we have heard, more than 1 out of every 10 earned dollars is lost to the government in this way.

Legitimate tax shelters are investments that give you tax benefits. In theory, most of them are set up by the government to accomplish some public good, but in reality they are often a response to special-interest pressures. As we mentioned, the range of allowable shelters has recently narrowed with the passage of the Tax Reform Act of 1986. For example, you can no longer treat losses on most real estate partnership investments as a reduction of your job-related income. Nonetheless, we are frequently offered all kinds of so-called tax shelters, ranging from investments in kiwi fruit to deals that claim to take advantage of a loophole in the tax law. Often the loophole is vague and subject to IRS or court interpretation, which puts the investor at risk. Even if that investor receives a favorable ruling, if the shelter becomes popular, our Washington tax legislators, hungry for new revenues, will move to close it.

Could you evaluate the leading tax-sheltered investments?

The leading legitimate tax-sheltered investments are pensions, your home, annuities, municipal bonds, life insurance, Series EE bonds, oil, and real estate investments. As you can see, there are legal tax-advantaged investments to meet most pocketbooks and circumstances. Here is our evaluation of the risks and rewards of each of these options:

Pension Plan. This is our "best buy." In our opinion, a pension plan is the best tax shelter available, so attractive that we don't mind singing its praises in many chapters. The government set up qualified pension plans as tax shelters to encourage and help people to save for retirement and perhaps to reduce their dependence on the social security system. While usually you use a pension plan for your retirement, you can also use it in other circumstances.

We view traditional corporate and small-business pensions, IRAs, and 401(k)s and 403(b)s all as pension plans. All give you the ability to deduct contributions from your income for tax purposes. As far as the Internal Revenue Service is concerned today, it is as if you hadn't even earned that money. At the same time that you are reducing current taxes, your money is being invested. If you are in the 28 percent tax bracket, it means that 28 percent more dollars are working for you than if you had saved your salary by putting it into a regular savings account. Another advantage is that you don't pay taxes on the income your investments earn while they are still in your pension. This gives you much greater compounding power. You pay tax when you withdraw the money, usually when you retire. The final major advantage is your ability to put your money in a selection of attractive investments without the high fees that sometimes accompany other tax-advantaged investments. As we discuss in the retirement planning chapter (Chapter 9), you can accumulate hundreds of thousands of extra dollars by using this method over many years. We easily give this tax-sheltered investment our value-oriented money planning award.

Because of the strong advantages, we sometimes recommend using pensions in nonretirement situations, despite certain penalties. In the example shown in Table 8-1, we placed $2000 annually in a regular savings account which is taxed yearly and compared it with a pension account taxed at the end of a fixed time period. Even though there is a 10 percent penalty for an early pension withdrawal, notice that you will have a higher after-tax amount by the end of 12 years, and the benefit will grow larger each year thereafter.

Your Home. Your home has important tax advantages. As with a pension, it will increase in value without being subject to income taxes until it is sold. And the mortgage interest cost used to finance the original purchase or later improvements is tax-deductible. Besides, your home is virtually the only nonbusiness or entirely investment-related asset that you can borrow against and for which you receive a tax deduction on that loan. As we mentioned in Chapter 2, interest on the first $100,000 you borrow for any non-home-related purpose using your house as collateral is tax-deductible.

Table 8-1. Comparison of Pension and Regular Savings

Year	After-tax ($), pension	After-tax ($), regular savings	Difference ($)
1	1,339	1,523	(184)
2	2,786	3,134	(348)
3	4,348	4,837	(489)
4	6,035	6,639	(604)
5	7,857	8,544	(687)
6	9,824	10,559	(735)
7	11,949	12,690	(741)
8	14,245	14,944	(699)
9	16,723	17,328	(604)
10	19,400	19,849	(448)
11	22,292	22,515	(223)
12	**25,414**	**25,335**	**79**
13	28,787	28,317	469
14	32,429	31,471	958
15	36,362	34,807	1,555

Furthermore, you can sell your home and buy another with no tax impact as long as the cost of the second is greater than the selling price of the first and you buy the second within two years of selling the first home. Finally, after age 55, the first $125,000 of profits on sale of your home is not subject to income tax. Note that you and your spouse are eligible for this $125,000 exemption only once.

Annuities. Deferred annuities run by insurance companies allow you to put money in investments in which income earned will not be taxed until it is withdrawn. Withdrawals cannot start until age 59½ without a 10 percent penalty. You can borrow a portion of the money, but you won't get a tax deduction on the interest paid on the borrowed amount. Keep in mind that the government periodically attempts to reduce or eliminate the tax advantages of deferred annuities.

There are two types of annuities: fixed and variable. Fixed annuities pay the rate of interest decided on by the insurance company, with current market rates a factor in the decision. The value of fixed annuities does not change, which makes them suitable for conservative investors.

Variable annuities allow you to place your money in bonds or stocks whose returns depend on how well those markets and the money manager performed during the year. These annuities, which change in value according to the insurance company's performance, often guarantee at least the return of your principal.

If you are not pleased with the investment performance of your annuity and want to transfer to another company, you can be discouraged by the large withdrawal penalties. Both fixed and variable annuities are apt to penalize you severely for early withdrawals; they often start at 7 percent and work down to zero over 7 to 10 years. Variable annuities also contain large yearly overhead costs that tend to offset the tax benefits. Certain new low-cost, direct-to-the-consumer, variable annuity policies (marketed by mutual fund companies) may create better opportunities.

In our opinion, annuities are best suited for you if you are a conservative investor and have a modest amount of money that you feel you will not need until retirement. Shop around to find an insurance company rated AA or better that offers a fixed annuity with a competitive current rate of return and a "bail-out" clause of no more than 1½ percent under the current rate of return. This clause allows you to transfer ("bail out") without penalty if the insurance company's annual assigned rate of return falls by more than 1½ percent. Not only will that preserve some options for you, but it can compel the insurance company to be more competitive in their assigned rates should interest rates fall.

Note that municipal bonds often offer higher after-tax returns than annuities for people in all but the 15 percent bracket. For a comparison of the tax advantages of deferred annuities with municipal bonds, see Table 9-3 in Chapter 9.

Life Insurance. Life insurance is sometimes marketed as a tax-advantaged investment. That is because the extra money you pay in early years—beyond what is necessary to insure you against your current mortality risk and to pay commissions to the broker who sold you the policy—is put in a cash account; the interest earned on the account is not subject to tax unless you withdraw it. While that is certainly a tax advantage, we don't believe in insurance as an investment. You generally don't receive the proceeds, your heirs do, and reinvesting the dividends may not add to the death benefits of the policy. You will pay non-tax-deductible interest charges if you borrow any of the buildup in the cash value of the insurance policy (which can take years to be meaningful). Furthermore, the amount you borrow will reduce the death benefit. Therefore, we don't recommend using insurance as a tax shelter.

Series EE Bonds. Series EE bonds—the ones that make nice gifts because the recipient sees $50 on the face but they can be bought for $25—qualify as tax shelters because taxes on the interest earned can be deferred until you cash the bonds in. And while U.S. government bonds of all types, including Series EE, are subject to federal taxes, they are free of state and city taxes. Cashing in can be postponed 30 years with tax-free compounding until that time. The rate of return improves the longer you keep the bonds. If you keep them more than five years, you will receive a rate of interest 15 percent below the rate earned on five-year U.S. Government Treasury bonds. That rate has recently been about equivalent to municipals, which have the added advantage of being tax-free instead of tax-deferred. With backing from the U.S. government, stable prices, and ease of purchase and sale, Series EE bonds offer an attractive investment for highly conservative individuals.

Oil. Oil partnerships—in which a general partner supervises operations while you invest as a limited partner—are one of the oldest forms of tax shelters available. The costs of drilling can often be partly or fully deducted on your tax return in the year you invest, even though the related revenues may phase in over many years. Any initial losses from drilling costs can be used to reduce your job-related income and taxes, providing you are willing to risk being a general partner with unlimited liability against all your personal assets if the partnership is sued. Many partnerships provide substantial insurance against that occurrence and some offer to switch you to limited partnership status within one year so that your risk will be limited to your initial investment. The revenues you receive each year are also tax-advantaged since a percentage of the yearly cashflows is not subject to income tax because of certain depletion allowances.

The most important factor in selecting an oil partnership is finding a reputable general partner. We talked to the president of an oil company with a history of successful deals and a remarkably stable level of return. We asked how he managed to be so successful, and he replied that when one partnership was having difficulties, he would shift cashflows into it from a more successful deal. Obviously, he was violating his responsibility to represent each partnership separately. His conduct also raised a question: If he would transfer revenues from one group of investors to another, how do you know he wouldn't transfer funds to a special structure consisting of only one investor—himself?

Other important selection factors include the record of the organization in previous partnerships and the percentage of your money that actually goes into the investment instead of into commissions and administrative costs; we prefer at least 90 percent. We also prefer that the general partners earn their income after you receive your original investment back and you both then share in the profits. As you can gather, there are a lot of factors to consider besides tax benefits. The outlook for oil prices and the likelihood of finding oil are just two. Actually, there are methods of reducing the risk of not finding oil—such as drilling in fields in which oil has already been found. Nonetheless, this is a relatively risky proposition to get into merely for tax benefits. We recommend that you try it only if you have a calm disposition and above-average resources. Even then it is best to diversify your investments in a number of oil partnerships to reduce your chances of disappointing results.

Tax-Oriented Real Estate Investments. Tax benefits for owning real estate properties are found in Chapter 7. Here we'll mention two types of real estate investments in which tax benefits are particularly important: low-income housing and historic rehabilitation.

Low-income housing projects are not good investments by themselves. They are costly to operate, and the possibility of appreciation in value is remote. Consequently, the government allows you certain tax benefits, including deductions against your taxable income even when you haven't suffered any out-of-pocket cash loss. We worry that you won't be able to recover your original investment when you try to sell the property, and we don't regard the tax losses in this form of real estate as sufficient reason to invest in these partnerships except in special situations.

Historic rehabilitations can be more promising. When you invest in real estate certified as historic structures, you are allowed to take a 20 percent investment credit for any outlays for improving the property. This tax benefit is a credit that can be taken directly against what you owe. You must be careful to receive regulatory approval for your improvements; they must be compatible with the original design and feel of the property.

Historical rehabilitation is a very popular tax shelter in certain places. It has been estimated that over half the rehabilitation in Philadelphia, for example, has been done with tax credits in mind. Obviously, this credit can be of substantial current value, but when you sell the property, your gain will be higher to reflect the total benefit.

The key here is to make sure that the potential tax credit has not already been included in the price you pay for the property. We had one excited client, Andy, show us a Philadelphia historic partnership with a fully executed drawing of what the property would look like after it was renovated. His smile said, "I am going to beat the government." Unfortunately, to achieve his historic tax credit of 20 percent, Andy had bought the property for 40 percent more than it was worth without the credit.

Contrast that with another client, Miriam, who bought a late-nineteenth-century period piece near the shore as a retirement home. She paid $75,000 (80 percent of which she borrowed) and applied for historic status. The rehabilitation reduced Miriam's income taxes substantially. Today the property is worth twice its total cost five years ago.

Municipal Bonds. We describe this alternative in the next question "Should I switch to municipal bonds to reduce my taxes?"

"Faux Thermal International." This is a "hot" energy deal. The promoter plugs the product as a good alternative to high-cost gasoline. Even if it isn't, the promoter will tell you, the investment will be profitable because of a tax write-off set up to encourage new energy sources.

The tax write-off part is true. In fact, we project a 100 percent write-off against taxable income. There will be no return of your original outlay, though, because the entire investment will be worthless. You may also be liable for IRS penalties for sinking money in investments that lack economic merit. The moral of this hypothetical story is to avoid shady deals brought to you by creditable-looking salespeople who have traded in their sharkskin suits for dark, striped, flannel ones.

There are very few tax shelters that are both legitimate and profitable. Yet you'd be surprised how many people are desperately seeking them. A client, Ivan, made his business profit about once every four years and tried, during that fourth year, to shelter it. Four years before we met him, Ivan found one partnership that "sheltered" all his income; when the IRS found out, Ivan's house was attached for nonpayment of taxes and penalties. When Ivan came to us four years later, guess what he was looking for? That's right; he was looking for another leaky shelter.

Should I switch to municipal bonds to reduce my taxes?

Investing in municipal bonds is one of the most attractive tax shelters available today. As a low-overhead, easy-to-implement, tax-advantaged investment, we give it our second value-oriented award in this area. If you buy the right bonds within your home state or Puerto Rico, you will not be subject to federal, state, or city income taxes. Bonds from another state will just be federally tax-free.

Many people we meet want to know about the risk in municipal bonds. It is true that they are going to have to be watched more carefully in the 1990s, given the increasing financial and operating burdens placed on the states by the federal government. However, we believe that municipal bonds rated A or better, particularly those that are general state obligations of 1 of our 50 states, as opposed to certain municipalities in those states, are of high quality.

Make sure that your municipal bonds are nontaxable (not all are), and that they are not subject to alternative minimum taxes if you could potentially be subject to it. Municipal bonds have great flexibility, are easily liquidated if you need cash, and carry no redemption charges (except a commission that is not shown but is built into the price you get when you sell them). For people in brackets higher than 15 percent, municipal bonds have generally provided the highest after-tax returns of any type of high-quality bond. With federal and state taxes projected to rise over the decade, they should become an even more appealing tax shelter.

When should stocks and bonds be sold for tax reasons?

There are rules about when to sell for tax reasons. The trouble with them is that they are too pat and look at only one side of the decision equation. The other side is the investment return side. Improper decisions about when to sell can sometimes dwarf the tax benefits.

First, we will give you our conventional tax-oriented wisdom. Then we will present our financial planning adjustments to it.

Rule 1. Postpone sales of securities that have large gains until you have held them more than one year. They then qualify as capital gains. Income from capital gains is treated separately for income tax purposes and taxed at a maximum rate of 28 percent as opposed to a maximum tax rate of 31 percent on regular income. The distinction between capital gains and ordinary income is likely to become more important as ordinary income tax rates increase while capital gains rates stay flat or decline.

Our Modification. Compare cash benefits from selling for a tax loss with any projected rebound in the price of the security. You may be surprised at what you find. The potential rise in the price of the shares can dwarf any tax considerations. For example, assuming you are in the 28 percent tax bracket and your common shares are selling 25 percent below your original purchase price, any price movement above 10 percent relative to market averages will make it profitable to hold the shares. A 20 percent move will make it twice as profitable as selling for a tax loss. For such reasons, in investment accounts we manage, selling for a tax loss is only one factor in the total picture.

Rule 2. Delay sales of securities in which you have gains around year end to the new tax year. That way you will postpone your tax bill for a full year.

Our Modification. Be aware of any factor that could result in a sharply lower price by the time the new year rolls around. For example, it may pay to sell your shares in the current year, as opposed to the next, if a rumored takeover bid has driven the price up and you have no confidence that an acquisition actually will take place.

Rule 3. Before year-end, sell any securities in which you have a loss before December 31. This will allow you to take losses currently. You don't have to sell the securities and take capital losses if you already have established $3000 of such losses for the current year. Only the first $3000 of short- or long-term capital losses—after deducting any capital gains for the year—can be applied against regular income. The balance can be taken against future income, again at the rate of $3000 a year.

If you are dealing in bond transactions, you can often swap—sell one bond in which you have a loss and immediately buy another. This will probably save you commission costs. Make sure, however, that the securities are not from the same issuer or the same coupon and maturity, which could result in the IRS calling it a sham transaction and disallowing the loss.

Our Modification. Think carefully about shares of common stocks that have dropped sharply before you sell them for a tax loss in October, November, and December. During this time of year other people are selling their shares for tax reasons, which can artificially depress the price of your shares. In January, shares that have declined because of tax-loss selling—particularly those of smaller companies—often rebound in price, a phenomenon known as the January effect. Ken, an accountant with a particularly sharp eye for tax angles, asked our opinion of selling a holding in Bethlehem Steel, one of the largest U.S. steel producers, in November. We told him to wait, and he sold the shares in early February after a January price rise of 33 percent. Ken took the tax loss in the following year. The transaction did postpone and lower his tax benefits but, more importantly, it also substantially increased the overall cash he received.

Rule 4. Sell securities that have losses to offset others that you have already liquidated at a profit. On the other hand, if you have already sold or expect to sell securities at a loss, search for others in which profits can be taken so that your capital losses beyond the $3000 yearly limit can help the current year's cashflows.

If you have a large gain on one investment and feel it is time to sell, it may pay to buy "put" options on that security. For a fee, the put will allow you to freeze your gain or loss without selling the security. You can then postpone the taxable gain to the new year when you close out the transaction.

Our Modification. There are two instances in which you can sell for the tax loss without considering price appreciation. The first is when the price of the investment has declined so much—80 percent or more—that later price increases aren't likely to make as much difference as the current tax benefit. The second is when your losses are in the bond area. Stocks have many individual characteristics in addition to their relationship to overall stock market movements that may make it unwise to sell solely for tax reasons. Bonds, though, are most affected by changes in interest rates. Selling your bonds to realize losses and buying others can allow you to realize current tax losses and still benefit from future changes in bond market interest rates.

Rule 5. You should give careful consideration to selling shares for tax reasons if not only your stock but the overall market has dropped sharply. Your negative feelings at that point may reflect only overall pessimism, which often precedes a rebound in the market.

Our Modification. Consider buying additional shares in November equal to the amount you already own. Hold the shares for the required additional 31 days to make the transaction legitimate from the IRS standpoint. Then sell the original shares. You will get a tax loss and will maintain your longer-term position in the shares. You will, of course, also be affected by the gain or loss for the 31 days you hold that extra position.

What should I do when I expect my tax rate to rise?

If you expect a tax rate increase due to an overall rise in federal or state income taxes or because you've moved into a higher income tax bracket, consider doing the opposite of the tax rule of thumb: paying expenses in the current year and postponing income until the next year. When you anticipate a rise in your tax rate consider postponing expenses until the next year and take all possible income in the current year. Whether you should make this exception will depend on the amount of your tax increase. Paying taxes one year earlier than you have to means you are giving money to the government that you could otherwise have invested for an additional 12 months.

Don't make the common mistake of exaggerating your shift to a higher bracket. The higher tax rate won't be applied against all your income, just against the part of it that exceeds the lower rate. For example, if you had taxable income this year of $30,350 and the cutoff for the 15 percent bracket was $20,350, the impact would not be to move you in the second case to a 28 percent rate for the entire $30,350; you would pay 15 percent on the first $20,350, and 28 percent on the additional $10,000.

If the amount of the tax bracket increase from this year to next year is large, as is the jump from 15 percent to 28 percent, it would pay for you to accelerate income to this year and postpone deductions to the new year. The exact breakeven mark depends on what rate of return you earn on the money you could invest for an additional year. Generally, if you are in the 28 percent bracket or higher, it is not worthwhile to decline income in the current year and pay taxes earlier unless your tax rates rose by more than 2 to 3 percentage points.

How can I be assured of a refund on April 15?

We seldom see more pleasure on our clients' faces than when they receive a large refund from the government. In fact, some of them plan for the refund, budgeting their living costs carefully during the year, sometimes deliberately overpaying their withholding tax; the refund represents a form of forced savings. Contrast this with a large taxes-due obligation on April 15. That can throw your budget out of kilter and may even force you to borrow money to meet the payment. One of our clients fired her accountant in April because he failed to foresee a large amount of tax due with the year-end return.

Although a tax refund may give you the feeling that you have somehow beaten the system, financially this feeling has no validity. You will pay the same total amount of money whether you get a refund or you don't. The only difference is that by withholding more than you have to, you sacrifice the investment income your money would bring over the period.

On the other hand, you can be penalized for paying the government too little money when it is due. Quarterly payments are supposed to reflect your estimate of income for the year, not what you think you can spare. But you are not subject to penalty if the payments are at least as much as those you made last year. (However, if beginning in 1994 you have earnings of more than $150,000, you must make minimum payments of 110 percent of the previous year's tax.) When your income has increased over the previous year, you can defer payment until April 15 and have the use of your money for a longer period of time.

Remember: Assuming an 8 percent return on your money, for every $1000 you can delay paying the government for six months, you will gain an extra $40 in pretax income.

How many exemptions should I take?

An exemption is the amount the government allows you to deduct from your income based on the number of dependents you have in your household. If a tax refund is your main goal, you might claim zero exemptions on your withholding forms. To have use of the money for a longer period, increase the amount of exemptions, but be aware that taking more than you are entitled to can result in a penalty if you owe more than $500 and if it is over 10 percent of the total tax paid for that taxable year including the final payment on April 15. No penalty is due if you pay the same or slightly more than your previous year's withholding and you paid quarterly estimated tax payments on time.

We explained the relative advantages and disadvantages of over- and underwithholding in the previous question. If you just want to pay the correct amount, usually taking the correct number of exemptions should result in a figure in which taxes due are offset by taxes withheld. If you have unusually large deductions and generally get a refund at year-end, you can increase your exemptions. If, on the other hand, you have income not subject to withholding, such as small-business or investment income, you should raise the number of exemptions so that you aren't subject to penalties. By raising the exemptions when other income is not too large, you can prevent having to file quarterly estimated returns.

Do you have any special tax strategies?

Over the years we have made tax planning recommendations of all types, including in one case a recommendation to stop tax planning and get a good accountant. Arnold was spending more time on tax planning than on his business, which was heading downhill. At the rate he was going, he would have had his tax planning perfected about the same time his business stopped showing a profit—at which point, it would no longer be subject to taxation.

Here are some general tax planning strategies. Choose those that are relevant to your circumstances.

1. *Take advantage of available fringe benefits and negotiate for more.* You must pay taxes on your salary, but you won't be taxed on certain fringe benefits such as the first $50,000 of group term life insurance and all medical insurance premiums. Corporate "cafeteria" plans (those that offer a larger menu of deductible expenditures to choose from than just the traditional deductibles for medical or other types of insurance) may also be negotiated with your employer, but they have some additional restrictions.

Medical expenses in particular are becoming a costly sum. Having your employer pay your medical costs can increase your after-tax cashflow without increasing the company's outlays; if necessary, consider trading this benefit for a raise in salary. In fact, the company can actually benefit since it will have lower expenses for its share of social security payments to the government than if you took a wage hike instead. Companies will probably not be able to discriminate by offering you a benefit package that they don't provide for other employees, so you and your coworkers may do better by negotiating together.

If you encourage your company to start a pension, profit-sharing, or 401(k) plan, you can provide a tax shelter for contributors. One of our clients, Holly, successfully bargained with her employer, ultimately receiving a portion of her annual raise in new fringe benefits rather than cash. In that circumstance, both parties profited.

2. *Donate stock to charity.* This is an example of avoiding taxes entirely. You can donate securities to qualified not-for-profit institutions—religious, educational, charitable, and so on. This is a good tactic when you have large gains in common stocks that you intend to sell. If you sell the shares on the open market, you will pay a capital gains tax. If you donate your shares to a charitable institution, you will get a deduction for tax purposes and eliminate any capital gains tax. Just make sure the not-for-profit institution is recognized and qualified by the government. There is a listing of these organizations in IRS Publication 78 (*Cumulative List of Organizations*); for newer organizations, call your local IRS office and ask if the charity you have in mind has been approved.

3. *Place your child on your payroll.* If you have a business or a job in which you could use some help, you can employ your child. The criteria is that the child perform genuine services that are useful and you pay him or her at a rate appropriate for the level of service provided. You receive a deduction on your tax return, while your child must report the sum as income. You have effectively shifted income from yourself to your child, who is most likely in a lower tax bracket for earned income even if he or she is under age 14.

4. *Start a part-time or full-time business.* It's not so easy to start a business. Why should you bother? You should because a business gives you more flexibility with regard to taxes. For example, the part of your home that you use solely for your business can be deducted currently if it doesn't create a business loss; you can start a pension plan with your profits; and you can deduct certain business-related travel and entertainment costs.

Your business, however, can't be just a tax shelter. To satisfy the IRS, you have to show that you intend to make a profit. If you don't make money in any three of five consecutive tax years, your business may be considered a hobby. But if you have high start-up losses in the initial years, they can serve to reduce your taxable income. It can be done.

Arthur converted his hobby—buying and selling antique watches—into a profit-making activity, with substantial use of tax-deductible expenses. We have even recommended to other clients that they get their employer's approval to restructure their jobs as a consulting business rather than as a salaried position.

5. *Donate clothes to charity.* Instead of throwing them out when you are finished with them, why not donate your clothes and other valuables to a qualified charitable institution? Make reasonable estimates of the resale value, based on original costs and other factors such as condition. Prepare a statement supporting your estimates. Some charitable institutions may supply you with a written estimate of value. In either case, ask for a receipt and keep this estimate for your tax records.

Under the tax act of 1993, beginning in 1994 you need more documentation and tax forms if you deduct over $250 per contribution. You can consider splitting up your contribution into parts that fall under the $250 limitation. If you donate property with a claimed value of over $5000 per year to charity, get an appraisal from an independent third party.

6. *Transfer money to your child.* Until your child reaches age 14, he or she will be taxed at your rate for unearned income (that is, income that does not come from work, for example investment income). However, even then the first $550 of unearned income is not taxed at all and the next $550 is taxed at the child's rate. When he or she reaches age 14, the child will be taxed at his or her own rate for the entire sum, which creates income-shifting possibilities. You might gift your 14-year-old some money. Giving money for college is one possibility, but keep in mind that once you gift the money, you cannot determine how your children will actually use it (see the question "Should I put assets targeted for college in my child's name?" in Chapter 6).

What are some tax deductions and tax credits I might have missed?

Lots of our clients search eagerly for deductions and credits. Allowable *deductions* reduce your tax bill, while *credits* are more powerful because they reduce your actual taxes dollar for dollar. For example, if you are in the 28 percent bracket, a $1000 deduction will reduce your tax bill by $280, while a $1000 credit will reduce your taxes by the full $1000. Check to see if any of the following credits or deductions apply to your situation. Choose methods that apply to you, and keep the others in mind for future years:

Child Care Credit. If both parents work, or if yours is a single-parent household and you have a job, or if one parent works and the other is a full-time student, qualified child care is credited for children under age 13, up to $2038 for one child and $2527 for two children or more. Beginning in 1994 the credit will not be available for children under one year. The total amount of credit will rise annually beginning in 1995. The actual amount of this credit is dependent on your child-related expenses and joint incomes. (Sorry, overnight summer camp expenditures do not qualify.)

Dependent Care Credit. Your dependents are not only your minor children, but also others whom you support financially. For example, if a member of your household is a disabled adult who earns less than $2150 annually, that person could be treated for tax purposes as a dependent. The same rules as those explained in the child care credit apply here. That is, the outlays necessary to allow you to work—such as caretaker fees—are subject to a tax credit of a maximum of $720 for one person or $1440 for two people.

Points on Mortgages. Write out a separate check for the points that you pay on the mortgage you initially take out to purchase or improve your principal residence rather than taking a loan with the points deducted. You can get a current tax deduction for the expenses instead of deducting the points in equal amounts over the life of the mortgage. Unfortunately, this doesn't work when you refinance an existing mortgage.

Moving Expenses. You can deduct certain of these expenses if you move because of a job change. The move must take you more than 50 miles farther than the distance between your old job and former home. Furthermore, you must work at least 39 weeks of the year after the move. The tax act of 1993 narrowed the range of expenses you are allowed to deduct, eliminating such items as searcching for a home and temporary living expenses.

Casualty Losses. Unfortunately, theft is on the rise in the United States. Your losses through theft and physical occurrences such as fire beyond those you are reimbursed for through insurance coverage are deductible, providing they are over 10 percent of your adjusted gross income. The first $100 of any loss is not deductible. If you have had a theft, report it to the police, file the proper forms, and document it carefully. If you can't recover the stolen items but you provide proof of the theft and the value of the items, you can receive a deduction for this loss. Remember, you must support both the occurrence of a loss and the amount of damages.

Expenses for Charitable Activities. You are probably aware that cash and items donated to charity are deductible. Did you know that if you volunteer for charitable work your expenses are deductible too? If you volunteer, keep records of your expenses, including transportation to and from the charitable institution. You can deduct car mileage, reasonable cost for meals, and other expenses related to your volunteer activities.

Miscellaneous Expenses. The following items are deductible only if they and other miscellaneous expenses together exceed 2 percent of your adjusted gross income:

1. *Uniforms.* You can deduct the cost of any required uniforms or protective gear such as goggles and hardhats. Keep all receipts for your tax records and remember that the uniform must be inappropriate for everyday wear. For instance, a standard three-piece suit would not be an allowable deduction. We remember reading that Gerald Ford was denied a deduction for the custom-made suits he bought when he was running for President.
2. *Job-related expenses.* If you are out of work or are looking for new work in the same occupation, your job-seeking expenses are tax-deductible. Job-seeking expenses include travel expenses, résumé writing, employment agency fees, and so on. Training to maintain or improve your performance at your existing job, such as classes, is also deductible.
3. *Home office expenses.* These are allowed if a portion of your home or apartment is used regularly for business purposes. You also have to establish that this space is used *only* for business activities.

If you are employed by a company, you can take this deduction if a home office is required by your employer, or in certain other cases. This item is a political football. The courts and the IRS periodically interpret the area differently. Taking this deduction can mean a greater chance of audit, so be careful about using it, particularly when the deduction isn't large.

4. *Home computer and cellular telephone expenses.* These are deductible if they are required by your employer and are used the majority of the time for business. Subject to certain restrictions, you can deduct a home computer used in investment-related pursuits.
5. *Fees for rental of a safe-deposit box that holds investments.* Your costs for a safe-deposit box are deductible providing it holds your investments such as stock or bond certificates.
6. *Advisory fees.* Fees paid for tax preparation, financial planning advice that is tax- or investment-related, investment management, and subscriptions to investment-related magazines, newsletters, or newspapers are all deductible.

What are good year-end tax planning techniques?

December is the month commonly used for year-end tax-related planning for both individuals and business. It is best to prepare for this event at the beginning of the fourth quarter—say, in October. Your goal is to defer taxes to the new year. (See the question "What should I do when I expect my tax rate to rise?" for an exception to this rule.) By planning certain transactions carefully, you may be able to favorably influence your tax situation. Some of our clients have found these tactics useful:

1. If you own a business that is operated on a cash basis, you can realize less income by not billing your customers for services rendered before year-end until after January 1. If you are on a cash basis, income is taxable in the year you receive it.

2. Defer bonuses and business income until the new year if your company allows you to do so.

3. Prepay state and city taxes with a bias toward the high end of what you might owe. That will give you an extra deduction on your federal return one year earlier. The next year the overpayment will be reported as miscellaneous income on your tax return. Be careful about overstating these tax expenses by too much because you can be penalized for it on your federal return.

4. Cluster expenses subject to a minimum level in the current year. For example, medical expenses are deductible only to the extent that they exceed 7.5 percent of your adjusted gross income. Instead of waiting until next year, plan for medical visits in December if you are over the 7.5 percent floor. Combine two years' worth of deductible miscellaneous expenses by seeing your accountant in January and December and paying for next year's business-related magazine subscription in the current year. This will bring you over the 2 percent limit for miscellaneous expenses.

5. Defer investment income. Buy three-month to one-year certificates of deposit and Treasury securities. Interest will not be credited for tax purposes until maturity, which you should structure to fall due the following year.

6. Plan year-end investment sales. Stock and other securities should be planned in part for their tax impact. The general tax rule is to take deferred sales on profitable transactions in the new year and liquidate securities with losses in the current year subject to the $3000 annual limit. For more information on this topic, including a discussion on when these rules should be modified, see the question "When should stocks and bonds be sold for tax reasons?"

7. Open a pension plan in the current year. If you are planning to start a Keogh plan, do it by December 31. While the money needed to fund the pension won't be due until the tax return is due (including extensions), you won't be able to take the deduction if the account isn't established in the year the money was earned. That isn't true for certain other pension plans, such as a SEP.

8. Keep your receipts for all goods and money you donate to charity as well as the written acknowledgment from the charity for gifts that don't benefit the donor. Contributions are deductible when paid, not when promised. If you want to deduct your contribution to your alumni association this year, it is not enough to pledge a certain

sum over the telephone. Make sure you actually send in your check before December 31.

9. Watch the dates for getting married or divorced. This can save you money. Your marital status on December 31 determines your status for the full year. The approach should depend on your relative incomes. If one person is earning a great deal more than the other, it will be better to get married in the current year. If you and your partner earn similar amounts, it will be better to postpone the marriage until January. The tax bill of 1993 substantially increased this marriage penalty. The difference in impact between the two examples is due to the way the tax tables are structured.

When the income of the two people is about equal, it also will be better to get divorced in the current year. If that puts ideas in your head about getting married every January and divorced every December, forget it. The IRS will disallow marital changes intended solely to get around tax laws.

Besides, are you absolutely sure you can trust your partner to complete the whole process? Think about it.

9

Planning for Retirement

People come to financial planners for a wide variety of reasons. Often what they are seeking, however, turns out to be either investment advice or a retirement plan. In fact, the two areas are often related. Most people invest their money with the goal of having enough funds to retire comfortably.

Some people begin thinking about and investing for retirement when they are in their twenties and thirties, but they are the exceptions. Our clients who own businesses say their younger workers would much rather have the cash than an investment in a pension plan that they cannot touch for many years, despite the tax benefits involved. We find that often it is not until people reach their forties or fifties that they start thinking seriously about retirement. And a good number of middle-income people never do plan seriously for retirement. They ought to—it takes a lot of money to retire comfortably.

Social security as a percentage of total retirement income is likely to decline in the 1990s. Retirement ages are scheduled to be raised, half of social security payments are already subject to taxes for people whose incomes are above-average (and taxation may be extended further), and every few years Washington lawmakers consider cutting back existing payments. (Cutbacks are encouraged by those who believe that retirees have a better standard of living than people who are currently working.)

If you have planned properly for retirement, you will have had a substantial burden lifted from your shoulders when the big day comes. You can look forward to many comfortable years pursuing interests of your own choice. If you have not started planning, or if you would like to improve your retirement planning procedures, you need to read further.

How should I invest for retirement?

Fortunately, for many Americans there are a variety of ways to save for retirement. The most attractive of these are "qualified" pension or profit-sharing plans that allow you a tax deduction for contributions. We discuss these in the question "What is the best way to save for retirement?"

Once you move away from qualified plans, practically anything can be thought of as an investment for retirement. In fact, you are likely to be bombarded with investment alternatives, some of which may be hazardous to your wealth. One widow we know was persuaded to put her entire retirement savings into two "unusually attractive" real estate limited partnerships. Even without considering the merits of the investments themselves, their purchase violated two basic rules of financial planning: (1) never put all your eggs in just a few baskets and (2) make sure you can get some eggs out of your baskets when you need them. Clearly, these investments were not suitable. The limited partnerships did not provide a cash payout, could not be sold, and are likely never to have their capital returned. The widow has been forced to drastically reduce her lifestyle.

A truly attractive retirement investment has most of the same characteristics as any other investment. The major differences are that retirement investments have more of an emphasis on longer-term growth prior to retirement, and should focus on income, liquidity, and safety thereafter.

However, be careful not to overemphasize this shift in investment focus. Too often, people view this planning as a race, with retirement day as the finish line. In reality, life goes on after retirement day, and your investments must keep on bringing in money. Your long-term return on investment can help determine whether or not you have a long, productive, and worry-free retirement.

When should I start planning for retirement?

There is no magic date at which retirement planning should begin. It depends on such factors as your current assets, the retirement benefits you will receive, and the standard of living you would like to enjoy upon retirement. Steve, a 28-year-old professional man, came to see us about retirement planning when his wife was expecting their second child. He was very specific about setting up retirement plans, college funds for his children (including three years of law school for a child not yet able to pronounce the word *lawyer*), financing the purchase of a home, and identifying the insurance he needed. Now at age 33, Steve's financial goals have been established and he is well on the way to realizing his ambitions.

If you didn't have Steve's foresight, do not be depressed. Although few financial advisors would object to such long-term thinking, most people will not choose to begin planning vigorously for retirement at such a young age. Steve had the resources, vision, and discipline to set aside funds while he was young, but a more popular tendency is to focus on immediate wants and needs.

Of course, the time at which you begin saving has side effects. For every dollar you save at age 35, it can take three dollars to compile the necessary retirement sum if you begin at age 55. This is particularly true if your goal is to have a substantially higher lifestyle than is possible on your social security income and corporate assigned pension plan. The moral is that saving substantial amounts at an early age makes retirement significantly easier.

Since in our experience most people tend to ignore morality tales and many will save only sporadically until middle age, we generally recommend that significant retirement planning begin 20 years before the anticipated retirement date. This date is typically age 65 but that is likely to rise as full social security payments start at age 67 or later in the 1990s.

Most people should begin programmed saving for retirement when they are in their forties. Contributions should be stepped up at about age 55, when for many families money has been freed up as college and other child-rearing expenses have been reduced or eliminated.

What is the best way to save for retirement?

Aside from social security, there are three assets that form the backbone of most people's retirement funds: pensions, personal savings, and homes. Your home is a tax-advantaged investment, and a few simple steps (see Chapter 7) can lead to large gains on sale at retirement. Does this mean that you should buy the largest, most luxurious house possible? You shouldn't unless it provides good investment value and you plan to sell it when you retire. Otherwise, a substantial investment in a home will not help in the planning process and can actually tie up a large portion of your assets.

In our opinion, a pension plan provides the best form of retirement savings for the average American. Your contributions to qualified pension plans, including profit-sharing plans, regular pensions, IRAs, 401(k)s, 403(b)s, and SEPs, are tax-deductible; even though this money is being invested for you, for current tax purposes it is treated as if you had not received it! Nor are earnings on the money subject to taxes while it is in the pension plan. The money will not be taxed until it is withdrawn.

A growing number of companies have established 401(k) plans that allow participants to put aside up to $8475 a year in 1992, with allowable contributions increasing annually by the rate of inflation. These plans have different rules, but most allow you to diversify your savings among several investment alternatives, such as money-market accounts, stocks, or bonds. Even if retirement seems far away to you now, you should think carefully before deciding not to contribute to the plans. True, you may have other pressing needs and you may be hesitant about "locking up" your funds, but do you really want to pass up this excellent tax benefit and retirement planning tool? In some cases, you may also be foregoing free matching contributions by your company. A matching contribution of 3 percent, for example, is really a 3 percent increase in your salary with no immediate tax consequences.

If you place $7000 (equivalent to $5000 of take-home pay for someone in the 28 percent tax bracket) into a qualified pension plan each year for 20 years at an 8 percent investment rate, your total assets at the end of the period will amount to $320,000. The same sum withdrawn from the company, taxed, and invested in taxable U.S. government bonds yielding 8 percent (5.8 percent after tax) would amount to only $179,000. Table 9-1 compares the two forms of investment for varying periods of time.

Even though the pension monies will be subject to income taxes over the years as the funds are withdrawn, the benefits are sizeable. Besides, since you cannot touch the funds without incurring a substantial penalty, the pension can help you withstand the temptation to borrow the monies "temporarily" for a nonessential item. In that way, the pension can also be a good form of enforced savings. The pension plan wins this chapter's value-oriented money planning award hands down.

When a pension plan is not available or when it is important that you keep the funds aside for possible use before you retire, you should maintain as many of the favorable characteristics of a pension plan as possible. That means, make regularly scheduled payments into separate savings accounts. If you are in the 28 percent tax bracket or higher, consider substituting municipal bonds or tax-

Table 9-1. Comparison of Pension and Personal Savings*

	Savings placed in U.S. government bond in pension	Savings placed in U.S. government bond in regular account
Pretax savings annually	$7,000	$7,000
Taxes at 28%	0	−2,000
After-tax savings annually	$7,000	$5,000
Total savings at end of		
5 years	$41,066	$28,051
10 years	$101,406	$65,166
15 years	$190,065	$114,275
20 years	$320,334	$179,252
30 years	$792,982	$378,985

*Individual is in the 28 percent tax bracket with an investment earning 8 percent annually.

deferred annuities for certificates of deposit and purchase government bonds as the lower-risk component of your retirement savings.

Should I contribute to an IRA under the current tax laws?

Before the Tax Reform Act of 1986, we strongly encouraged all of our clients to set up allowable IRAs ($2000 for each working family member or a $2250 total where only one spouse worked). The 1986 act eliminated this tax deduction for single people making over $35,000 and for couples making over $50,000, if they are currently enrolled in a pension plan.

The tax deduction on the old IRAs was very important because, in effect, Uncle Sam was financing a portion of each payment by providing a current tax credit for the money deposited. The remaining advantage, tax-free compounding of income until withdrawal, may still be effective when amounts are kept in for periods of 14 years or longer even if they undergo penalty for withdrawal prior to age 59½. (The penalty is 10 percent over the normal tax.) Like corporate pension plans, IRAs can be a good form of forced savings. Moreover, there are a wide array of investment alternatives that can be used within an IRA, ranging from certificates of deposit and bonds to growth equity mutual funds. Therefore, while we no longer press our clients to contribute to IRAs, we do believe they are advantageous.

How do I plan for medical outlays and nursing home expenditures?

One of the greatest fears of people considering retirement is that they will be faced with a large medical or nursing home bill that will devastate their savings. The medical part can be taken care of fairly easily. Medicare pays about 75 percent of the approved cost of physician visits and other medical services and supplies. The annual deductible you pay before Medicare benefits begin is currently $100. (See Chapter 12 for a fuller discussion of Medicare.) In order to avoid a gap between the Medicare approved amount and actual costs, use doctors and suppliers who accept assignment (that is, take Medicare as full payment). In addition, you should buy a comprehensive major medical policy to pay the balance not covered by Medicare. Check the upper limits of the policy, which should be at least $1 million for each illness.

The nursing home situation is more complex. Medicare does not pay for custodial care in a nursing home (and most nursing home care is custodial), but it will contribute toward skilled nursing or rehabilitation care in a participating nursing home for up to the first 100 days. The first 20 days of stay will be completely covered by Medicare, and the next 80 days will be paid by Medicare with a contribution by the patient ($81.50 daily in 1992). Of course, certain requirements must be met. For example, you must enter the nursing home after at least three consecutive days in a hospital, you must have your physician's authorization that the skilled nursing home care is necessary, and your condition must be the same one that was treated in the hospital.

Nursing home insurance is available. However, people with modest incomes cannot afford the annual cost for a truly comprehensive policy including home health-care benefits, which can be $2000 or more for people aged 55 and many times higher for people in their seventies. If you have enough income to cover the sizeable ongoing nursing home costs, you do not need this insurance. It is the middle-income person who is most affected by nursing home costs. While policies are improving steadily, in our opinion, nursing home insurance has not yet been perfected to the point that it represents good value. If you would like the peace of mind of at least partial coverage, begin to buy this insurance by age 50 or 55 when the premiums are at a relatively low and affordable level.

Statistics indicate that relatively few individuals spend more than five years in a nursing home. Those who do can be reassured that the government will pick up the cost when their money runs out. In fact, you can take advantage of the government subsidy for nursing homes and protect your estate by transferring most of your money out of your estate and into the hands of your beneficiaries. This strategy is allowed if it is done two-and-a-half years or more before you enter the home. (For further information, see Chapter 12.)

How do I know if I have enough funds to retire comfortably?

This question and "Is my money invested properly?" are the two most frequently asked by our clients. There is no easy answer to determine the amount of funds you will need when you retire. Basically, it depends on your own idea of "comfort." The two following, widely differing anecdotes illustrate this point.

One of our clients, Mark, always felt that the future would bring better fortune than the present. Not that the present was bad; Mark's manufacturing business provided him with $125,000 per year in profits, but his personal expenses consumed the entire sum. We were flabbergasted when Mark told us that his idea of a comfortable retirement was $250,000 a year in today's dollars. Since his business did not appear capable of expansion, his goals and his resources were clearly in conflict. It took all of our and Mark's wife's powers of persuasion to convince him to scale down his concept of comfort.

This was in sharp contrast to another couple, the Petersons, who came to us for a retirement plan. Throughout their marriage, this husband and wife had maintained an extremely conservative standard of living. They had never bought a home or a car and seldom took vacations. The Petersons told us that they were "depression babies," brought up in the 1930s when having a job and food on the table was often a large-enough goal. Partly because of their low standard of living, by the time they were ready to retire they had accumulated investable reserves of over $600,000. It was clear to us that their existing fears of being wiped out were—under any foreseeable circumstances—unwarranted, and their idea of a comfortable retirement could be expanded. But first, we had to show Mr. and Mrs. Peterson in our detailed, year-by-year computer forecasts that they could, in fact, buy a home, take annual vacations, boost their overall spending, and still not run out of money even if they would live to be 130! While the Peterson's lifestyle has improved noticeably, we wonder if the wife secretly puts aside some of the spendable income for what she would term a rainy day.

In Table 9-2, we have outlined the cumulative amounts you would need to save by various ages to fund retirement from age 65 to age 90. The figures are broken down by different costs of living and assume a 6 percent after-tax return, a 5 percent inflation rate, and social security benefits for two people living to age 90. Let's assume your retirement cost of living, including taxes, totals $25,000. Savings of $215,000 at the retirement date—age 65—currently returning 6 percent after tax, plus social security should be sufficient to cover your needs from age 65 to 90. A good sum in pension savings or a corporate pension payout at retirement would reduce the required savings figure. For example, a $10,000 annual corporate pension payout after retirement would lower this required figure by about $100,000.

Keep in mind that it is not enough to fund for average mortality dates, which at retirement are around 80 for men and 84 for women, since many people live well beyond the average age. Actually, 10 percent of men and women live well into their nineties, and longevity is increasing.

If you have not achieved the level of savings indicated by Table 9-2, have a higher cost of living or a lower investment return, or want to fund for a longer life span, you should plan to save more each year prior to retirement. For example, saving an additional $5000 per year at a 6 percent after-tax return can total $50,000 in only eight years.

Do not base your decision about whether you can retire comfortably on your calculations of your retirement income and cost of living at the date of retirement. Inflation will result in a steady increase in your cost of living, but your pension payments and investment income may not rise accordingly. Most large corporations, for example, provide fixed-level pension payments for their retirees. Your retirement income will grow measurably only if it is indexed for inflation (as is social security), if you save money each year, or if you place your savings in growth investments. With expenses increasing faster than income, the majority of people are forced to dip into savings over the years to support their lifestyles. This is fine as long as the savings will last over your life expectancy. Whether your savings are adequate depends on such factors as your rate of return on investment savings as compared with the inflation rate, whether your pension will climb with inflation (most do not), your assets, and how long you live.

Table 9-2. Retirement Savings ($) Needed at Various Ages and for Various Costs of Living

	Expenses, $									
Age	15,000	20,000	25,000	30,000	40,000	50,000	60,000	70,000	80,000	100,000
25	35,000	85,000	145,000	210,000	370,000	525,000	675,000	825,000	980,000	1,280,000
35	40,000	95,000	160,000	230,000	410,000	575,000	740,000	910,000	1,075,000	1,410,000
45	45,000	105,000	180,000	255,000	450,000	635,000	815,000	1,000,000	1,185,000	1,550,000
55	50,000	115,000	195,000	280,000	495,000	695,000	895,000	1,100,000	1,300,000	1,705,000
65	55,000	125,000	215,000	305,000	545,000	765,000	985,000	1,210,000	1,430,000	1,870,000

Figuring out how much money you need to achieve a comfortable retirement under your personal circumstances is complex and can cost thousands of dollars if done in a truly professional manner. We have simplified the process and in Appendices A and B we provide the means by which you can attain an approximation of your needs.

What will happen to my living costs after I retire?

Retirement living can bring significant changes in costs. On the one hand, your job-related expenses are eliminated. These include business clothing, lunches, and transportation. Many couples find they can get by with one car instead of two. Taxes are likely to decline appreciably. If your mortgage is fully paid up at retirement, your living costs could also go down by a large amount.

On the other hand, expenses no longer supported by an employer, such as medical costs beyond Medicare and major medical insurance, will rise. Because you have more leisure time, you might run up higher annual costs for vacations, food, and entertainment.

Still we find that many retirees are able to cut their cost of living by 30 percent or more without feeling that their standard of living has changed.

What if I don't have enough money to retire?

Don't get upset if you cannot afford retirement yet. You have a lot of company. A significant percentage of middle-class Americans will not have enough money to retire comfortably when they want to. Kevin came to our office and announced that he was 66 years old and flat broke. Just as important to him, his wife, Jenny, knew nothing about his financial setbacks and lack of retirement income beyond social security. With our encouragement, Kevin told his wife that he had spent their retirement savings. Jenny was more understanding than Kevin had feared; by successfully relieving himself of the burden of secrecy, our client probably added a few years to his life. Kevin was forced to continue to work in an effort to accumulate money for retirement. Fortunately, he has remained healthy and productive and has maintained a fairly high income level. Under our guidelines, the couple has cut back substantially on trips, gifts, and expensive clothes. While they are not yet out of the financial woods, their retirement future looks considerably brighter.

Here are some measures you can follow to avoid a similar emergency situation:

1. *Save more each year prior to retiring.* Many people find they can save a few thousand dollars each year without really cutting into their standard of living. For the average American family, saving an additional 5 percent of salary each year for 15 years before retiring, combined with social security income, can finance 4 more years of a comfortable retirement.

2. *Earn additional income.* Take an extra part-time job either before or after retirement. While a preretirement second job is usually taken just to earn extra income, a job after retirement can represent good physical and mental therapy.

3. *Postpone the retirement date.* The country has recognized that people can be productive to an older age than was thought 50 years ago. Mandatory job retirement is often age 70 now instead of 65. For many people, each two years' additional work can add two-and-a-half years to the age at which resources would run out.

4. *Liquidate underutilized assets.* Sell or otherwise develop cash-flow from those assets that do not provide meaningful income. Most commonly this involves the home. Your home can be partially rented out, a new mortgage that does not require principal payments can be acquired, the home can be sold to your offspring in return for lifetime occupancy, or it can just plain be sold outright with you moving to an apartment.

5. *Reduce retirement expenditures.* Moving to a lower-cost location is the easiest way to reduce expenses. The sale of your home can provide a healthy nest egg, with the first $125,000 of gains tax-free one time only after age 55. Shifting to planned retirement communities, or to a lower-cost or lower-taxed area (certain southern states, rural areas, or college towns) can save you money without impairing your

standard of living. Otherwise, by watching outlays more carefully, many retirees can reduce their retirement costs without noticeably affecting their standard of living.

6. *Raise investment returns.* Increase the income from your savings. Often that means assuming greater investment risk. You can take money out of bank savings accounts or money-market accounts and place it in nongovernmental, guaranteed lower overhead, mutual fund money-market accounts.

You can buy government Treasury bonds that are not subject to state income taxes or municipal bonds from your state that are not taxable at all. Or you can take a harder step—buy conservative stock mutual funds and resolve to hold them for five years or more (see the discussion of investments in Chapter 3).

It is sometimes possible to raise expected returns without a real change in the overall risk level of your assets. First, though, we recommend a careful analysis of your discomfort level before venturing forward with a change in investment risk. Many times, it is preferable to modify your noninvestment alternatives instead.

How do I decide whether to take early retirement?

Recently, many corporations have been giving their employees the option of retiring early. From a lifestyle standpoint, the decision depends on your desire to embark on new activities. Often people under 65 choose early retirement, assuming they have the financial means to do so, because of discontent with their current positions. We have found that frequently people who do leave soon shift to other full- or part-time positions, sometimes in new career areas.

From a financial standpoint, the first thing you should do is establish the ability to support yourself in retirement. Take into account any minimum sum you want to leave your children or other heirs. If your corporation is offering an incentive to leave in terms of extended salary and pension benefits, make sure that you are not being given a subtle message that you have no future with the firm. Then relate the package to normal retirement income and, when appropriate, to potential employment income in other attractive positions that are available to you.

Marilyn was offered a severance package equivalent to one year's pay and three years additional credit for pension purposes. However, when she looked into getting another job, Marilyn found that she would have to take a 40 percent pay cut. The option of rejecting the retirement offer and staying on was genuine, and she did so.

When the figures are not compelling and the desire to leave is not pressing, it is better to stay on and thereby be able to fund additional years of a comfortable retirement.

Should I take a lump-sum pension settlement or roll over my funds?

When you leave your job or retire, you may have to choose between taking the cash out of the pension plan in a lump sum or rolling it over by transferring it to a special rollover IRA account. We will look at the advantages and disadvantages of both choices.

If you are over age 59½, taking a lump-sum distribution will allow you to withdraw the money without the extra 10 percent tax on premature withdrawals and will also qualify you for special income averaging. Under current regulations you can exclude all other types of income, and for tax purposes the sum can be treated as if it were spread equally over 5 years; if you are over age 50 as of January 1986, you have an additional choice of spreading the monies over 10 years. In most instances if you are eligible for 10-year averaging, taking it will be better than choosing the 5-year method for all distributions under approximately $400,000.

Rolling the money over, on the other hand, provides you with a tax shelter by allowing the funds to compound free from income taxes and postpones the time you begin to pay taxes until you actually need the money or until age 70½ (when you *must* begin to withdraw the monies). You must deposit the funds with a qualified custodial institution such as a bank, a brokerage firm, or an insurance company within 60 days of receipt. The costs of maintaining such an account are generally no greater than those for a regular IRA. Many institutions allow you to invest the funds in a wide variety of investment vehicles.

The special tax rates applying to lump-sum investments were more important prior to the Tax Reform Act of 1986. Now if you have more than $100,000 in settlement funds, you will be taxed at a higher bracket even under 5-year averaging. Postponement of taxes through a rollover is generally more beneficial than those special lump-sum tax rates. Exceptions are when a large portion of the money will be needed in a few years or if you believe there will be a severe increase in future tax rates. In most circumstances, we recommend rolling it over since doing so can add a good sum to your retirement nest egg.

At what age should I start withdrawing money from my pension or IRA?

Aside from those plans that require you to pay a fixed sum as long as you live, most pensions (corporate retirement plans, Keogh plans, SEPs, or IRAs) allow withdrawals without penalty at retirement age 59½ and require it by age 70½. At age 70½ withdrawals are made actuarially by Internal Revenue tables based on life expectancy. When should you begin? Your instincts may tell you to begin withdrawing as soon as you retire. Isn't that what you worked so hard to do?

Don't do it. While taking out your money at retirement may satisfy your emotional needs, the withdrawals will come at a financial price. As we have said, money taken from a pension plan is subject to taxes on withdrawal. Leaving it in the pension and living from your regular savings for as long as possible will allow the money in the plan to continue to grow tax-free and postpone the date taxes are paid. This is no small matter. Postponing taxes on withdrawals of $10,000 a year for seven years and then paying taxes on the entire sum can add as much as $5000 to your overall assets! More gradual withdrawals would add even further to the savings.

Ideally, you should wait to begin withdrawing from your pension until you reach 70½ years old and take minimum required payments thereafter. Use your non-IRA, nonpension assets first. Be assured that after you retire, most plans in which you have control over the assets allow you to take out as much money as you need. In case of emergency, you can always remove the money from your pension savings. It is no less your money whether it is in your personal savings account or in your pension savings account.

How attractive are annuities as retirement investments?

Annuities are often marketed as retirement investments. Income earned on annuities, as with pension plans, is deferred from taxes until it is withdrawn. You can begin withdrawals at age 59½ (10 percent can be withdrawn per year before age 59½ without IRS penalty), but you do not have to start withdrawing by age 70½ as you do with pensions. Also unlike pensions, an unlimited amount of money can be placed in annuities. The key advantage for qualified pension plans is that you get a tax deduction for pension deposits whereas payments to an annuity generally cannot be deducted.

Many companies offer variable annuity alternatives. Money deposited in these annuities are invested in a variety of investment vehicles that can go down as well as up. (Variable annuities are similar to mutual funds and are discussed under tax-advantaged investments in Chapter 8.) The largest proportion of annuities outstanding, however, are fixed annuities whose return is assigned by the insurance company based on returns in their own investment portfolios. The principal does not fluctuate and therefore cannot decline, and the return is often comparable to certificates of deposit; furthermore, like banks offering certificates of deposit, certain insurance companies provide higher returns than others.

Some people are drawn to annuities because of the very feature we dislike—the annuitizing feature. Annuitizing converts your annuity investment into fixed annual payments based on life expectancy often beginning when the person retires. We counsel against annuitizing for a number of reasons. Frequently, the insurance companies' mortality assumptions are overly conservative—which means you may get lower payments because the insurance company assumes greater longevity than may be appropriate. Then, you should realize that the fixed annual payments will look progressively less attractive as inflation reduces their purchasing power. In addition, your offspring will almost certainly be poorer, since, with few exceptions there will be nothing left to give to them when you die, whether in 6 years or 60.

Tax-deferred annuities are often seen as substitutes for conservative investments such as certificates of deposit or bond mutual funds. As such, they are perhaps most appropriate for individuals in low tax brackets. Of course, IRAs also offer this tax-deferral feature, and without the sizeable redemption fees you can have with annuities should you decide to switch investment managers.

For people in higher tax brackets interested in finding retirement investments, the true alternatives for fixed annuities are high-quality municipal bonds and municipal bond funds. Annuities offer a moderately higher annual pretax return and your investment value will not move up and down; however, qualified municipal bond returns are permanently tax-free in contrast to the tax-deferred status for annuities. (The value of your municipal bonds will fluctuate with changes in interest rates, but you can expect to receive the anticipated rate of return if you hold these bonds to maturity.)

Some people are uncomfortable buying a security that fluctuates in price, and others are put off by the $10,000 to $25,000 size generally necessary for municipal bond purchases and lack of maturity dates for municipal bond funds. For these people, annuities represent attractive investment alternatives, particularly because of the annual savings beyond the $2000 to $2250 IRA limit. When these factors are not of concern, we recommend municipal bonds rather than fixed annuities as the better retirement investment for our clients in 28 percent and higher tax brackets for the fixed-income portion of their portfolio. A comparison of municipal bonds with tax-deferred annuities is shown in Table 9-3.

Table 9-3. Comparison of Annuities and Municipal Bonds

	Tax-deferred annuity		Municipal bond
Amount of deposit	$20,000		$20,000
Pretax return	8%		7%
	Cumulative pretax savings	Cumulative after-tax savings	Cumulative after-tax savings
End of 5 years	$29,387	$26,758	$28,051
10 years	43,178	36,689	39,343
15 years	63,443	51,279	55,181
20 years	93,219	72,718	77,394
30 years	201,253	150,502	152,245

What is the best age at which to start taking social security?

First make sure you are covered by social security. Those not covered by social security include police officers with their own retirement systems, federal government employees who were hired before 1984, farm and domestic workers with irregular employment, low-income self-employed people, some Americans working abroad, some children who work for their parents, and some students. If you are not sure whether you are entitled to social security, check with your employer or with your local social security office.

Most people are currently entitled to retire and take social security at age 62. If you do this, you will permanently receive 80 percent of what you would get at age 65. The amount moves up steadily to 100 percent if you start collecting at age 65 and can become 3 to 8 percent more for each year you postpone retirement beyond age 65, depending on when you were born. For most retirees, the question is whether to start social security at age 62 or delay until age 65. The answer depends on such questions as whether you need the money immediately, how your health is, and what return you can receive on the government payment if you invest part or all of it. As we show in Table 9-4, the point at which many people would begin to benefit financially from postponing payments until age 65 would come if they lived beyond age 77. It assumes a 6 percent after-tax return on the monies received and a current benefit of $9600 at age 62 (80 percent of an assumed $12,000 benefit at age 65). For most of our middle-income clients already resolved to take early retirement, because of the often strong emotional desire to receive income as early as possible, and in the absence of ancestors who lived well into their nineties, we recommend taking the money at age 62.

How can I prepare for lifestyle changes in retirement?

Retirement is likely to be the biggest change in the second half of your life. It involves making many decisions, both financial and nonfinancial. Although retirees and preretirees frequently feel pressured, don't expect to make all your major changes at once. Arriving at one major lifestyle adjustment a year is great progress.

The first decision facing you may be whether to move or to stay where you are. Factors to consider involve your willingness to leave your friends and family, the availability of interesting leisure-time activities, weather conditions, and the cost of living in your present home versus the cost of living in a retirement home or community. Before you decide, visit the area you are considering moving to. If possible, live there for six months. Mix your seasons, and try to visit in different climatic conditions. For example, Florida is very appealing when it is warm there and cold up north, but have you visited Florida during the hurricane season? We suggest you stay over a holiday period, and see what it is like spending Christmas, Thanksgiving, or other holiday times without your family around you. Subscribe to the local newspaper and get a feel for life in the new community.

Table 9-4. Choosing When to Take Social Security

Age	Age 62, cumulative benefit, $	Age 65, cumulative benefit, $	Difference in balance, $
62	9,600		–9,600
63	20,256		–20,256
64	32,055		–32,055
65	45,092	13,892	–31,200
66	59,466	29,311	–30,155
67	75,287	46,385	–28,901
68	92,669	65,249	–27,419
69	111,737	86,050	–25,687
70	132,625	108,942	–23,683
71	155,475	134,094	–21,381
72	180,441	161,687	–18,754
73	207,687	191,912	–15,774
74	237,388	224,977	–12,411
75	269,733	261,104	–8,630
76	304,925	300,529	–4,396
77	343,178	343,508	330
78	384,724	390,313	5,588
79	429,811	441,236	11,425
80	478,703	496,589	17,886

If you decide to move, compare costs in various areas. You might want to rent while you look around for your new home. That will enable you to shop around at your leisure and gain perspective on a community before committing your funds. Call several movers and ask what they would charge to move you to your new home. Do their costs include insurance? What is their policy on breakage and loss? How long will it take to get where you're going? How experienced are their drivers and movers? Betty hesitated before buying moving insurance. Luckily, her moving company talked her into it. During the move, several pieces of Betty's fine furniture were damaged. The insurance company's first response was to send a furniture repairer to her new home. When Betty objected about the quality of the work he intended to perform, the insurance company issued a large check to her, which more than covered the cost of the furniture restorers she hired.

One way to lessen the cost of moving is to dispose of things you won't need. Have a garage sale before you go, or call an auction house and ask what you can get for the furnishings you plan to leave behind. Do they offer one price for all your items, or is it contingent on the proceeds of an auction?

Decide before you retire how you will fill your days. Some people like structure, others prefer flexibility in their schedules. Consider new hobbies, but try them out before sinking hundreds of dollars into golf clubs, thousands into a new boat, or spare cash on sportswear for a hobby that may not last. One of our clients, Rick, actually went out and bought his dream boat before discovering that his wife got seasick every time they boarded it. Guess what question Rick asked us the last time we saw him? "Know anybody who'd like to buy an almost-new boat?"

Consider part-time work for extra income or for diversion. Local malls or offices might be glad to have the extra help, and the funds could add nicely to your retirement budget. Volunteer at a local hospital, library, museum, or organization for the needy. Cynthia works weekly in a literacy program at her local library with a middle-aged woman who never learned to read. Cynthia's willingness to share literacy skills has opened doors to a different and exciting world for this new reader, and given great satisfaction to Cynthia. As a volunteer, you can use your old skills or learn new ones.

Now that you are retired, and beyond that certain age, you are eligible for many discounts. Take advantage of them. If you intend to travel, ask about discounts for seniors at airlines, trains, buses, car rentals, and hotels. Consider taking college classes at your local college (some of these are offered for free) or participate in the travel and learning programs offered through Elderhostel in the United States (75 Federal Street, Boston, MA 02110; 617-426-7788) or Interhostel abroad (6 Garrison Avenue, Durham, NH 03824; 800-733-9753). Rhoda, a widow who had never had time to travel during her working years, took the opportunity of her retirement to travel to Alaska with an organization she belonged to. Although she was initially nervous about going so far from home without a companion, Rhoda made many friends on the trip and enjoyed the new experience. She is currently contemplating a visit to Australia.

Carry your Medicare card (which you can get when you reach age 65) and your American Association of Retired Persons (AARP) membership card (which you can get after age 50), and—on the theory that nothing ventured, nothing gained—ask for discounts everywhere. You may find that if you are willing to shop on certain weekdays or at early hours you can get reductions in grocery stores, drugstores, museums, movies, local transportation, and even restaurants. Just remember to ask what the discount is and when it is available before you place your order. This is the time you have worked, saved, and planned for. Make decisions that suit your style, be flexible, and welcome new challenges.

10 Setting Up Your Estate

The term "estate planning" has always bothered us. It makes you think of financial fine-tuning for elderly people who live on large estates and drive in limousines. It isn't. Estate planning in its broadest sense is appropriate for all people—whether age 25 or 65, with assets of $10,000 or $10,000,000. It lets you decide who inherits what and under what circumstances after you pass away. You can also clear up legal and financial matters while you are still alive. As a result, you can reduce your estate taxes as well as protect your assets and your loved ones.

If estate planning is so important, why is it that over half the people we interview don't have simple wills? Can it be because of cost? Then why did we read somewhere that more than half the estate attorneys in the country don't have wills? Clearly there is something else at work here. We call it legal inertia. It may be the same sort of reasoning that brings about medical inertia—delays in going to the dentist, for example, even though people know that they will have to go eventually, and that delay can cause harm. It may be painful to confront your own mortality. However, we can categorically state that, no matter how unpleasant the subject of wills may seem, you will not live any longer because you do not have one.

We suggest you divide estate planning into three parts. First, focus on building up your estate. You do this by saving and investing, two refrains you have heard frequently in this book. If you are fortunate, you also can increase your estate by material gifts and inheritances from others. Second, actively maintain your estate. Give proper attention to actively managing your portfolio—otherwise after adjustment for inflation you can find yourself poorer even if the value of your assets goes up each year. In addition, if you are in a higher estate tax bracket, tax matters can become very important. Finally, prepare for the transfer of your assets to your chosen heirs. You can do this while you are still alive by gifting your monies to individuals or to charitable institutions. Alternatively, in your will you can arrange for the transfer of your money at your death.

This chapter focuses on the methods of transferring assets to those you wish in the shortest time possible after death, on minimizing costs, and on incorporating tax saving techniques. Our goal is to put the usual maze of legal jargon in simple terms and to keep your assets and peace of mind intact.

Do I need a will?

I am not interested in estate planning and I don't need a will because

1. I don't care if my heirs pay from 37 to 55 percent in taxes on my estate
2. I don't care if the state I live in determines which of my relatives inherit my assets
3. I don't care if my children get all of my money when they reach age 18 if my spouse and I die before that

If you honestly agree with the answers above, you can skip this section. If, on the other hand, those answers are untrue of you, or if they disturb you, read further.

If you care about where your assets go, you need a will. In fact, we give the simple will one of the two value-oriented money planning awards in this chapter. The will specifies who receives what when you die, but it only becomes effective upon your death. If you die intestate (without a will), the state has the right to decide which relatives will receive your assets and in what proportion. Your possessions will be split up according to a rigid formula which may not be what you wanted. For example, one state may have 50 percent of your assets go to your spouse and 50 percent to your children. If you have no children, 50 percent may go to your spouse and 50 percent to your parents. You, on the other hand, may want to leave your spouse 100 percent of your assets. Moreover, if both you and your spouse pass away in an accident, depending upon who dies last, even if only by a matter of minutes, a whole different set of people may become beneficiaries.

One client recently came to see us after the death of her husband. She and her husband had discussed her inheriting all his assets "one day," but he wasn't sick and thought "one day" would be far in the future. Therefore, he never got around to drawing up a will. After his death, our client was awarded one-third of her husband's estate (the rest went to their two grown children), and she has had to greatly reduce her standard of living.

Additionally, you may want to give certain items of sentimental value to specific relatives. For example, many women give their jewelry to their daughters instead of splitting it among the entire family. If you die without a will, the jewelry would likely be split evenly among various heirs. Alternatively, you may have a favorite charity that you would like to bequeath your money to. It is difficult to have your wishes executed if you haven't stated them legally.

There's a range of financial reasons for having a will. Yours could include the ability to choose who will benefit from your assets after you are gone, to set up trusts and select trustees, to appoint suitable executors, to make gifts or, even to disinherit certain people. Also, you can potentially save your heirs tens of thousands of dollars that might otherwise have gone to Uncle Sam if you didn't properly prepare this part of your estate. And, you shouldn't overlook the fact that if you die without a will, your heirs might automatically incur costs such as fees to lawyers, appraisers, accountants, realtors and the court-appointed executor whom the legal system may assign to help supervise and wind up your affairs. Because of the number of professionals involved, this process, called probate, can be very expensive in some states. Not only will charges on your estate rise, but it can take much longer to distribute your money. This can be a particular problem when your heirs need the money to live on. Also, the probate process will open your records to public scrutiny, exposing your private affairs to anyone who chooses to read about them.

In addition, if you have young children, you can make sure that they will be well looked after by guardians whom you have chosen if something should happen to you and your spouse. It pains us that so many young couples who are determined to plan for their children's education, and are obviously concerned about their well-being, have not taken steps to appoint guardians to raise their children and control the inheritance in the event of a double disaster.

If you don't have a will, make a date with a lawyer. In preparation for your visit, compose a list of your assets and your beneficiaries as well as any personal wishes you have. If you are married and both you and your spouse are setting up wills, try to iron out difficult items such as who will be the guardian for your minor children, who will be in charge of executing the terms of the will (executor), and who will supervise the assets and terms of the trust (trustee) if you are establishing trusts. (We will discuss trusts later in this chapter.) By going to the estate attorney with a good idea of your assets and wishes, you can save time and money.

Despite new do-it-yourself computer estate planning software this is one area we do not believe people should handle themselves, since the way you word your will can be as important as your intentions. A visit to an experienced estate attorney now can save a lot of aggravation for your heirs later.

Does my will need to be updated?

Your will should be reviewed regularly. Revisions should be made when your circumstances change. You may have gotten divorced, had additional children, seen your children grow up, or gained or lost considerable assets. Many divorced people unintentionally continue to list their former spouses as prime beneficiaries, even after bitter divorce settlements just because they haven't gotten around to changing the will.

Julian, a retired gentleman who came to see us, told us that he had a will and he believed there was no need to discuss it. When we questioned him further, Julian mentioned that his will was over 30 years old, but had been updated "recently." When pressed, Julian admitted that it had been updated 15 or 20 years before; he couldn't remember the exact year. We told him that in terms of tax and estate laws that was not recent enough.

Realize that new laws concerning inheritances, trusts, and taxes make whole portions of your will obsolete. In fact, if your will has not been examined by a qualified attorney since 1985 or earlier, and if you have over $600,000 in assets (including your house, life insurance, and pension plans), it is time for a review because of tax changes that occurred in 1986. And, if your will was written before September 1981 your spouse can be in danger of not receiving your assets estate tax–free. A regular review of your will with a competent attorney can provide peace of mind for you, and can ensure a smooth transition for your heirs.

If your changes are minor, your will can be modified by just adding a new codicil—that is, an amendment—instead of rewriting the entire document. Adding codicils can be a cost-effective way of keeping your will up-to-date. However, if you add a series of codicils to your will, you can create confusion and difficulty in interpreting the terms of the will. Try to use the same lawyer who drew up the will, if you found him or her to be qualified. We have yet to find a lawyer who will accept a will drawn up by another lawyer without suggesting major revisions.

How can I reduce estate and income taxes?

If you have accumulated material wealth, estate taxes (taxes levied following your death) can be a substantial burden. While estate taxes vary among different states and are often credited under federal levels, federal estate taxes beyond exempted amounts—the first $600,000 of assets owned per person are not taxed by the federal government—are levied at a whopping 37 to 55 percent of your estate's value. Many people, middle-aged and older, don't realize that with their pension, house, and insurance proceeds they are already beyond the $600,000 level. If your assets aren't at that level yet, don't worry. If you continue to save and earn investment income over time, with the effects of inflation and the possibility that the $600,000 benchmark may be lowered, you have a good chance of passing that mark some day.

The tax savings on the federal level become important once your assets move past the $600,000 mark. Assets pass to the surviving spouse tax-free after the death of the first spouse. Given an estate of more than $600,000, the assets would be taxed at a minimum of 37 percent upon the death of the second spouse. After the second spouse dies, the minimum tax to your heirs on the next $100,000 (above $600,000) is $37,000, and the rate increases from there. Obviously, it pays to consider tax reduction techniques.

To reduce estate taxes, you can gift the money directly to an individual or a trust while you are alive. We discuss this approach further in the next question. An alternative we find worthwhile for married people is a bypass trust (also called a credit shelter trust). In a typical situation, the first spouse to die—statistically more often the husband—leaves the surviving spouse all the assets in his or her estate. There is no tax on this transfer, but by leaving the survivor the assets, the decedent—the person who died—has lost the $600,000 exemption. Instead, the first spouse could leave $600,000 or less tax-free by giving it directly or in trust to a third party, most often the children.

If you set up a bypass trust you can have income from the $600,000 given by the trustee to your widow or widower. The basic $600,000 will become the property of your heirs (other than your spouse) after your spouse dies but the principal could be used for the surviving spouse's medical needs or, some attorneys advise, to maintain his or her standard of living. Many lawyers suggest you make your spouse one of the trustees who supervises the assets, but not the sole trustee.

Nonetheless, it is our experience that creating a trust sometimes makes the surviving spouse uncomfortable. While it provides considerable flexibility, it doesn't allow your spouse to have full control over the assets. You sacrifice your spouse's control for later tax savings for your ultimate heirs. In our example in Table 10-1, the husband and wife each have $600,000 in assets. Notice the difference in estate taxes made by the bypass trust, which in this case amounts to large tax benefits. Because of these large tax benefits, we give the bypass trust our second value-oriented money planning award in the estate planning area.

We have found that as total assets move up beyond $1,500,000 and savings increase proportionally, people are less concerned about the question of having full control and come to like this approach better.

Table 10-1. Bypass Trust Example

	Without bypass trust			With bypass trust		
	Husband	Wife	Children	Husband	Wife	Children
Total assets	$600,000	$600,000	$0	$600,000	$600,000	$0
Husband dies	(600,000)	600,000	0	(600,000)	0	600,000
Tax at first death	0	0	0	0	0	0
Total assets	0	1,200,000	0	0	600,000	600,000
Wife dies	0	(1,200,000)	1,200,000	0	600,000	600,000
Tax at second death	0	0	(235,000)	0	0	0
Net estate	0	0	965,000	0	0	1,200,000

Strictly from a financial standpoint, the bypass trust begins to make sense when you significantly cross the $600,000 threshold.

In addition, keep in mind that passing your money to a younger generation as opposed to someone in your generation can save on estate taxes. That is because you can skip one generation of estate taxes. But don't let tax questions determine your estate planning. Use them to support your wishes. If your principal concern is caring for your spouse, instruct your lawyer to that effect so that he or she can construct your legal documents to reflect your wishes.

Should I gift money now or leave it in my name?

We believe gifting is the simplest way to transfer assets by removing them from your estate before death. You can gift in order to avoid estate or income taxes or to provide someone with money he or she can use now. Furthermore, neither the person donating the gift nor the person receiving it has to pay a current gift tax. You can gift a maximum of $10,000 to the same individual each year. You can, moreover, give an unlimited number of $10,000 gifts to different people. You can also gift an unlimited amount to each person for medical reasons or education if you make the check out to the medical or educational institution, not to the individual. (You can gift assets to your spouse at any time, in any amount, without being subject to estate taxes.) If you are married, you and your spouse can gift $20,000 per year jointly to each individual on your list.

If you transfer assets worth more than $10,000, you still will not pay a tax. Instead, the amount over $10,000 will apply against your now combined estate and gift tax exemption of $600,000. Only when you exceed the $600,000 level will taxes apply. There is also an advantage to giving away assets that will grow rapidly; it freezes their value and prevents what would have been an even greater estate tax burden at death. Finally, if you gift to people in lower income tax brackets than yours—your children, for example—less of the income from the assets will go to Uncle Sam.

Whether you should gift money to your minor children depends on what you can save in income taxes, whether you will need and qualify for college aid (if you put money in your child's name, you may significantly reduce the aid your child will receive), and finally, whether you trust your children to use the money in the way you intended. As a general rule, we recommend keeping your options open by holding onto your assets and investing the money in municipal bonds for income tax savings.

Gifting your money to others later on in life, to reduce estate taxes, is more complicated. First, look at your financial situation and make certain you have enough money for your own retirement. Be sure to include a sufficient cushion for the impact of inflation on costs, potential medical bills, and perhaps even nursing home or at-home nursing care. Remember that a gift is final—you can't get the assets back if you change your mind.

Next, look at the impact the gift can have on your beneficiary. Extensive gifting can have a negative impact on industriousness and family relationships. Warren Buffett, the famed investor who has accumulated billions of dollars, intends to give almost the entire sum away, presumably so that it won't strongly influence his children's lives. Most important of all, we believe that gifting should be done only when you have enough monies for the rest of your life.

Will my foreign-born spouse be protected by my will?

Possibly she or he will not. To protect a foreign-born spouse who is *not* an American citizen, you may have to take special precautions. If you die before your spouse and your estate has more than $600,000 in assets including your home, the government will not allow you to pass that excess along to your spouse free from estate taxes as it would for a spouse who is a U.S. citizen. The amount above the $600,000 will be subject to estate taxes starting at 37 percent.

We recommend a way around this that may suit some couples. Set up a qualified domestic trust (Q-DOT) for your noncitizen spouse, and appoint someone in whom you have confidence—your adult children, a reliable relative, a trustworthy friend, or a professional advisor—to administer it. The trustee must be a U.S. citizen or a U.S. organization, such as a bank. Your spouse will then benefit from the income from the trust, but will be unable to touch the principal that in most cases will revert to your children after the death of your spouse. In certain instances the trustees will be able to take money out for the special needs of the survivor spouse, such as health care. Your money will be protected from the high taxes that can be levied currently against a noncitizen spouse.

Discuss this arrangement with your spouse, and see if it is something that he or she can live with. Then consult your estate attorney. Alternatively, consider gifting monies to your spouse now (if you are not concerned about divorce). A noncitizen spouse can be gifted up to $100,000 annually. Money that is already in the foreign spouse's name will not be taxed upon death of the American spouse, and may save considerable money in estate taxes.

Of course, if your spouse dies first, and you are an American citizen, you should have no special problems with assets that are in the United States. Also, if your spouse becomes an American citizen after your death but before the tax return for your estate is due, and your spouse was a resident of the United States following your death until becoming a citizen, no extraordinary measures will be necessary.

Should I have a living will?

A living will indicates your preferences should you become incapacitated, with no hope of recovery. Very often family members have to decide whether loved ones should be kept alive as long as possible through mechanical or medicinal means, or whether nature should be allowed to take its course. This area has become a very sensitive one. Your doctor and the hospital may be concerned about legal and ethical matters. Your family members may become very emotional, and may even be divided in their thinking.

In our opinion, a living will can save families anguish and ongoing concern about whether they made the right decision. You can clearly state under which conditions you would want someone to "pull the plug"; or you can express your desire to be kept alive as long as possible under any circumstances. In addition, the document can state any wish to donate your organs after death.

What do I do if my spouse, who handles our finances, dies?

This is a situation that we deal with very often. We tell our clients to take their time. Many decisions can be delayed, and the emotional upheaval that you're experiencing may prevent you from making wise choices. As soon as you are prepared to do so, try to assemble all the factors in your financial life. Locate your investment assets. Find out how much insurance you have and which company it is with. Contact your accountant as well as other financial professionals who have worked with your late spouse.

If possible, make up a list of questions, set up an appointment with these advisors, and go down your list one by one. In most cases, these professionals will be understanding and try to help. Don't hesitate to ask for copies of all documents relating to your financial affairs. (About once or twice a year we are called by an attorney who is trying to locate all the assets in an estate. Even when these calls concern people we only met once five years before, we gather whatever information we have in our files to help the family.) Also, contact your spouse's company and talk to the employee benefits person about pensions, insurance, and other death benefits you may be entitled to.

If liquidity is not a problem, pay bills as they come in; leave long-term decisions for at least six months after the death of your spouse. That will give you time to locate all necessary materials, talk to professionals and begin to get back on your feet. Then decide what changes will be necessary to meet your needs. If you are working and have a regular income, you can afford to make investment changes slowly. If you are dependent on income from investment assets to support you, you may want to get professional advice soon.

As you begin to understand your spouse's system of doing things, you may acquire valuable information. Yet, what worked in the past may not be the best alternative in the future. Sometimes when a spouse is ailing, financial matters remain untended for long periods of time. It may be appropriate to make changes.

Some people who come to us are unable to alter any decisions made by their spouses for purely emotional reasons. Lisa, a widow who came to see us, had been on her own for 18 months. Her husband had invested their substantial assets, but she did not know what they were, what they were worth, or what to do with them. All Lisa's assets were in stock certificates in a safe-deposit box that her husband had obtained almost 30 years earlier. When we suggested that she make a list of the assets, that we would review them for her and tell her which we believed she should hold and which she should sell, Lisa was horrified. The very thought of removing them from her safe-deposit box was abhorrent to her. Since that time, Lisa calls us every few months to "discuss" whether she should go ahead with this portfolio review, but as yet—two and a half years after her husband's death—she has done nothing.

Before you make any major financial decisions, take a deep breath. Realize that there are people out there who thrive on the emotional susceptibility of the recently bereaved and may call and offer you deals. Sometimes the deal benefits the salesperson most. Don't be pressured into doing anything that doesn't sound reasonable, or that you can't check out. Take your time; most worthy investments will not disappear overnight. (For more information about protecting yourself from questionable practices, see the question "How can I prevent my parents falling prey to scams and unscrupulous sales pitches?" in Chapter 12.)

Don't switch your investments because a friend tells you he or she has his or her money in a great place. Even well-meaning friends can unintentionally mislead you. Also, what works well for a friend may be inappropriate for you due to differences in your personal situations.

Art came to us on the recommendation of his friend, Dorothy. When we set up his account we customized it for Art. Later that week, when he called asking why he was invested in different things than Dorothy was, we couldn't tell him that Dorothy had almost double the amount of money that he had, that she was willing to take more risk than he was, or that she was 12 years younger than he was. Nor could we tell him that she had different retirement goals than he did, planned to leave less to her heirs than Art did, and wanted to spend more while she was alive. Art had to take our word for the fact that his portfolio was suited to his particular needs and circumstances.

It is important to remember that there is more than one way to handle a financial situation. Although your style may be different from that of your spouse, you can learn to handle your own finances. You may already know more about them than you think. Were you responsible for keeping the family budget, for balancing the checkbook, for paying monthly bills? Did you contribute to decisions on large purchases, such as vacations, remodeling your home, and purchasing a family car? Do a little at a time, handle the daily matters first, and take your time deciding about anything you do not completely understand.

Are trusts a good idea?

Trusts are separate entities designed to hold assets for your benefit or for the benefit of others. These assets are managed by a trustee or trustees who have a legal responsibility to conform to the wishes of the person who creates the trust (the grantor).

We recommend trusts often, because they have distinct advantages. They allow the grantor to set certain ground rules for use of the money which wouldn't be possible through outright gifts. For example, if you set up a trust for the benefit of your child, you could specify that the money is to be given to your child at age 30 and in the interim be used only for college payments.

Diana, recently divorced and not in good health, structured her will so that a trust would be set up to handle all her proceeds. The beneficiaries were her two young children. She didn't want her former husband who loved the children but was careless in financial matters to have control over the funds, so she designated our firm as trustee. Her instructions were specific, generally restricting withdrawals to educational expenses for the children. Diana was a strong believer in not giving her children access to the funds until they reached their late twenties. By setting up a trust through an estate lawyer as opposed to a bank custodian account, which would have required distributions at ages 18 or 21, Diana was able to reflect her wishes exactly. When Diana passed away, the financial arrangements went smoothly.

There is a type of trust for almost any form of transfer of assets you can think of that doesn't run contrary to public policy. Trusts have a great deal of flexibility and can provide professional supervision. For example, the trustee can be a legal or financial person who has a responsibility to target a rate of growth for the assets that exceeds inflation.

You can use trusts to organize your assets in one easy structure so they can quickly be transferred upon your death. They can escape some probate costs and make it extremely difficult for your creditors to have access to your property. Finally, as we showed before, you can use trusts to reduce estate taxes, as in a bypass trust, and to lower income taxes by transferring money to someone in a lower tax bracket while you maintain some control over the use of your assets.

The disadvantages of trusts are that they can cost $500 to thousands of dollars to establish, and can require filing separate trust tax returns—which involves another cost and much paperwork in transferring and supervising assets. Unless the reasons for setting them up have to do with limiting control, a need for professional supervision, a desire to bypass high probate costs because of a complicated estate, or unusually high probate costs in that state, these costs generally make trusts unattractive for people who are transferring less than $100,000. There are, however, some simple bank trusts that can be set up and administered for a nominal cost.

If you decide to establish a trust, be very careful about choosing trustees, just as you should in selecting an executor for your will. Naming your spouse as sole trustee can result in paying unneeded estate taxes and can restrict the ability of the trust to transfer after-tax income to him or her. Naming a bank will bring in professional management with no problem if a trustee dies. However, individual trustees such as lawyers, accountants, and financial advisors can often provide more individual attention to your needs.

Naming a close friend or relative can offer the advantage of a personal understanding of your wishes but sometimes at the expense of professional expertise. Be careful in choosing someone as trustee—even a son or daughter—as he or she may be tempted to use the assets for their own purposes. Also keep in mind that some children could limit withdrawals so that they would eventually inherit more money. However, if you are sure of your children's honest intentions and interest and if they have business experience or can learn quickly, they can be a good choice. Alternatively, you can name cotrustees, selecting from relatives, banks, and individual advisors. When anyone other than a son or daughter is involved, we recommend your estate pay them an annual fee for managing the account.

Should I set up a living trust?

Whatever the reason, this is the most common trust question we are asked. A living trust has nothing to do with a living will which, as we explained previously, determines your choices concerning medical treatment during critical illness.

A living trust is simply a trust you set up while you are still alive. It can be distinguished from testamentary trusts that can be set up by wills and take effect upon your death. The living trust accumulates part or all of your assets in a separate trust structure. It shares the advantages of other trusts—professional management, organization, and flexibility.

There are two ways of constructing many trusts, including living trusts: revocable and irrevocable. You have greatest flexibility in establishing a revocable living trust. You can have your assets organized under one trust umbrella and change the beneficiaries or other terms whenever you wish.

In order to get the living trust's estate tax reduction benefits, however, you have to set up an *irrevocable* living trust. That means that if you change your mind, you cannot regain control of your money. If, on the other hand, you were able to exercise any material control over these assets, they could be considered a part of your estate and you could lose the benefit of keeping the assets out of your estate. The assets bypass administrative costs in probate because the trust—not the individual—is the owner of the assets and you are ensured that your finances will not be open to public scrutiny. Some attorneys say that this can make it difficult or impossible for your creditors to attach the property in the trust.

We have recently helped set up a living trust for a client who became disabled after an accident at a very young age. Instead of becoming depressed, he has one of the brightest dispositions of anyone we know. He has made great physical progress, and will be looking for a job soon. In the event that he passes away without a spouse, he would like most of the income on his money to go to his parents and most of the principal to go to charity. The living trust will facilitate his care in case his health worsens and will ensure that the beneficiaries of his choice receive his assets in the event of his demise.

If these advantages aren't compelling, you may not need a living trust. It can be expensive to set up and administer a living trust and difficult to transfer assets into it. Many of our clients cannot get over the fact that they will lose control over the assets in the irrevocable trust forever. After we explain the advantages and disadvantages of these trusts and the ability to get similar tax savings through bypass trusts which come into existence at death, most of our clients agree with our recommendation to provide for trusts to take effect at death.

Should I grant a durable power of attorney?

A power of attorney allows the person you select to act on your behalf to perform certain activities. It can be a very powerful instrument, so it should be used with care. You may want someone to act for you in a different location, for example, when you are out of the country, or in a situation in which they have specific knowledge that you lack. In that case you would grant a limited power of attorney.

A power of attorney can be most useful when you are incapacitated. In that event, the power will allow your delegated representative to act on your behalf without being challenged. We often recommend that our clients grant durable powers of attorney which provide broad powers (limited only by your own wishes) and remain effective in the event of incapacity or disability for just that reason. These powers remain in effect until canceled by the grantor or until the death of the grantor. Keep in mind, however, that as one sharp estate lawyer told us, granting durable powers is like giving away signed blank checks. Be careful about whom you give them to. A more restrictive alternative is a "springing" power of attorney which is recognized in most states and which springs into effect after some predetermined occurrence, such as an illness.

People who are elderly, ill, or disabled are particularly good candidates for a durable power of attorney. For the power to have legal bearing, the person granting the power must be competent at the time of the assignment and all parties to it must be of legal age.

These powers are now recognized in some form in all states. We remember one case in which a woman was suddenly incapacitated and her daughter had to go to court; after considerable delays and thousands of dollars that the daughter could ill afford, she was granted permission to make financial and legal decisions on behalf of her mother. Meanwhile, the mother's assets had substantially decreased in value. A durable power of attorney could have avoided that.

It bears repeating that you must have full confidence in the person or persons you grant the power to. Limit the power to those areas in which you feel you may need help. If all you need to do is grant a simple power, you can buy the form in a stationery store for a few dollars. To assure that it is valid, be certain to have your signature notarized. If your needs are complex or if you are unsure of the consequences, you should consult a lawyer about drawing up a power of attorney that fits your circumstances.

You should also consider a medical power of attorney (sometimes referred to as a health-care proxy) which will assign to others the power to make critical medical decisions for you using your established ground rules in the event of your incapacity. This issue is not covered by the durable power of attorney.

Should we put our assets in joint name?

It is common practice for couples to put their assets in joint name and for elderly individuals to have their assets shifted to joint name with sons or daughters or other beneficiaries of their estates. Putting your assets in joint name with right of survivorship allows your beneficiary to have access to those assets immediately upon your death. Assets held in joint name bypass the sometimes costly and cumbersome probate process.

On the other hand, having the assets pass to your spouse at death can result in extra taxes for estates valued over $600,000. Even if your estate is under $600,000, in many states you may be subject to a state estate tax. Moreover, if one spouse is much more likely to die first, it is often best to have that person own 100 percent of the property. That is because the property will receive what is called a "stepped-up basis." Instead of valuing the property at its cost for income tax purposes, it is valued at its current market price. Thus, if a couple has a $325,000 home which cost $25,000 and if the home is in the deceased spouse's name and is sold by the surviving spouse, there will be no gain on sale and therefore no income tax due. On the other hand, if it is in joint name, 50 percent of the gain after adjustment for the one-time $125,000 exemption (available only if one spouse is over age 55) will be subject to a substantial income tax. Also, keep in mind that assets that are in joint tenancy with right of survivorship (JTWROS) will pass to the joint owner even if your will says otherwise.

Your feelings of sharing your assets with your spouse may lead you to put your assets in joint name. A better idea, particularly when assets are beyond the $600,000 level and children are involved, can be to take assets out of joint name, set up equal-sized estates separately, and use a bypass trust. (Separate restrictions apply in the community-property states of Arizona, California, Idaho, Louisiana, Nevada, New Mexico, Texas, and Washington.)

How can I best leave money to a charity?

If you donate modest sums to charity on an ongoing basis, the simplest way to do so is by means of an outright gift. You will receive a deduction on your tax return, providing that you itemize your deductions.

Some people choose to leave a significant portion of their assets to a charitable institution for any number of reasons, such as a lifelong affiliation with an educational institution, religious beliefs, or a desire to aid in the common good. Sometimes charities benefit from those who have no relatives to leave their money to. In our practice we see a number of people who are in that category.

Donald, single and in his fifties, for whom we did a retirement plan, comes to mind. When we presented our plan to him, we detected as much amusement as interest in the results. Although Donald had asked us how much he could afford to spend per year, since he had a substantial amount in assets, we'd assumed he had no intention of using all the money up over his lifetime. With a wide grin Donald asked us who he should leave his money to. We asked what his charitable interests were and he said he had none; nor did he care where the money went as long as the government didn't get it. We gave Donald a list of charitable institutions that we felt were worthy and would cater to his need for attention.

You can make donations while you are alive or after your death. If you gift money when you are alive, you can, of course, donate the entire sum to a charity outright. More likely, however, you will want to consider putting the money in trust. Under a charitable remainder trust you give the assets to a charity and receive an income equivalent to at least 5 percent of the value of the assets annually. This charitable method is particularly useful if you have an asset that doesn't supply you with income you could use but you don't want to sell it—for example, the house you are living in. If you are married and the charitable gift will take place upon your death, you probably will want income to go to your spouse and the principal to charity when he or she passes away.

The second method you can use is a charitable lead trust in which the income goes to the charity for a fixed period or during your lifetime and the asset can be left to your heirs upon your death. Both of these types of trusts provide a tax deduction for the calculated amount of the donation. This amount must comply with governmental guidelines and can be different from what the gift is truly worth. If, instead of using a trust, you donate money during your lifetime, you will receive a charitable deduction subject to a maximum yearly amount that is based on a percentage of your income. The amount of the donation in excess of the yearly maximum can be carried forward to apply toward future tax years. If you donate outright at death, your estate will receive a deduction which will result in no tax to your estate on the amount you donated.

Charitable trusts can be a good tax savings tool, sometimes even without charitable intent, although the government can challenge your deduction if it appears you made the donation to save on taxes. Make sure you are giving to a group that the government recognizes as a charitable organization for IRS deductibility purposes. (For information about obtaining a list of qualified organizations, see the question "Do you have any special tax strategies?" in Chapter 8.)

How can I avoid probate?

Many people wish to avoid probate. However, the more relevant question may be, "*Should* I avoid probate?" A probate is the state's process for verifying who is entitled to the proceeds of an estate. The probate process can be extended and expensive. It is also public. During the probate proceedings, your assets will be open to public scrutiny.

Can you benefit from probate? It does provide a legal finality on estate matters when completed. Consequently, it can protect your estate against subsequent claims by creditors. Also, contrary to some people's beliefs, it permits allowances for family living. Despite these factors, on balance, in most instances avoiding probate will save your estate money.

There are three main types of property that will not go through probate:

1. *Joint property.* Property held in joint name with right of survivorship will bypass the probate process. Making your spouse or child a joint owner of an asset won't keep the property that is in your estate free from estate taxes, but you will not be subject to probate costs. As we discussed previously in the question about joint property, make sure it won't result in higher estate taxes.

2. *Trusts established during your lifetime.* By placing all your assets in trust, you are in effect transferring them to a separate entity: the trust. Upon your death they will go directly to your chosen heirs. As we discussed before, be sure that the cost and inconvenience of the living trust are not greater than the benefits you receive.

3. *Life insurance and pension and bank proceeds.* Life insurance, pension proceeds, and bank accounts with named beneficiaries will go directly to whomever you have designated.

Be sure to keep the documents up to date. We would like to have a nickel for every person who is divorced from his or her spouse with intentions never to see them again, yet has neglected to take the ex-spouse's name off a pension or life insurance policy. In most instances these documents will take priority over wishes stated in your will.

Should I use life insurance in planning my estate?

Clearly, life insurance has a role in estate planning for many people. In its simplest form it provides money to your heirs in the event of your untimely death. As we pointed out in Chapter 5, when you have sufficient assets built up you no longer need life insurance as a hedge against mortality risk.

Life insurance is also billed as a way of providing ready cash to survivors who have sufficient other assets. There are cases in which life insurance cash proceeds are needed, but in most cases it is an overrated feature. Generally cash is available for living expenses through the liquidation of other assets, even before estates are settled. Often, where estate taxes are a heavy burden for an illiquid estate, the IRS will accept a delay in payment.

Finally, there is the guilt trip element. If you are leaving over $600,000 or have a substantial state estate tax, you may feel that you have to give your heirs a way to receive their monies free from estate taxes. Therefore, as the insurance salespeople advise, you might feel compelled to buy enough insurance to cover the tax. Of course, this can be an emotional response. Most people have no particular amount they want to leave their children, with or without taxes. Besides, the dollars saved in insurance costs can be used to build up a larger estate to divide among your heirs.

It is true that life insurance proceeds that aren't payable to the estate can escape estate taxes. (We will soon explain how to arrange that.) But this should be a concern principally for those with estates over $1.2 million. Those people should not make insurance proceeds payable to the estate to pay taxes since they will then be included in the estate and be subject to estate taxes. Besides, outright gifts of $10,000 a year also escape estate taxation.

However, there are often times when you wish not to gift monies directly to your heirs or, alternatively, to gift them your existing life insurance policies directly, for example, if you want the income to go to your spouse and the principal to your children when your spouse dies. Another instance is if our first choice of $600,000 in a bypass trust has already been accomplished but more than $600,000 remains. In either case a life insurance trust can be an attractive alternative. You can gift your existing life insurance to a trust set up for that purpose and name the trust your beneficiary. The proceeds can be used to pay off estate taxes and administrative costs, and the balance can be managed for the beneficiary by the trustee. Be sure to eliminate any signs of remaining ownership such as the ability to change the beneficiary. To be free of estate taxes the gift of your existing policy must take place at least three years prior to death;

otherwise, the transfer will be unsuccessful and proceeds will be included in your estate. The trust must be irrevocable, not subject to change by you.

If you have no life insurance or want to add to it, you can consider purchasing some "second-to-die" life insurance that pays off when the second spouse dies. However, there is a widespread incorrect belief that these policies are cheap. While it is true that they have low current payments, you will be paying their annual costs for a longer period of time (until second death) and you can expect the ultimate payout to occur at a later date than normal first-to-die insurance.

If you are sure you have no need for money at first death and that the surviving spouse can afford the annual payments of the policy, these policies can be attractive. Follow our directions on selecting policies in Chapter 5. Whether you gift existing policies or establish new ones, you can continue to make required yearly payments to keep the policies current with the first $10,000 free from estate and gift taxes. Just make the amounts payable to the trustee.

In sum, insurance is often *not* needed in estate planning once payments to the surviving spouse or children can be covered through other means. If you are one of the fortunate ones who has assets over $1,200,000, the amounts from $600,000 to $1,200,000 can be covered by a bypass trust. You can compare a life insurance trust with a gifting program of cash or donations of existing life insurance policies. If owning life insurance with a guaranteed cash payout to your heirs attracts you, you can of course use it instead of other investments that provide higher returns. But recognize that you are generally sacrificing efficient financial terms for emotional comfort.

What family trust is best for me?

You have read the trust question and have decided that trusts are attractive. Aside from the living trust and the charitable trust, each of which is discussed in separate questions, we will focus here on the two most popular trusts that can be set up through your will to benefit your heirs upon your demise: bypass trusts and Q-TIP (qualified terminable interest property) trusts.

The bypass trust discussed earlier allows the decedent to take advantage of the $600,000 exemption. It eliminates the large estate tax bite by naming a beneficiary other than the spouse—generally your children—to receive this sum of money. Income is given to the spouse, and the trustee can pay out (invade) principal. The decedent, not the surviving spouse, controls who ultimately receives the bypass monies.

The Q-TIP trust gives the surviving spouse the income but he or she never owns the property in this trust. The money in this trust could comprise the entire amount of assets in the estate. The decedent decides who will ultimately receive the principal, not the surviving spouse. It also qualifies for the marital deduction of no estate taxes upon the first death. There are two important requirements. The spouse must receive *all* the income of the trust during his or her lifetime. And, the executor of the estate must choose the Q-TIP election or else the money will be included in the decedent's estate, subject to taxation.

In sum, the Q-TIP trust takes care of the surviving spouse, but control over the entire estate is given to (vested in) the decedent. Clearly then it can be used in second marriages in which there are differing priorities about heirs as well as in unstable marital situations. It is also effective when the decedent had been concerned either about the financial responsibility of the spouse or the possibility that the spouse will become negatively influenced by a new partner in a potential second marriage.

The two types of trust don't have to be thought of as either/or alternatives. The bypass can be used together with the Q-TIP. The bypass can save estate taxes on amounts up to $600,000 while the Q-TIP can be used to control the remainder of the assets. If you decide to use a bypass trust separately or with a Q-TIP, remember that it is not good enough to state so in a will. You must have sufficient assets in your own and your spouse's name to fund the bypass amounts intended.

Which trust is best for you depends on your particular circumstances. In many instances, no trust at all, just leaving the money to your spouse, is an attractive alternative. If your estate is above $1.2 million, you should consult a financial planner, an estate attorney, or both to make sure you are getting what you need.

The bypass trust alone is the one we recommend most. As we mentioned, the principal can go to your children while the income goes to the surviving spouse. In addition, payments of 5 percent of principal or $5000, whichever is greater, can be made annually. Principal can be taken by the survivor for medical reasons or just to maintain an established standard of living. We find that many of our clients can live comfortably with this trust. It is the trust of tax reduction choice (that is why we gave it our value-oriented award) in which the surviving spouse can adjust to a relatively modest loss of control as compared to that of an outright transfer of assets.

Although Sean had always handled the family's finances, he began to encourage his wife, Merle, to become familiar with financial matters many years ago. He took her to meet their lawyer and accountant. Recently they came to see us together for more formal estate planning advice. We recommended updating their wills to reflect their changing intentions regarding beneficiaries. We also recommended that they set up a bypass trust of $300,000 for each of their two children for the $600,000 exemption equivalent. Then we assisted them in transferring half of their marketable securities to Merle so that estates could be equalized and sufficient assets set up in each estate to fund the trust wishes stated in their wills. We then referred them to a lawyer who specializes in estate planning and subsequently reviewed his work. Then we invested most of their assets in no-load mutual funds.

When Sean passed away 16 months later, the restructuring of his estate enabled his heirs to save over $250,000 in taxes and probate costs. Just as important, Merle did not have to worry about financial matters. After she came to terms with her emotional loss, she was able to take full control of her finances.

11
Relationship Planning

Financial planning is normally divided into neat little areas. When we started our business, we thought of planning in terms of a "typical" life cycle: you grow up, get married, buy a house, and raise and educate two children. Then you retire and make sure your estate is in order.

Was this white-picket-fence view of life ever really representative? It certainly hasn't been since the 1950s. The sixties began an overhaul of traditional concepts that has extended to the present time.

Now nothing surprises us. We see traditional families, divorced couples, young couples with different last names who are married, couples with children who aren't married, retired couples who prefer to live together rather than to marry, and same-sex couples who have long-standing relationships but can't marry.

Hilda and Victor, a retired couple, came into our office together. They had different surnames but the same address and joint bank accounts. They discussed their shared hopes, plans, and finances freely. We assumed they were married. When they mentioned "his" children and "her" children, we asked if this was a second marriage. Hilda and Victor were taken aback; they had assumed that we would know they were not married. Since that time, we do our best not to assume anything.

The divorce rate has risen sharply in recent decades. The number of divorces per 1000 married people has almost quadrupled from 42 per 1000 in 1960 to 166 per 1000 in 1990. For most people divorce is still an emotionally wrenching experience and one they choose only after much thinking and planning. Sometimes, though, the decision to separate or divorce can come as a surprise.

Joel, the middle-aged owner of a small business, and Phyllis, a homemaker, came in for investment and retirement planning. They were an unusually attentive couple, calling each other "dear" and "sweetie," and displaying a considerable amount of physical affection. Members of our staff who were at the meeting remarked on how nice it was to see that a couple who had been married for 18 years could still be so much in love. Personally, we thought the romantic display in a business office was a little overdone.

Sure enough, a week later Joel phoned to tell us that he was considering a divorce; he hadn't told Phyllis yet because she would be devastated. The big surprise, though, came afterwards—a call from Phyllis asking us to treat her assets separately because she had finally made up her mind to file for divorce. But, she urged, don't mention anything to Joel. She had to find the most tactful way to broach the subject because he would be devastated.

Relationships are not without consequences. In fact, from a financial viewpoint, there are real differences involved in being single, married, remarried, or divorced. But we will say more about that later in the chapter.

We just got married. What financial arrangements should we make?

Getting married represents a significant change in your lifestyle. Now each of you has responsibilities to the other. The financial part of the equation can be a true partnership in which both people contribute to maintain their standard of living.

Have a frank discussion about money with your new spouse. Put all your assets on the table, decide about joint and separate responsibilities such as who will pay the bills, who will balance the bank statements, and who is going to make investment decisions; then institute savings and spending habits that will suit your joint lifestyle.

Decide whether separate or joint bank accounts are for you. Although the majority of first-married couples we meet do not distinguish between his and her money, we find a growing trend in first marriages toward separate accounts, particularly if one spouse has inherited money from his or her family. Couples who have been married before and may have children and assets from previous marriages often prefer to keep their funds separate.

Your budgeting needs are likely to change. Before you may have spent with a "what me worry" abandon; now you may have longer-term goals, including raising the down payment for a home or putting away money for children's education. We recommend that you try to save at least 10 percent of your combined incomes. While this may be hard in the beginning, we find that most couples can do it when they have a particular goal in mind and set up a separate account for their savings.

We also notice that a new seriousness takes over the investment policies of recently married couples. Trading in speculative stocks, options, and futures often gives way to more conservative investing in growth and income mutual funds. Take the time to review both spouses' investment assets and assign the more adept one to handle your accounts.

Ask your new spouse about his or her credit rating. In some instances, your own credit rating can be affected by that of your spouse. If you apply for a mortgage and two incomes are necessary to qualify, both spouses will be investigated. On the other hand, it is against the law to reject an application by one spouse for his or her separate credit, which should be based on his or her own credit history and income capabilities. An exception is made in community-property states, where the credit of both spouses can be checked. Any judgments creditors receive against assets for amounts owed are limited to the assets owned separately by the spouse with the problem or to those owned in joint name. If you are concerned about your spouse's credit rating, keep your assets separate and think about transferring assets out of joint name to your own account. However, since there will be instances when the transfer to your name will not be recognized as a barrier to being sued, it may be wise to consult a lawyer for serious problems.

Family responsibilities bring new needs for protection. If you plan to have children soon, make sure you have adequate life insurance. Review your will and see if you want to update it, change the beneficiaries, or make a new one altogether. Now is a good time to choose new beneficiaries for your pension plans or life insurance policies, too.

If you are uncomfortable discussing these issues, remember that they don't go away; they affect your day-to-day living situation and should be ironed out as soon as possible.

Are there financial reasons to marry?

If you are looking for a financial reason to marry, try one of these: savings in income taxes, living expenses, insurance coverage, and estate taxes. Because of these financial benefits, we give the institution of marriage a value-oriented money planning award. Let us explain.

Tax Savings. If you and your partner have substantially different incomes—say, $70,000 for one and $15,000 for the other—marrying and filing jointly will save the higher earner money in taxes because of the way the income tax tables are set up.

We confess to a more romantic view of marriage, and prefer that you choose to marry or not marry for reasons other than financial ones. However, in all fairness we feel obliged to point out that getting married can actually penalize you financially; if both you and your spouse work and earn about the same amount of money, the federal tax on your joint return can be appreciably higher than it would be for two single people who file their tax returns separately. The tax act of 1993 made marriage an even greater tax burden.

Living Expenses. While it isn't exactly true that two can live as cheaply as one, you can save on the housing expenses because now you are sharing. Perhaps you can save on restaurant and entertainment too, because of your new incentive to spend time at home.

Insurance Coverage. A growing number of corporations are allowing employees to refuse fringe benefits such as health insurance. Instead, the employees can take extra pay. If your corporate plan provides family coverage, and you utilize it, your spouse may choose not to be covered by his or her company's group insurance plan. Your spouse may then receive cash in lieu of this benefit, and you can bank your extra money. Give careful consideration before doing this, though. Suppose, for example, that you are covered under your spouse's policy, you develop a health problem, and your spouse leaves his or her job; you can then be left without coverage.

Estate Taxes. You can take advantage of the unlimited marital deduction which allows you to transfer assets between husband and wife during life or at death without gift or estate tax payments. In contrast to married couples, couples who live together without marriage have assets fully subject to estate taxes if one member passes away.

What if we live together and are not married?

Marriage is actually a form of contract that is recognized not only by our society but also by our legal system. It's a contract that may make each spouse entitled to property in the event of divorce or the death of a partner. For example, your spouse is entitled to certain pension benefits whether you want to share your pension or not. And, unless he or she waives that right, a surviving spouse can take over your lump-sum qualified pension (roll it over) without paying income tax until he or she makes withdrawals.

A person who is involved in a relationship outside of marriage usually has few or no rights to the partner's property. Yet there are several ways to protect yourself. You can establish rights by contract if you both agree to the terms. Aaron and Molly had lived together for over 10 years. Molly told us that she worried that she had no protection if Aaron, who was considerably older, died first. But even though Molly had been Aaron's confidant all those years, she feared upsetting him by asking him to find a way to protect her after his death. We encouraged Molly to discuss her fears with Aaron, and together they worked out the terms of a contract that gave Molly the security she wanted.

A contract is legally recognized if there is some form of goods or services (called "consideration") rendered by each party. If each of you brings something to the relationship—for example, property and, in some states, companionship or domestic services—then you are candidates for an extramarital agreement. To draw one up, consult your attorney.

If you want to leave a substantial amount of your assets to the person you live with, draw up your will carefully so that it can withstand a challenge from your family members. If you think you are protected by your partner's will, keep in mind that a will can be changed. It would be better for you in many circumstances if your partner set up an irrevocable trust with you as beneficiary; you would be more secure because the trust can't be changed. Or you can put property into joint ownership, with the entire amount going to the survivor after the first partner dies. Taking out insurance policies on the life of a substantial money earner is another way to cushion the effects of a sudden death.

Assets that you hold in your own name, medical coverage, and other insurance benefits can be the best form of safety. A relationship that suits you and your partner today can change dramatically over time. For example, ask yourself, would anything happen to your relationship if you became disabled?

Unless you have written contracts or trusts in place that will withstand permanent separation from one another (irrevocable), it is best to think of yourself as a single entity. Do your own financial planning and provide for your own future as well as you can.

Do we need a prenuptial agreement?

A prenuptial agreement is a premarital contract that establishes separate assets which will *not* be part of marital property. It can also help you set up guidelines for conduct and duties of both spouses during marriage and determine property rights in case of a breakup. You can include more personal factors as well. (A postnuptial agreement is the same type of contract, but it is drawn up *after* the marriage.)

We recommend you think about this type of agreement carefully, since it can be a source of friction when you least need it—when preparing for your marriage. Prenuptials are used most often in cases of second marriages when one or both individuals have substantial wealth and want to leave their money to the children from their first marriage. Most commonly, one spouse agrees to leave a sum of money to the other spouse outright or to provide for the transfer of assets in a trust in exchange for a release of claims against the donor spouse's estate.

Michael and Audrey exhibited the kind of stress a prenuptial agreement can put on a couple. Michael, a middle-aged businessman who had saved over $400,000, planned to marry Audrey, who had no money of her own. Michael had always intended to leave his money to his nieces and nephews. His attorney suggested a prenuptial agreement, but Audrey was very hurt and angry when Michael told her his plans.

We advised Michael to draw up an agreement that provided only a small sum to Audrey if they should divorce before two years were up and a larger sum to her if they divorced before five years passed. The agreement would dissolve after the seven-year mark, at which time Audrey would have all a spouse's usual rights to her husband's assets. Audrey agreed to this arrangement and invited us to their beautiful, old-fashioned wedding. Last time we saw them Michael and Audrey had just celebrated five happy years of marriage.

Know what you are getting yourself into before you sign the agreement. This is our advice, and it is the law. It is important to use separate qualified lawyers to represent each party. Given the horror stories that financial advisors hear, we can't stress that enough. Both parties to a prenuptial agreement must enter into it freely and in good faith, without excess pressure from the partner. Each person must understand what he or she is signing and must disclose full assets to the other person. Check your will for any possible conflict with the prenuptial agreement.

Even with all these precautions, if you move, investigate the validity of the agreement under the laws of your new home state. For example, whether you have a prenuptial agreement or not, when one party is the principal earner, many states will not allow him or her to be relieved of supporting the spouse following divorce.

Money or property that is transferred to one of the parties in exchange for the release of marital rights is considered a gift and therefore subject to combined gift and estate taxes. If the transfer occurs *after* marriage, the gift will not be subject to estate taxes because assets can be transferred between husband and wife tax-free.

If substantial assets are involved, you can set up a trust in addition or as an alternative to the prenuptial agreement at any time, for example, at the beginning of your marriage, when you are planning a divorce, or in your will. Often the Q-TIP trust, which can provide income for your spouse and have someone else ultimately inherit the principal, is an attractive way to accomplish your goals. (For more information on Q-TIP trusts, see Chapter 10.)

Make sure that your pre- or postnuptial agreement provides for your spouse to forgo the proceeds from your retirement plan, if that is what you want. Remember, your spouse has to sign a waiver to effect this change.

Are there special considerations for second marriages?

In our experience, second marriages sometimes lack the youthful enthusiasm of the first one, but husband and wife have a more sober understanding of what it takes to make a relationship work. Each spouse brings good and bad experiences to the table. Each also brings financial assets, debts, furnishings, personal possessions, and other items to the marriage.

Children are often part of the second-marriage package. If first marriages are based on optimism for the future, second marriages tend to be based in part on businesslike relationships. Children add to the considerations, resulting in a new "his, hers, and theirs" arrangement. In other words, you and your spouse may want to maintain separate property with your own set of beneficiaries. In any case, you are under no legal obligation to support a stepchild or to put that child in your will.

Given past experience, you and your spouse may choose to maintain separate checking and savings accounts and contribute separately for household expenses. One couple, Steve and Bonnie, even made personal loans to each other—with the terms of the loan outlined in written documents—when one couldn't pay his or her agreed-upon share of expenses for a particular month.

Your situation can become more complicated if you and your second spouse have children together. It can be hard to decide how to divide assets between the old and new families. We recommend that you and your spouse openly discuss these matters and, if necessary, bring an objective advisor, such as a good friend, to your discussions. If it helps, draw up a pre- or postnuptial agreement.

If minor children are involved, you might want to take out additional insurance made payable to the children from your second marriage. If your assets reach the $600,000 figure, it may be best to give your child money to buy the policy just to keep the insurance out of your estate. To accomplish this, you can use an irrevocable life insurance trust in which your child is the beneficiary. We often recommend trusts for minor children. These can be inexpensive bank trust accounts or others that lawyers set up, called 2503(b) or 2503(c) trusts.

When children from the first marriage are grown, there are other considerations. This is particularly true if the marriage takes place when both parties are in their senior years and the marriage's timespan is likely to be limited. People often ask us who should be the principal beneficiary—the new spouse, or the children? Clearly, it depends on your own wishes and often results in compromises.

We have talked more than once to children of divorced or deceased parents who worry that a new marriage could result in a loss of their share of their parent's assets. In such cases, we sometimes recommend pre- or postnuptial agreements and Q-TIP trusts to take care of the new spouse and allow the children to be ultimate beneficiaries. We often find both sides agreeable to these trusts.

Jack, aged 71, was happily married and living in a retirement community when his wife of 43 years suddenly died. No sooner was the funeral over than the widows in his neighborhood began ringing Jack's doorbell and bringing him blueberry pies—his favorite. Jack, a shy man, was lonely. He began to develop a relationship with an exceptionally outgoing woman. His three children were worried that Jack, who was in poor health, would leave his wealth to this woman, who he was marrying more for companionship than for love.

We recommended that Jack see a lawyer about a prenuptial agreement. Jack was nervous about bringing the topic up with his intended and was surprised to find that she had terms of her own. She was concerned about conserving her assets for her children and grandchildren. They struck a deal that satisfied all parties, those who were directly concerned and those who were indirectly involved.

What are the basics of divorce planning?

The last thing you want to talk about at this time may be your finances. Your thoughts are probably elsewhere—the future, how you will get along after the divorce, how you will relate to other people—not on financial matters. Yet you do want to structure your affairs as well as possible in the period beyond your legal breakup. Consider the following "big three" concerns of divorce planning: alimony, child support, and property settlements.

Alimony. Alimony is the amount of money that one ex-spouse is legally bound to give the other. If you are paying or receiving alimony, you need to rethink your tax situation. You can't file joint tax returns after divorce, which can be a plus if you and your former spouse earn about the same or a negative if one of you has a more modest income. For tax purposes, the person writing the alimony checks can deduct the payments. The person who receives the money must declare it as taxable income. Usually the person paying alimony is in a higher tax bracket than the receiver, so this works out well—for the alimony payer, anyway. (If both parties agree to not declare it for income tax purposes, the cash outlay or the cash received will have no tax effect). The payments must be given in cash form, the individuals cannot live in the same house after divorce or separation, and the money cannot be specified for anything other than alimony. Payments must stop when the person receiving the money dies or remarries.

Depending on the terms of the divorce decree, life insurance payments can also be deductible as alimony providing the person who owns the policy is the one paying the alimony and the beneficiary is the person who receives it.

Be careful in constructing alimony payments. If the payments decline by more than $15,000 in the first three years after separation for reasons other than death or remarriage, then you will have to include in taxable income a portion of the amount you deducted in the two previous years. Your spouse can also deduct that same amount he or she previously included as alimony income.

Child Support. When you are drawing up your divorce agreement, consider that alimony will end upon your former spouse's remarriage or death; payments to support your children, however, will probably continue until the youngest child is 18 or 21. Child support payments are neither tax-deductible by the giver nor taxable for the receiver. The person paying may prefer tax-deductible alimony, while the person on the receiving end may like nontaxable child support.

If property is transferred as child support, taxes come into play. If the property is transferred to the guardian, income from the property is taxable to the person who supports the child if it is meant to be used as support. If the property is transferred to your child directly, income from the property will be taxable to the child who, if over age 14, is likely to be in a lower tax bracket than you are.

Property Settlements. These settlements are one-time transfers of cash or other assets upon divorce. You may be interested in how they are determined. In most states, the assets accumulated during your marriage are treated as contributions by both parties and they split the property equitably upon divorce (equitable distribution), even if the larger wage-earner paid most of its costs.

The days of deciding who is at fault for the breakup of a marriage and penalizing that person financially are pretty much over. Certain states, known as community property states, even require you to split all marital assets fifty-fifty. Any gifts or inheritances that one person received during the marriage or assets accumulated before the marriage are excluded, but growth in these assets may be considered marital property if the spouse contributed significantly to that growth.

Judges consider the length of the marriage, the number and ages of the children, the age and health of the divorcing parties, and their projected future financial outlook. Their rulings can vary depending on the judge and your state.

If you transfer assets to your spouse during marriage or pursuant to a decree within one year after your divorce, neither of you will be taxed, and this tax exemption may even be extended under special circumstances. In these transfers, the receiving spouse's cost for purposes of calculating taxable gains on later sale of the property is the same as the cost for the donor spouse.

Keep in mind that your spouse has rights to your pension assets as part of the divorce settlement. Normally, transfers out of a pension plan are taxable, but in the case of divorce you can roll over part or all of the amounts without paying taxes.

Finally, make sure you have enough cash income to pay for your spouse and children's support, or to cover your living costs if you are not working. Proper cashflow planning will help smooth the financial aspects of your divorce.

What strategies should I consider in divorce planning?

Where there is little money, it may be wise to compromise with your spouse because it can save you both legal bills. In any case, your goal should be to reach a full and lasting settlement. Get separate attorneys; this is one time it doesn't pay to skimp. Make full disclosure of all your assets. If you violate this rule, you risk opening up a settlement claim years down the road.

Take a tip from our friend Fred. He says that it is important to have a good attorney to negotiate a settlement, a knowledgeable appraiser to evaluate your possessions, and a few good friends to see you through rough times. Above all, Fred adds, be fair, and hope your ex-spouse will be the same. Fred should know; he's been married and divorced twice. (Fred is still optimistic about marriage. He is considering another walk down the aisle with his new girlfriend, who has also been divorced several times.)

Here are some specific strategies for you to look into.

Assessing Your Property. Under equitable distribution, you and your spouse can decide how your property will be split. First find the fair market value. If you own stocks, look in the newspaper for their prices. If you have other assets that cannot be valued easily, such as a house or a business, you can bring in experts to appraise the property. Expect your spouse to bring in another set of experts to arrive at their own figures. You know what that means: there will be two valuations. One appraisal may be unusually high, the other unusually low. The judge won't necessarily have enough familiarity with the objects to decide which appraisal is more accurate. Our advice is to try to settle before you are forced to see a judge. This is your property, and you know what it's worth to you, emotionally and financially. Your best course is to strike an agreement that suits you and your spouse.

Deciding Between Alimony and a Property Settlement. From the recipient's point of view, if your income is lower than that of your ex-spouse, a property settlement may be preferable to alimony. The assets yield income that can be used. Even more pertinently, a bird in the hand is worth two in the bush. You don't want to know how many alimony agreements are not followed through after the first few years. Besides, alimony ends upon remarriage. A property settlement—

whether in real estate or cash or some other asset—can last forever; if it is managed correctly, it can also help you keep ahead of inflation.

On the negative side for the recipient, debts to your spouse arising from property settlements are eliminated in case of bankruptcy, whereas alimony and child support payments are not.

Deciding Between Alimony and Child Support. From the payer's point of view, maximizing alimony and minimizing child support brings a large tax deduction. You can still have some of the payments go for child support. For example, you can have some of the money go for college payments, with the alimony dropping down after college is over. But the IRS will probably call a portion of the payment child support if there is a linking of the decline in alimony from the divorce settlement to the decline in college costs. Keep in mind that the payments you make for alimony don't have to go for your child's support. You have to trust the spouse who has custody of the child to finance the child's living costs.

From the recipient's point of view, you may want to have more money treated as child support, which will continue if he or she expects to remarry soon.

Watching Tax Angles. Legal costs for divorce are not usually deductible. But tax advice for the spouse who pays the legal fees is. Consider having the lower-income spouse pay all legal fees. Make an agreement that the alimony payments for the next year include the amount of these fees. In that way, the alimony payer gets the alimony deduction and the payee gets to deduct his or her accountant's fees over the 2 percent of adjusted gross income floor, which for him or her is easier to achieve than it would be for the higher-income spouse. Also, the payee can deduct advice that leads to taxable income or, in this case, taxable alimony.

Similarly, there is often a fight over who will take the exemption for a child. This exemption phases out gradually if income exceeds a threshold amount which depends on marital status, so that it may be better for the exemption to go to the lower-income person. If you can't reach an agreement, the exemption will go to the spouse who has custody of the child for more than half the year.

When property settlements are involved, remember that transfers of property that have greatly jumped in value since you bought them will cost the owner higher capital gains taxes when they are sold. You should think about this when you decide who gets what. Ella was offered one of two pieces of property in her divorce from Hal. Each one was worth $75,000, but one had cost $25,000 and the other $70,000. Since Ella was going to sell the property, we recommended she take the one with the $70,000 cost, which would have only a small tax due on the gain, a net savings in taxes to her of over $10,000.

Actually, in deciding on property settlements, it is best to plan so that assets are equitably distributed on an after-tax basis.

Adjusting for Inflation. Watch your annual alimony payments. Most alimony payments are made for a fixed sum. As a reader of this book, you are aware that inflation cuts into the purchasing power of those payments so that their real value declines over time. If you are the recipient, you should try to negotiate a schedule of payments that increases along with the cost of living (as given in the Consumer Price Index). If the payer is nervous about this, an alternative can be to share in the annual job-related increase in income he or she receives.

Buying Insurance. Where alimony or child support is sizeable, it may be a good idea for the payee (the person who receives alimony income) to have insurance on the life of the payer (the one who extends alimony). Make sure that the policy and annual payments are kept in force by having the payee hold the policy but the payer remit the annual fee to the payee. Remember, as long as the payee fully owns the policy, the alimony payer can deduct the premiums.

If you have children and you can't rely on your former spouse to look after them, you may need either term or ordinary life insurance. Consider disability insurance as well. If possible, also have your ex-spouse carry disability on him- or herself so that alimony and child support payments will continue even if he or she is disabled. Make sure you have proper medical insurance; people who don't have it can face potential bankruptcy if there is a serious illness in the family. Review your coverage to make sure it reflects the changes in your circumstances.

Disposing of Your Home. Be careful about accepting your house as an asset if you plan to live in it and don't have enough income to maintain it. Negotiating for marketable securities instead of the house could provide you with the income you need to support your cost of living.

In addition, if you and your spouse decide to sell, are over 55, and have large gains on your house, sell it *after* the divorce. If you were to sell before the divorce, you would receive only one $125,000 tax exemption on the gain. If you sell the house after the divorce, you and your spouse can *each* take a $125,000 exemption.

Benefiting from Social Security. Divorced spouses are entitled to their ex-spouse's social security benefits based on their ex-spouse's payments provided they were married at least 10 years, divorced for 2 years, and didn't remarry before the spouse's retirement or death. Normal social security eligibility requirements must be met, and you will receive half the benefits of your spouse.

Don't worry about your wage-earning spouse; he or she will still receive the same full social security benefits he or she would have received if you had not gotten divorced.

What changes do I need to make after my divorce?

If you are recently divorced, you know how traumatic such a major change can be. You are on your own, perhaps for the first time in many years. If you are like Judy, you have a loss of confidence, a feeling of betrayal, and an inability to make financial decisions, in part because they have always been made with a partner.

It may take some time, but the sooner you begin to think of yourself as a single person instead of a couple, the better. Emotionally, it can help you get back on your feet to have your spouse remove all of his or her belongings from the family home, if you continue to live in it.

Financially, there are many changes that you should make as soon as possible:

1. *Insurance.* Is your ex-spouse named as primary beneficiary in your policies? Call your insurance agent and have the beneficiary changed to your children or other heirs. Reconsider the amounts of life insurance and disability insurance you need now. While you may need more to support your children, if your main reason for having insurance was to provide for your spouse, you'll need less.
2. *Pensions.* Fill out a change of beneficiary designation form and send it to your pension administrator.

3. *Trusts.* Review any trusts you have and, unless they are irrevocable and therefore you can't make changes in them, make sure they reflect your wishes under your new single circumstances.
4. *Wills.* Similarly, make an appointment to have your will updated. Change your beneficiaries if that is appropriate.
5. *Powers of attorney.* If you've given your ex-spouse these powers, destroy the original documents and decide if you want to give someone else the powers instead.
6. *Joint accounts.* Do you and your ex-spouse have joint checking, savings, brokerage, or other accounts that were not part of the settlement? Take your spouse's name off them.
7. *Safe-deposit box.* Does your ex-spouse still have access to your safe-deposit box? Is this what you want? If not, remove his or her name from the list of authorized users. If necessary, close the box and open another one in your name only (or jointly with one of your children or other trusted relatives).
8. *Credit cards.* If there are joint privileges on your cards, call the companies and have them issue you new cards (and new account numbers, if necessary). Your ex-spouse should get his or her own cards. We learned this lesson from Adam, whose ex-wife ran up $8000 worth of debt on his credit cards right after their divorce. Unfortunately, Adam's ex-wife refused to repay the debt, and Adam was legally responsible for it.
9. *Phone cards.* These are credit cards in another form. Your ex-spouse can continue to use them unless you change the accounts.
10. *Other companies.* Notify all companies with whom you do business—for example, your employer—about the change in status.
11. *Social security.* Call social security when you are about to apply for benefits, or if you are currently receiving benefits.
12. *Spread the news.* Some couples feel officially divorced only after they tell their friends and relatives. If you are in this category, you might also want to inform your religious leaders, children's teachers, landlord, and others.

Lastly, keep your plans flexible. You may swear off marriage now, but statistics show that the majority of divorced people enter the marriage game again.

12

Caring for the Elderly

In our practice, we have found that caring for the elderly is a matter of growing concern. It is commonplace now for our clients to ask us for helpful planning strategies for this group.

The reality is that in many cases caring for the elderly can be highly stressful. You may watch helplessly as people you love and respect diminish in their abilities. Sometimes they even begin to resemble children: self-centered, demanding, with little patience for others. Given your limited time, finances, and other priorities you might feel unable to meet all their needs and feel guilty if you can't. It helps to realize that you *are* making a difference and are repaying the person for his or her past kindnesses.

Caring for the elderly can also be prohibitively expensive. These days you are likely to face high medical and nursing home costs. If you do not plan carefully, your own assets could be jeopardized. This chapter will explain how to assist others in this stage of their lives.

Proper planning for this time can help those you care about reach a comfortable later period of life. Ideally, like George Burns in his eighties and nineties, your parents, other relatives, or close friends will be cheerful, optimistic, and well cared for, with a quick wit and an interesting outlook on life.

How can I prevent my parents falling prey to scams and unscrupulous sales pitches?

As our population ages, many elderly people fall victim to pressure from unscrupulous salespeople who try to profit from their fears and uncertainty. They find themselves saying yes to deals they don't understand to avoid hurting a salesperson's feelings, or simply to get out of an uncomfortable situation.

Remind your parents of the following rules:

1. Don't do business with anyone you don't know. Ask for credentials and proof of any claims as well as objective measurements of past performance. While Mrs. Morgan was in a retirement community in the Southwest where she spends three months each year, she was urged by a salesperson to purchase an emergency alarm system that would alert medics if she became ill while living in the retirement community or in her home in the Northeast. Mrs. Morgan deferred, and said she would check further. When she got home and followed up, she found that, despite the salesperson's assurances, the system would have been ineffective in the Northeast.

   If you aren't sure about something, check with local consumer protection agencies or your Better Business Bureau.

2. Don't let people who ring the bell unannounced into your house. One woman we heard of let someone into her house to be polite, and four hours later was still listening to his sales pitch. Eventually, when it was late and she wanted to have her dinner, she signed the papers he handed her just so he would leave and she could regain her privacy.

3. Whenever possible, don't make snap decisions. Take your time, analyze your decision, and tell the salesperson you will get back to them. The most important thing is to give yourself breathing space. Your response may be different after you've stepped away from the situation.

4. Discuss all financial decisions with your family or other advisors before completing the transaction. Tell the salesperson that you can't make a decision until they give you their opinions. We recently saw a client who said she couldn't make a decision without consulting her attorney, her daughter, and her son-in-law. We would rather she did all that than make rash decisions she might later regret.

5. Don't buy anything over the phone. Ask to see all proposals in writing.

6. Don't divulge your credit card information or other personal data to strangers.

7. Remember our rule of not investing in anything you don't fully understand.

8. Think carefully before revising your will, especially if you are considering establishing a new beneficiary. Is this person someone you have known for some time or someone you have recently met? How do your friends and relatives feel about this person? Speak to an estate attorney privately, without the new beneficiary present, before you take this step.

9. Don't remove money from a bank or other account to give to someone you have recently met. Don't take strangers with you when you withdraw funds. Pay for all transactions by check, so you will have a record of the arrangement.

10. Never feel too foolish to ask for more information or to say no. You have a right to control your own finances. Examine all the pros and cons and make sure you are comfortable with your decision.

How can my parents plan for medical outlays?

One of the greatest fears people have is that they will be faced with a large medical bill that will wipe out their savings and that they will become a burden to their children and grandchildren. If your parents are over 65, the medical part can be taken care of fairly easily.

Medicare insurance—a program of the U.S. Department of Health and Human Services—is available to people over 65 and some younger disabled people. It is based on their own or their spouse's past employment. Your parents will probably qualify if either of them has worked for 10 years. They can apply for Medicare coverage at their local social security office.

Medicare consists of two parts: hospital insurance, known as Part A, and medical insurance, Part B. Most people do not have to pay for Part A coverage, which includes inpatient care in a hospital, care in a skilled nursing home (one that provides medical care) after a hospital stay, home health care, and hospice care (that is, care for the terminally ill).

If your parents are eligible for Part A coverage, for a monthly premium ($31.80 in 1992) they can also enroll in Part B. Under Part B, Medicare pays about 75 percent of the approved cost of visits to doctors, a second opinion, outpatient care, ambulance services, diagnostic tests, blood transfusions, some drugs, and other supplies and services that are not covered under Part A. Even if they don't qualify for free Part A coverage, if your parents are over 65, they may be able to buy either Part B coverage or Parts A and B coverage by paying monthly premiums.

The annual deductible before Medicare benefits begin is currently $100. Note that Medicare Part A, which pays for hospitalization, has a deductible of $652 per benefit period, which begins when a person enters the hospital and ends when they have been out of the hospital for 60 days in a row.

In order to avoid a gap between the Medicare approved amount and actual costs, suggest that your parents use doctors and suppliers who accept assignment; that is, they take Medicare as full payment. Alternatively, your parents can buy a comprehensive major medical policy (known as Medigap) to pay the balance not covered by Medicare. Such policies used to be restricted to the healthy, but under recently approved congressional legislation, if a person subscribes to Medicare insurance, Medigap insurance must be sold to him or her regardless of physical condition if he or she applies within six months of first qualifying for Medicare Part B (at age 65 for people who are retired, and for others when they retire and sign up for Medicare Part B). Be sure to avoid policies with high deductibles, and check the upper limits of the policy, which should be at least $1 million for each illness.

The nursing home situation is more complex. Medicare Part A will contribute toward skilled nursing or rehabilitation care in a participating nursing home for up to the first 100 days. The first 20 days' stay will be completely covered by Medicare, and the next 80 days will be paid by Medicare with a contribution by the patient ($81.50 daily in 1992). For him or her to qualify certain requirements must be met. For example, he or she must enter the nursing home after at least three consecutive days in a hospital, not including the day of discharge; the physician must authorize that skilled nursing home care is necessary; and the condition must be the same one that was treated in the hospital.

Medicare does not pay for custodial (activities of daily living) care in a nursing home—and most nursing home care is custodial rather than medical.

Should my parents take out nursing home insurance?

The simplest way to guard your parent's assets is to have nursing home insurance, which includes custodial care in their own home. However, as we mentioned in Chapter 9, for people with modest incomes, the costs for comprehensive coverage of $2000 per year for people aged 55 and progressively much higher as they age (with costs of $10,000 to $20,000 per year for those in their late seventies) is prohibitive. If people are rich enough to handle the sizeable ongoing nursing home costs, then they do not need this insurance. If they have no assets, the government will cover them. It is the middle-income person who is most affected. While policies are improving steadily, in our opinion nursing home insurance has not yet been perfected to the point that it represents good value. (The just-announced experiment in Connecticut of joint state aid and private nursing home insurance may be a step in the right direction.) If your parents want the peace of mind of at least partial coverage, they should begin to purchase the insurance by age 50 or 55, when premiums will be relatively low and more affordable.

Most elderly people do not have nursing home insurance. They are vulnerable to large bills for at-home care or nursing home costs. In some instances, local community charitable organizations or the city or state have programs to help needy people. Aside from that, bills can mount rapidly. Nursing homes can range from poorly kept chambers of horror to efficient centers of learning and companionship. The latter can cost as much as $85,000 per resident per year. Statistically, relatively few individuals spend more than five years in a nursing home. Still, it doesn't take much to figure out that most people's money will be exhausted before then.

Will the government help with nursing home bills?

There is another way to afford nursing home care that is actually meant for the poor or the "medically indigent." You and your parents have to decide whether you feel it is appropriate. The government will pay all nursing home costs at virtually any nursing home in the country if your parents have run out of money. They can qualify by transferring their assets into an irrevocable trust, also known as a Medicaid trust. The income from the trust can be used to help pay for their upkeep; the principal will go to their children or whomever they choose.

Understand that the trust cannot be undone. In other words, your parents will not have access to the money and they will be dependent on the trustee they select, often their children, to look out for them. Remember, the more money the trustee issues to them from the trust, the less he or she will ultimately have for him- or herself. Also, if there is any ability to withdraw principal on their behalf, then the principal can be assessable by the government; any income withdrawn may also be assessable. For that reason, your parents may want to wait until they have an extremely high probability of going into a nursing home before setting up an irrevocable trust. They might also consider appointing an objective nonfamily member, such as a bank, as trustee.

Note that the government will not pay for nursing home care up to the first two-and-a-half years after the trust has been set up. It is possible to buy nursing home insurance for the interim period of time.

When it is set up and operated as intended, a Medicaid trust, giving the trustee some discretion, can protect your parents' assets either for their spouse, children, or other heirs. (Spousal resources can also affect eligibility for government aid.) If your spouse will not be going into a nursing home, he or she will be allowed to keep the house if it is in his or her name; in certain circumstances, the house can also be transferred to a brother or sister or children.

Another way of disposing of your parents' assets is to gift them directly to their heirs. This method costs less than a trust, but it doesn't allow them to have an objective trustee to look after one or both spouses.

In either case, this is a high-risk situation; your parents should be careful about giving their money away prematurely.

Are there financial strategies in caring for my parents?

You may feel guilty even asking such a question. Many of us feel we should be selfless in our dealings with our elders, especially our parents. After all, didn't they sacrifice for us? At the same time, caring for the elderly can cost large sums of money, and there are ways to ease your financial burden without harming anyone.

Elder care can be mutually advantageous. For instance, if you pay more than half the support for an aging family member, you can claim the cost of that care as an income tax deduction. Buying aging relatives a house or an apartment can be an advantage for them if they don't own one already. They then pay you rent equivalent to what they would otherwise pay, while you receive the ultimate benefits of holding an investment that should grow over time. The rent that your parents must remit to make this a bona fide transaction may also give you some immediate cashflow beyond mortgage and maintenance costs. In addition, you can write your investment off over 27½ years (the value of the building only, excluding the worth of the land) in the form of annual depreciation charges. If you have a reported loss on the home—including allowable depreciation—for tax purposes, you can use that loss to reduce your other reportable income. The loss is gradually phased out for incomes between $100,000 and $150,000.

If your parents are better off financially than you are yet don't own their home, you might agree upon slightly different arrangements than those outlined above. You still purchase the house for them. In addition to paying the rent, however, have each of your parents gift you as much as $10,000 (for a total of $20,000 per year) to meet annual interest and mortgage payments. As we mentioned above, make sure that you set the rent on the property at the going market rate.

Alternatively, should your parents own a home and need capital, you can buy the property from them. In return, you can give them lifetime rights to live there at a market rent. The procedures are the same as though you had bought them a new house, with potential tax benefits and prospective growth. Gifting by the parents may once again be a factor in whether you can afford the bank payments to finance the purchase.

The benefits of such a purchase should be carefully weighed against leaving the property in your parents' name until their deaths. At their deaths you would receive a stepped-up basis for the property. That means that if you were the beneficiary, you would receive the property at the then-current market value as opposed to the potentially much lower cost figure your parents had based on their old purchase price. If your parents sell their house, they benefit from the one-time $125,000 tax exemption for people over 55. If the actual gain in price is substantially over that sum, it may pay to skip this method and wait for the stepped-up basis at death, which can save a tidy sum in capital gains income taxes; if they had purchased their home many years ago, chances are your parents would have to pay a large capital gains tax if they sold the home to you.

Other, more complex approaches that are beyond the scope of this book—such as transferring a family business to the next generation or selling it to employees or outsiders—are possible for people who have private businesses or large assets.

If you are contributing more for your parents' care than other family members are, don't hesitate to tell them that your contributions should be reflected in their wills. If you anticipate problems, you may even want to ask your parents to gift you some money while they are still alive. Keep a careful record of the amount of money you have invested in their care. Be sure to include interest in the interim. Those records are not for their benefit; rather they are to help you make a claim against the estate if the will designates that the expenses of the last illness be paid by the estate, or to avoid any later controversy with your siblings about the distribution of your parents' assets.

How can I best plan for the terminally ill?

We know that, first and foremost, looking after the needs of a terminally ill relative or friend can bring you much emotional pain. We have found that it helps to understand the range of feelings the terminally ill might go through. According to research, they may start off by denying the situation, progress to anger, move to bargaining to prolong life by good behavior, then become depressed and ultimately come to terms with reality. If time permits, it is best to wait until you and the terminally ill person have accepted reality, before you initiate discussions about financial strategies.

From a financial standpoint, planning for the terminally ill actually can be more definitive than other planning because normal life cycle uncertainties are eliminated. Often you can facilitate financial planning through a durable power of attorney, which will allow one or more of the people involved—for example, the spouse, the children, a close friend, a relative, or a lawyer—to act on the sick person's behalf when necessary. You can buy a form for a simple power of attorney in a stationery store; drawing up a more complex one requires an attorney. If the person is mentally competent, the power should be put into effect as quickly as possible because he or she may not continue to be lucid and legally competent to sign it. The alternative, in the event of mental incapacity, is to have the court appoint a guardian or conservator. This often takes considerable time and costs more money.

Make sure the power of attorney is durable, meaning it will not expire upon incapacity. Also, have the person sign a separate medical power of attorney (health-care proxy) to allow you to make medical decisions on his or her behalf. Because these powers of attorney are readily obtainable and can provide savings in cost, time, and effort, we give them a value-oriented money planning award.

If you have complications with the terminally ill person's assets or heirs, or have questions concerning his or her competence, consider a living trust as described in Chapter 10. Also, when assets are substantial, it is often easier to have the courts recognize personal wishes with a trust document instead of a power of attorney.

The planning tool we use most often for the terminally ill is gifting. As a general rule, gifts (except for life insurance and possibly those from a revocable trust), even at deathbed, are excluded from the dying person's estate and therefore not subject to an estate tax. They won't be subject to gift tax, either, if they are limited to $10,000 per recipient, or $20,000 if both husband and wife gift at the same time. (Interestingly, you can gift an unlimited amount of money for medical or educational purposes—for example, you can pay an institution directly in advance for someone's four-year education.) This will reduce the size of your estate and federal estate taxes if the estate is over $600,000.

If the terminally ill person is your spouse, you can gift an unlimited sum to him or her. It's beneficial to transfer to a terminally ill spouse investment assets that have grown considerably and that you expect to sell within a few years. In this way, you can take advantage of the stepped-up basis on death and avoid income taxes on the growth of the assets. However, you must do so at least one year prior to death or leave it to someone other than the person who owned and transferred it to the terminally ill spouse.

Let's say you own a home worth $300,000. You paid $90,000 for it. You could transfer the home tax-free to your terminally ill spouse. When he or she passed away, the cost for income tax purposes for the home would be $300,000, not $90,000. At an assumed tax rate of 33 percent, if you were the beneficiary, you would save $70,000 in income taxes on sale. You could reserve the one-time $125,000 credit—it wouldn't have covered the full gain anyway. Because of the large amount of money that can be saved with relative ease of transfer for many types of assets, we give this strategy a value-oriented money planning award.

From an income tax standpoint, the opposite is true for assets in which the ill person has material losses. Sell these now. That way, the losses can reduce income taxes; delaying sale until death will result in losing the tax benefit.

Urge the ill person to review and update his or her will, sign a living will that gives directions on when and if to "pull the plug," and prepare or update his or her list of assets and their location. Now is the time to institute an informal, nonlegal, written description of his or her wishes and information procedures to be followed. Include in the document such facts as funeral and burial arrangements; where to reach the lawyer, accountant, and financial advisors; what money is to be collected and bills to be paid; and items of a more personal nature.

Make sure that your parents' estate has enough cash or marketable assets to cover living needs and estate taxes. When assets are held in the sick person's own name only, it might be a good idea to change them to joint name or close them out. If they are in one name only, it is sometimes difficult to get access to them for some time after the death of the account holder, particularly if they are kept in another state. You don't want to be forced to sell your parents' home and other assets at fire-sale prices.

What should I know about paying for care for the terminally ill at home?

Many people prefer to spend their last days at home. Still, they may require costly care. Home visits by medical professionals following a hospital stay will often be paid for by Medicare.

For a terminal illness, contact your local hospice for advice on handling your family's medical situation. Often hospice care can be arranged in the home, not in a hospital, and sometimes free care is provided. (Contact the National Hospice Organization at 800-658-8898.) If care is given in the hospital, Medicare should pay for all covered services (there is no deductible for hospice care) for two 90-day periods and one 30-day period, and sometimes an extension beyond those periods. If your parents prefer home care, visiting nurses, social workers, and volunteers often make home visits. Find out if your parents qualify for home-delivered meals or homemakers services. If you are providing most of the hands-on care yourself, try to connect with an organization that will give you a respite from caring for your parent. Every effort should be made to ensure that the terminally patient is comfortable and relieved of pain, and to involve relatives in the care and counseling services.

Depending on state law, certain insurance companies now allow a terminally ill patient to draw down on his or her life insurance while he or she is still alive. This can be very useful for financially strapped individuals or those who would like to upgrade their living costs.

During this trying period someone with a cool head, a grasp of the important factors, and an understanding personality can be of great help. In our experience, either someone close to the terminally ill person or a professional advisor can be a good choice. In one case, Zachary, the youngest of four brothers who was considered a rebellious, immature member of the family rose to the occasion and assumed the role of family financial and health-care coordinator. In our opinion, a better job couldn't have been done by a professional for the business items, and the emotional ones were handled by Zachary as only one who truly cares could have done.

How can I get help in caring for my parents?

Today there are many professionals who deal mainly or solely with the elderly. Many organizations were created as recently as the 1980s to deal with just such issues.

If you are wondering where to turn for help, start with advisors you already know and trust—your family doctor, your attorney, your financial advisor, or your accountant. If they feel you need more specialized help, they may be able to recommend a colleague.

If you are on your own and don't know where to start, try calling the associations that represent specialists in the fields you need, for example, your state medical society, state bar association, or your local branch of the National Association of Social Workers. Follow up their referrals, however, with a check of the credentials of the person you are thinking of hiring. Conduct an interview on the phone or in person; ask how they would go about helping your family and how much it would cost. Ask about their education, training, and experience. And then weigh the costs of their services with the benefits you or your family would receive.

Following are some elder-care professionals, the services they provide, and how you can reach them:

The Eldercare Locator. This service is currently available to callers in the Northeast and expects to be available in almost all states by January 1993. It is sponsored by the National Association of Area Agencies on Aging. Callers are referred to a local organization that will assess their needs and recommend appropriate nonprofit public or private facilities. Call them at 800-677-1116.

Geriatric Care Managers. These people can help you find appropriate care for your relatives. Their services include home care, counseling, information, and crisis intervention. For referrals, call the National Association of Private Geriatric Care Managers (602-881-8008) and tell them you would like to be given the names of some Category A members—those who have at least two years' experience, meet certain educational criteria, and are the principals in an elder-care practice. Then check their credentials yourself.

Elder Law. This is a new legal specialty. The National Academy of Elder Law Attorneys (655 North Alvernon Way, Suite 108, Tucson,

AZ 85711; 602-881-4005) will send you a brochure about how to find an attorney who specializes in this field. It is up to you to ask about that person's expertise, how long he or she has worked in this field, and what percentage of time he or she spends practicing elder law.

What financial planning is appropriate after the death of a loved one?

You might think that financial planning ends with death. That is not quite true. After someone's death, the survivors can deal with a wide range of financial planning issues ranging from redistributing the estate to reducing estate taxes.

Probably the first thing you should do is to make an accurate list of all assets and liabilities of the decedent. Then determine where the assets are. Open the decedent's safe-deposit box which, depending on the state you live in, you may have to do in coordination with a state government official or armed with a qualifying court authority. Make a broad estimate of the cashflow of the estate. Have the assets of the estate appraised and analyzed. When assets are widespread or complex, call in an advisor.

In many instances your next step will be to liquidate the assets. As value-oriented advisors we recommend that you or others such as the lawyer take care not to allow the assets to become subject to an "estate sale"—that is, a below-market sale price intended to move the assets quickly.

In other instances the assets may be divided and given out instead of cash. We have many clients who meet with the other beneficiaries and agree to apportion stocks, bonds, and real estate or to retain proportionate ownership in the assets according to the terms of the will.

There are many tax-related questions such as how long to keep the estate that files a separate tax return functioning, whether the filing of a joint tax return allowed for the year of death is the best alternative, how to apportion income and expenses between estate and individual tax returns, and whether to select as the date of valuation of the assets the date of death or six months thereafter. When these returns are complex, it is a good idea to have an accountant or tax attorney file the estate and final income tax returns.

You may be concerned about the need for liquidity to cover living costs for the surviving spouse and for estate taxes. Don't make too much of the need to keep the estate liquid. You can sell marketable securities such as common stocks and bonds to raise cash. Pension and insurance proceeds may become available. Sometimes it is possible to borrow money from the beneficiaries. The federal government can grant extensions for tax payments in cases of hardship. "Hardship" includes the estate's need to provide income to the spouse and family and to pay off claims. Extensions can range for up to 10 years.

You might also think it is impossible to change the beneficiaries—doesn't the will state absolutely and finally who gets what? No it doesn't, in the sense that a beneficiary can refuse the gift ("disclaim" it). If he or she does so properly, there will be no ill effects. It will be as if the item was never given to them. For example, if the decedent has left money to his or her spouse with the children named as contingent beneficiaries and the spouse disclaims it, it will immediately go to the children. The disclaimer must be in writing and received by the person transferring it or by a representative, not have any part used, and not be disclaimed with any qualifications.

Keep in mind that if the spouse does not get a required minimum percentage of a decedent's estate, he or she can contest the will and get a higher share. The minimum percentage will vary by state.

The surviving spouse should be aware of the rollover provision of a spouse's pension plan or IRA. If the decedent had a qualified plan, the amount can be transferred to the spouse without him or her losing the pension's tax-sheltered status. The surviving spouse can make withdrawals based on his or her age, with minimum payments beginning at age 70½.

Norma was the recipient of her recently deceased husband's pension plan. When she spoke to us, Norma was in fragile emotional health and had difficulty making decisions. We arranged for the pension to be transferred (rolled over) to Norma's IRA. Norma had been thinking of buying an annuity with the proceeds, but by rolling over the money we probably saved her over $100,000 in income taxes. Once we had taken care of Norma's most pressing concerns, we suggested she leave her other financial decisions, such as where she should invest her money, until she was emotionally ready to deal with them.

Be sure to find out if the spouse of the decedent is entitled to medical insurance with the spouse's employer for a fixed period (often three years). And investigate if it is inexpensive and worthwhile to keep the medical insurance for a while. In any event, using it up may be advisable until the spouse has had time to look at outside policies. Think about canceling life insurance policies and investing the cash value if there is really no need for the spouse to provide funds to anyone now. It may be a good time to revise the spouse's will to take into account the new realities.

Finally, remember that social security payments can begin at age 60 for widows or widowers whose benefits are based on the earnings of their spouse, as opposed to an age 62 minimum for retired persons. However, if the spouse's payments begin at age 60, he or she will receive just 71.5 percent of the maximum amount the decedent spouse was eligible for instead of the 82 percent he or she would receive if they waited until age 62.

13

Putting It Together: Solutions for the 1990s

In this book we have given you the basic tools necessary to do your own financial planning. But there is a problem. If you are like most people we meet in our practice, you probably don't know exactly what personal financial planning is. It's not your fault. There has been much confusion about this field.

What is financial planning? It's a way of handling your finances to achieve the goals you set for yourself. It covers six main areas: (1) cashflow planning and budgeting, (2) risk management and insurance, (3) taxes, (4) investments, (5) retirement, and (6) estate planning. A comprehensive financial plan must integrate these six areas because decisions in one area affect the others; for example, the cash that you spend on life insurance will no longer be available for retirement. The financial plan helps you to decide how to best use your funds according to your own priorities. As one client put it, financial planning is like taking a trip. First you find out where you are. Then you find out where you want to be. Financial planning helps you navigate to get there in the smoothest way.

Most people don't think in terms of an overall financial plan. One financial planner told us his clients usually come to him to cure a specific "hurt." They want to solve one problem, such as how much money they should put away for retirement, how to afford a home, or which investments to select for growth and safety. The preceding 12 chapters addressed and helped you find solutions for specific hurts.

Physical health requires a proper balance of sensible diet, exercise, a favorable physical and emotional environment, and a periodic medical checkup. Similarly, financial health requires your attention to all six planning areas; the relative amount of resources devoted to each depends on your age, your goals, your lifestyle, your risk tolerance, your income, your assets, and your personal desires. The aim is to guide available cash into those areas that need it most. The outcome can be financial security—the feeling that you have no financial hurts, and a reality that backs up the feeling.

After we had eliminated her how-to-structure-her-investments hurt and explained how a financial plan works, Elizabeth—who knows we both have earned Ph.D.'s—proclaimed us "financial doctors." But rather than spend the additional money required for our full planning services, Elizabeth asked us to get her started building her own financial plan. We did.

In this chapter we will do for you what we did for Elizabeth. We will give you some overall planning advice, go over our own Money Ladder concept, and present a real-life example, all of which will help you to build a plan yourself, according to your own personal financial goals.

What are the key money factors for the 1990s?

Gazing into our crystal ball, we predict that during the 1990s business and the economy will move at a slower pace than in the roaring eighties. Conspicuous consumption will be less conspicuous. Instead, people will be seeking greater value in their purchases and practices.

Our low personal savings rate and our government and trade deficits will get more attention. You will see the government becoming more involved in raising the quality of education, rebuilding the country's infrastructure, improving the environment, and bettering the quality of life for all Americans. Unfortunately, these government practices and our governmental and trade deficits will necessitate raising taxes on both the federal and state levels. Those in the highest income brackets will be paying larger percentages of total tax revenues than in the recent past, thereby erasing some of their benefits from the Reagan tax cuts. Legislators will try to disguise the higher taxes.

You will notice clearer distinctions between higher- and lower-quality organizations in insurance, municipal bonds, and in the international arena. With other Americans, you will learn not to put blind financial faith in any institution, with the possible exception of the federal government. You will continue to find inflation a force to reckon with—the country lacks the resolve to contain it permanently. The tax code will continue to shift toward rewarding savings and penalizing consumption, and the process will be hastened by the recognition that the population is aging and has not saved enough for retirement, and by the full taxability of social security payments except for the lowest-income groups. Longer life spans brought about by medical breakthroughs, gene therapy, physical fitness, and better nutrition will mean that you will need to save more money for your retirement.

You will see new financial instruments emerge; some of them will be painful duds. Limited partnerships will become popular again, perhaps with improved economic underpinnings, to take advantage of the rebound in real estate prices. Mutual funds will continue to make gains over individual stocks and bonds for individual investors who recognize their appeal and the inability to make money through short-term trading. (Did you know there are more mutual funds than stocks on the New York Stock Exchange right now?)

As the quality of the profession continues to improve, more people will use financial planners. At the same time, cheap computers and easy-to-follow software will make many techniques that until now were unique to financial advisors newly available to all. You will be able to perform the mechanics of your own financial plan more simply.

Modern investment theory practices will be established throughout the investment industry. This will make it more difficult to do better than stock market averages. Diverging from consensus thinking will continue to provide the easiest way to outperform the market.

If you ignore the drumbeat of group thinking and pick the right time and place to invest, you will see that the momentous economic and political changes going on in Europe and the Pacific are creating opportunities for holding international securities.

This country's own economic ride, meanwhile, won't be nearly as smooth as it was in the eighties. Nonetheless the United States will successfully find a new balance between adopting attractive Japanese techniques and traditional American entrepreneurial activity and emphasis on the individual. Economic rewards will further shift from those who use finance as a path to wealth to those who make our products more competitive in the international arena. Any unresolved problems the country has will be handled in the peculiarly American way of denying the difficulties of the situation and making the new practices fashionable.

Finally, given these changes, the idea that people don't have to plan at all and that things will take care of themselves will virtually disappear. Instead, you will find that good financial planning practices will be even more important, mandatory for some and amply rewarding for all. At decade's end the stock market will be appreciably higher, the average American's standard of living will have improved greatly, and the United States will still be the number-one industrialized nation.

Should I act on advice from my friends and relatives?

Beware. Friends and relatives who are not financial service professionals may not be reliable sources of financial advice. Even if they mean well and don't tend to exaggerate, what may have worked for them in the past may no longer be a good investment. In addition, do you have about the same amount of assets as your friend or relative? Are you at the same stage of life? Do you like to take the same amount of risk? Do you have similar goals? Chances are that you can't answer many of these questions because you have never discussed these personal details. A financial planning strategy that has been good for your friend may be inappropriate for you.

Usually we tell people that if they hear the name of an investment whispered at a cocktail party, forget it. That is not a good way to get your investment information. Potential investments have to be researched, analyzed, and compared in the context of risk, return, the economy, and market conditions.

Frequently, clients call up with the name of an investment that they heard was going to be a winner. When we track down the company, which sometimes involves considerable resourcefulness, we often find that it isn't public and so shares are not available; or it is barely in business, has no information to dispense, or has questionable assets, management, or prospects. If you can't do your homework and research an investment fully, you are better off keeping away.

Furthermore, if your friend tells you that he has shares of "Speculative Investronics" which had been selling at $5 and now are going for $12, he may have neglected to tell you that he bought them when they sold at $48 in the early eighties. With hindsight, we all can think up impressive investment war stories.

Since it is difficult even for professionals to properly research new investment opportunities, it is that much more difficult for individual investors who don't have access to major research sources to judge their merits. If you have doubts, there is probably good reason. Your relationship should not depend on whether or not you follow your friend's suggestion. In other words, don't listen to friends and relatives unless you are convinced they have special knowledge or a sharp investment eye and a keen understanding of your needs. Don't be pushed into anything that doesn't sound right to you.

Can I handle my own finances?

Our first inclination was to say yes. We wrote this book with a you-can-do-it-yourself approach in mind. But on reflection, we feel that it depends on your financial personality, which includes your skills, experience, needs, temperament, and ability:

Personality 1. You or your spouse are well informed financially and like to manage your own finances. You are willing to take the time to research topics that can be useful to you and to supervise your investments, either directly or through mutual funds. You don't need a financial planner.

Personality 2. You have no experience financially. You are capable overall, but when you try to tackle financial matters you get hopelessly confused. Common stock to you means similar-looking cattle. You are easily influenced by the latest idea you hear. You have trouble with mathematics. You need a financial advisor. If your situation is simple, a yearly consultation may be enough.

Personality 3. You have high family income and substantial investable assets, or own a business or professional practice. The relevant question may not be whether you can handle your own finances, but whether a good financial planner can do it better. There are approaches to improve investment returns, decide how much insurance you really need, reduce taxes, plan estates, prepare for retirement, and integrate business and personal financial planning that a professional could help you with.

George, a 58-year-old businessman, came into our office to check on whether he had been doing things correctly. His expression said, "My situation is too complex. I bet you can't help me." We analyzed George's business and personal finances and combined our recommendations into what we call our integrated financial plan. Sometime later he walked away with a pleased look because his entire business salary was sheltered from taxes and he was able to raise his target living standards for retirement.

Personality 4. You have trouble keeping up with your bills and can't figure out how to save money. Truthfully, you are more concerned about living for today than in saving money for tomorrow. You expect the future to take care of itself. You could use financial guidance. Read this book through once and refer to it again for specific issues. Unless you change your habits, consulting a financial planner won't help.

Personality 5. If you don't recognize yourself in any of the other categories, you belong here with most people. You *can* handle your own finances. You don't have to be a financial genius; if you can read this book and understand the concepts, you qualify to help yourself.

Weigh the benefits of hiring a financial planner against the cost of $50 to $300 an hour and the cost of commissions, if applicable. If your situation is simple, periodic consultations can be enough.

If you are lucky, you may get professional advice as an employee benefit: a growing number of corporations provide planning and retirement services to employees on the theory that relieving their workers of financial worries makes them more productive on the job.

Make good on your promise to devote the time necessary to educate yourself and to supervise your financial activities. This is particularly important as you reach middle age and get closer to retirement. In the 1990s, changes in taxes and investments in particular will require close analysis.

Most people can manage their own money matters. Only when situations get complicated or when people do not have the time or are not disciplined enough to follow through on their own do they really need an advisor. For your usual planning needs, follow our instructions and don't put things off. On the other hand, some find it reassuring to contact an advisor when they face major changes in their lives, while others prefer to hire an expert to help improve their financial situation, to further organize them, and to check their progress. Also, there are those who would rather spend their own time on more leisurely pursuits. As we mentioned before, it is likely that more people will choose to use planners in the 1990s. Many independent surveys have targeted this as a growth area for the future.

How can I find a qualified financial planner?

There are four principal qualities to look for in choosing a good financial planner: educational background, experience, professional practices, and impartiality. The planner's educational background should include a college degree and completion of a specialized program in financial planning. The best qualifying program is the Certified Financial Planner program offered in a number of colleges throughout the United States, or by self-study through the College for Financial Planning. Experience should consist of full-time work in personal financial planning for a minimum of three years and preferably longer.

A financial planning professional should be willing to perform a full (comprehensive) financial plan or any of its six component parts at your request. If you wish, that plan should be supplied to you in writing. Make sure it is tailored to your personal needs and that it is not a standardized computer plan that simply has your name and figures printed in the appropriate blanks.

The final qualification, impartiality, measures whether a planner will truly be working in your best interests. Pay attention to this item because, in the absence of national certification standards, some individuals who call themselves planners are really salespeople, eager to get you to invest in some product of theirs. Ask yourself, and consider asking them, whether they can and will choose the best products and services for you, or whether their own interests will take priority in their recommendations.

The easiest way to avoid this conflict is to select a fee-only financial planner. True fee-only financial planners collect all their revenues from their clients, both for their advice and for subsequent implementation of that advice. None of their income comes from commissions on products they recommend. Since they receive all revenues directly from their clients, there is no reason for potential conflicts of interest to arise. Fee-only advisors *do* implement their recommendations.

Since fee-only advisors have no axe to grind, and can choose from the entire universe of both load and no-load (sales commission–free) products and services, they can offer clients a greater range of selections and can also save clients a lot of money. Because they give impartial advice and can often improve returns and cut commission and other expenses, we give our value-oriented money planning award to fee-only advisors. We should know; that is the way we choose to operate our own planning practice.

There are relatively few planners who operate on a true fee-only basis; without sales commissions it takes a long time to build up a practice and achieve a reasonable income. There are many fee-and-commission planners—the largest category of planners in the United States—who are knowledgeable and place their clients' needs first. They charge fees for their financial planning work and give the clients the option of whether or not to implement their suggestions through their affiliated broker-dealers. (Fee-based or fee-basis planners or planners who suggest they are fee-only but are actually affiliated with a broker-dealer for implementation purposes are considered fee-and-commission planners.) On average, fee-and-commission planners make three to five dollars in commissions for every one dollar in fees.

Be careful about using the third category of advisors—commission-only planners. Many are too sales-oriented to provide impartial advice and are tied to particular products. The planning information they provide "for free" and the commissionable investment products they recommend often end up costing you much more money than you save on fees.

Sally and Edward were interested in having financial planning done when Edward was about to receive his retirement plan distribution. After 20 years of working for the same employer, he had accumulated $300,000. This was the first time they had a material amount of funds to invest. Sally and Edward interviewed several advisors and mentioned that they wondered why they had to pay for our advice when other advisors offered them advice for "free." We explained that like other professionals we are compensated for our time and our expertise and that our fee-only approach ensures a wider choice of investment alternatives and services as well as impartiality in reaching a final decision. We believe what most persuaded Sally and Edward to become clients was that our fee seemed small compared to the $18,000 in commissions they would have paid ($300,000 times an average 6 percent sales fee) if they had gone elsewhere instead of investing in the no-load, sales commission–free mutual funds that we (and other fee-only advisors) recommend.

There are many organizations that will be glad to provide you with a list of planners in your area. If you want a fee-only advisor, contact the National Association of Personal Financial Advisors (NAPFA) at 800-366-2732. They will send you a list of fee-only planners in your area who have a minimum of three years' experience and have submitted a sample financial plan. It is then up to you to contact some of those planners and inquire about their services and fees.

If you want names of fee-only, fee-and-commission, or commission-only planners, call the Registry of Financial Planning Practitioners, which is part of the largest organization of financial services professionals, the International Association for Financial Planning. They can be reached at 404-395-1605. Members of the Registry must have three years' experience, have passed a practice-oriented exam, have met certain educational standards, and supplied recommendations from at least five satisfied clients for admission.

Another organization that will give you names of planners is the Institute of Certified Financial Planners, or ICFP. As you can guess, all members of this organization must have passed the Certified Financial Planners (CFP) exam. The organization also has a registry, but admission to it is available to all members of the ICFP who sign an affidavit attesting that they hold themselves out to the public as a financial planner and that they are willing to disclose how they are compensated. The CFP designation has significance today and is likely to continue to grow in importance as requirements for membership are tightened further. Again, these planners may be fee-only, fee-and-commission, or commission-only planners. The ICFP can be reached at 303-751-7600.

You can also check with the International Board of Standards and Practices for Certified Financial Planners (IBCFP), the regulating agency for CFPs, to see if anyone who tells you he or she is a CFP truly is. Call them at 303-220-0917.

Accredited Personal Financial Specialists (APFS) are certified public accountants who have passed a written exam and have submitted references from clients and colleagues. They tend to be strongest in taxes and in impartial opinions, and weakest in investments—some won't provide investment advice at all. Given the emphasis the American Institute of Certified Public Accountants (AICPA) is placing on this new designation, the APFS has future potential as a mark of financial planning expertise. For members in your area, call the AICPA at 800-966-7379.

The Chartered Financial Consultant (ChFC) is a financial planning designation given principally to life insurance agents who take financial courses and pass exams beyond the Chartered Life Underwriters Exam.

The Chartered Financial Analyst degree (CFA) is given to investment specialists who pass a rigorous three-part exam and have at least three years of practical investment experience.

It's up to you to interview several planners and exercise due diligence in selecting one. First, decide on the qualifications that are important to you. Perhaps you want an advisor who lives within a two-hour drive. (Don't overemphasize location. We do financial planning and investment management for people throughout the country. Most or all of the work can be accomplished by phone, fax, or mail.) You may, as we suggest, look for several years' experience or a certain educational level. Some people feel more comfortable with planners who have graduate degrees in business, such as an MBA, or professional accreditation, such as a CFP (Certified Financial Planner), CPA (Certified Public Accountant), APFS (Accredited Personal Financial Specialist) for accountants, ChFC (Chartered Financial Consultant) for life insurance agents, or CFA (Chartered Financial Analyst—an investment specialist).

Finally, any financial planner who offers services to the general public and gives investment advice is required to be registered with the Securities and Exchange Commission, but some are not. Make sure that yours is.

What should I ask my financial planner?

The National Association of Personal Financial Advisors has drawn up a Financial Planner Interview form (shown below) for clients to take with them to a first meeting with a planner or mail in advance. Have any planner you are considering fill out the form. It asks about the planner's education, level of experience, range of services, compliance with regulatory laws, and method of compensation. It takes only a few minutes to complete. Avoid any planner who refuses to answer your questions or complete such a form. You can get interview forms from NAPFA; their number is given in the response to the previous question.

Many financial planners offer an initial meeting at no charge. Find out when you call for an appointment. Your initial meeting should serve three functions:

1. *It allows you to find out about the planner's background and experience.* Ask where the planner has worked in the past and whether he or she has experience with your specific problems and working with people like you. For example, if your interests are improving investment returns and retirement planning, look for planners who have an extensive background in those areas.

2. *It permits you to learn more about how the planner operates.* For example, some planners give advice only and you carry out the decisions. Others will give advice and are also prepared to manage your investments on an ongoing basis, as we do. You should deter-

Financial Planner Interview

How to Choose a Financial Planner

BACKGROUND & EXPERIENCE

The backgrounds of financial planners can vary as much as the services offered. The planner's education and experience should demonstrate a solid foundation in financial planning and a commitment to keeping current. In addition to the following questions, ask the planner to describe his or her specific financial planning work experience.

1. What is your educational background?
______College degree
Area of study: ______________
______Graduate degree
Area of study: ______________

Financial planning education & designations:
______Certified Financial Planner (CFP)
______Chartered Financial Consultant (ChFC)
______Registry of Financial Planning Practitioners
Other: ______________________

2. How long have you been offering financial planning services?
______Less than 2 years
______2–5 years
______More than 5 years

3. What continuing education in financial planning do you pursue?

______1–14 hours of professional education each year
______15–30 hours of professional education each year
______At least 30 hours of professional education each year

4. Are you a member of any professional financial planning associations?

______Institute of Certified Financial Planners (ICFP)
______National Association of Personal Financial Advisors (NAPFA)
______International Association for Financial Planning (IAFP)
______Registry of Financial Planning Practitioners
Other: ______________________

5. Will you provide me with references from clients?
_____Yes _____No

6. Have you ever been cited by a professional or regulatory governing body for disciplinary reasons?
_____Yes _____No

THIS FORM WAS CREATED BY THE NATIONAL ASSOCIATION OF PERSONAL FINANCIAL ADVISORS (NAPFA) TO ASSIST CONSUMERS IN SELECTING A PERSONAL FINANCIAL PLANNER. IT CAN BE USED AS A CHECKLIST DURING AN INTERVIEW OR SENT TO PROSPECTIVE PLANNERS AS A PART OF A PRELIMINARY SCREENING. NAPFA RECOMMENDS THAT INDIVIDUALS FROM AT LEAST TWO DIFFERENT FIRMS BE INTERVIEWED.

(*Continued*)

COMPENSATION

Financial planning costs include what a consumer pays in fees and commissions. Comparison between planners requires full information about potential total costs. It is important to have this information before entering into any agreement.

1. How is your firm compensated?

______Fee Only
______Commission only
______Fee and Commissions
______Fee offset

How is your compensation calculated?

______Fee only (as calculated below)

Based on hourly rate of $_____
Flat fee or fee range of _______
Percentage (_____%) of ______
Are fees capped? ____Yes ____No

______Commission only (from securities, insurance, etc.) that clients buy from a firm with which you are associated.
______Fee and commission ("Fee based")
______Fee offset. You charge a flat fee against which commissions are offset. If the commissions exceed the fee, is the balance credited to me?
_____Yes _____No

[Note: the Securities and Exchange Commission (SEC) requires that this information be disclosed.]

2. If you earn commissions, approximately what percentage of your firm's commission income comes from:

______% Insurance products
______% Annuities
______% Mutual funds
______% Limited partnerships
______% Stocks and bonds
______% Coins, tangibles, collectibles
______% Other (explain) _______________
100%

3. Does any member of your firm act as a general partner, participate in or receive compensation from investments you may recommend to me?
_____Yes _____No

(Continued)

SERVICES

Financial planners provide a range of services. It is important to match client needs with services provided.

1. Does your financial planning service include:

______A review of my goals.

Advice on:

______Cash management & budgeting
______Tax planning
______Investment review & planning
______Estate planning
______Insurance needs in the area of life, disability, health and property/casualty
______Retirement planning
______Other

2. Do you provide a written analysis of my financial situation and recommendations?
_____Yes _____No

Is the analysis tailored to my personal needs and goals?
_____Yes _____No

3. Does your financial planning service include recommendations for specific investments or investment products?
_____Yes _____No

Do you offer assistance with implementation?
_____Yes _____No

4. Do you offer continuous, on-going advice regarding my financial affairs, including advice on non-investment financial issues?
_____Yes _____No

5. Do you take possession of, or have access to my assets?
_____Yes _____No

REGULATORY COMPLIANCE

The SEC requires if an individual or firm hold out to the public as providing financial planning services, that under most circumstances, they are required to be registered with the SEC.

1. Are you or your firm registered as an Investment Advisor with the U.S. Securities and Exchange Commission?
_____Yes _____No

If NO, please indicate which SEC allowable reason for nonregistration applies:

______Fewer than 15 clients
______Do not provide generic or specific advice on securities
______Do not provide financial planning advice for a fee, but only as a registered representative or broker/dealer

2. Is your firm registered with your state securities office?
_____Yes _____No

If NO, please explain:

____
____
____

PLEASE PROVIDE A COPY OF YOUR REGISTRATION WITH THE SECURITIES AND EXCHANGE COMMISSION (ADV Part II), AS REQUIRED BY THE SEC UNDER THE INVESTMENT ADVISORS ACT OF 1940.

____
Signature of Planner

____
Firm Name

____
Date

mine at this first meeting whether there is a fit between your needs and the planner's style.

3. *It establishes whether the planner is right for you on a personal basis.* Do you feel that the person understands your situation, and are you comfortable discussing it with him or her? Communicate your concerns. Think about the reasons for your visit. Ask how the planner would approach such problems. If you aren't at ease with the planner—perhaps you feel he or she isn't interested or isn't taking your concerns seriously—take that as a sign of a poor match, and look around some more.

Arrive prepared. Think up your own questions. Don't be embarrassed to read from a list. No worthy planner will fault you for doing a thorough job of researching the professional advisors you seek. Besides, he or she has probably been asked many of those same questions before. Your questions might include general ones about style of investment or how involved the planner gets in educating a client, to more specific ones about your personal circumstances. Don't expect the planner to offer particular answers to your personal financial concerns at a free initial consultation.

Questions to Ask a Financial Planner

1. How long have you been in business?
2. How many clients do you have?
3. How do you handle your client load?
4. Who will work on my plan?
5. Who will be my primary contact at your firm?
6. Do you use standardized computer programs?
7. How long do you typically spend on a plan?
8. What is a usual relationship after the plan is completed?
9. Are you available for phone calls during the day?
10. How long does it take you to return clients' calls?
11. How are you compensated?
12. Do you sell any products?
13. How much might commissions be in my circumstances?

14. If there is a fee, what does it include?
15. Do you make specific recommendations of investment vehicles?
16. How many of your clients are in my income (asset, age) category?
17. Are you registered with the Securities and Exchange Commission (SEC)?
18. Can I have a copy of SEC advisor registration Form ADV Part II?
19. Can I see a copy of a sample plan your firm has done for someone like me?
20. What professional organizations do you belong to?
21. Can you give me names of clients to call as references?

Financial planning at its best is a very personal business. You want someone nonjudgmental whom you can talk to with ease. Some people prefer to go only to members of their own ethnic group, or planners over 50, or males, or females. That is their prerogative. Although professional qualifications are of the highest priority, your sense that someone is tuned into your way of thinking and feels right should not be ignored.

Olivia, a retired office worker, made an appointment with a financial planner. The planner, whom a friend had recommended, was perfectly charming. He told her that most of his clients were women, the majority of them elderly widows. He knew how to get along with them, he said as he held her hand. He invited Olivia to lunch but, preferring to go to someone with a more businesslike approach, Olivia quickly declined the invitation and left the office.

How often should I review my finances?

Review your finances whenever significant changes are anticipated or occur in your life: changes in marital status, new offspring, death of a family member, an inheritance, change in job, relocation, a material modification in income, and so on. One couple in their thirties came to our office with a common story—they hadn't been serious about their finances and now wanted a top-to-bottom analysis of their current situation and help in setting up a structure for their financial future. We developed a comprehensive financial plan, but on the day of our arranged meeting only the husband showed up. He informed us that they were getting divorced, paid our fee, and left with the plan but without our usual presentation. We subsequently performed additional services for him at no extra cost. Clearly, due to the major change in their circumstances, what the couple needed now were two financial plans, not one.

Once or twice a year you should review the investment part of your plan if you have professional help or invest in mutual funds—more frequently if you are managing your assets yourself. Don't look at your investments too often, though. Daily study of stock prices can lead to anxiety and overreaction to near-term events, instead of appropriate focus on the longer term.

Review the other parts of your financial plan at least once yearly.

What can I do to broaden my financial knowledge?

No one is born with the ability to make financial decisions; you generally acquire it through years of education and practical experience. This book has given you a basic foundation in financial concepts. For many readers, that may be enough. We also provide a list of further readings and other sources of information for each chapter.

If you would like still more information, why not take an introductory course in financial planning or investments at a college in your area. Many offer a variety of finance courses in their adult education divisions. One word of caution: sometimes the lecturer has a hidden agenda, a point of view or reason for providing the course other than education. That's normal, but you should be aware of a potential bias before acting on the advice anyone gives you.

Read a newspaper's financial pages; *The Wall Street Journal* and *The New York Times* are particularly good choices. You can select from a variety of personal finance magazines that deliver straightforward advice, including *Money, Kiplinger's Personal Finance Maga-*

zine, and *Worth*. There are a number of magazines that cover overall business, investment, and financial topics, including *Barron's, Business Week, Fortune,* and *Forbes*. You also can become a member of the American Association of Individual Investors (312-280-0170), which offers a monthly journal and has seminars throughout the country.

All of these sources will help keep you up to date with the changing economic conditions in the 1990s. As you broaden your financial knowledge, be aware of current opportunities. For example, if the government offers tax incentives to encourage further savings, think about how you can shift your assets and savings pattern to take advantage of the opportunity.

How do I prepare a financial plan that helps me reach my goals?

Do you have goals in the back of your mind that you hope to achieve over time? Most people do. We believe that in most cases these goals *can* be reached. Frequently all that is needed is a plan and the desire to stick to it. You have to supply the desire. We'll show you how to construct a plan that can help make your goals a reality.

We have a new way for you to handle your planning that we call the "Money Ladder." It is our framework for organizing and reaching your financial goals. There are three main parts to the money ladder approach—identifying your goals, calculating their costs, and deciding how you can achieve them. The Money Ladder brings your goals together so that you can see how they relate to one another and how you can reach those that are most important to you. (A sample Money Ladder Goals Identification Worksheet is given in Appendix A.)

Here's how you can develop your own Money Ladder:

Step 1. Establish Your Goals. Goals aren't always apparent. Joan requested that we do a financial plan for her. When we asked specifically what her goals were, Joan said she had never really thought about it. We explained that a plan should be constructed around particular goals, and helped to identify hers in the six major planning areas: cashflow, insurance, taxes, investments, retirement, and estate planning. Real estate and education were handled as separate areas because they were particularly important to Joan. With her goals firmly established, we were in a position to proceed with Joan's planning.

Determine your goals. Here are some goals that you, like many of our clients, may hope to achieve:

- *Lifestyle:* To maintain or improve the way you are living currently.

  Planning for the 1990s: Target lifestyle improvements along with your savings program. It won't be easy, but in many cases it can be done.

- *Taxes:* To reduce taxes to the lowest amount legally possible without sacrificing income.

  Planning for the 1990s: Over the long term, taxes are going up. Take this into account in your planning.

- *Investing:* To earn the highest return possible at the level of risk you are willing to accept.

  Planning for the 1990s: Begin to use true diversification techniques, including a shift to investing on a global basis, using asset allocation techniques.

- *Real estate:* To purchase a home you enjoy living in that also becomes an excellent investment.

  Planning for the 1990s: Place emphasis on real estate. It should be an unusually attractive investment opportunity for this decade.

- *Debt:* To borrow and repay in a responsible way, or to stop borrowing altogether.

  Planning for the 1990s: Use credit carefully. Debt will be your enemy almost as often as it will be your friend.

- *Education:* To provide enough money to fund your child's college of choice or your own extended education needs.

  Planning for the 1990s: Plan carefully. College costs will continue to exceed the inflation rate. On the positive side, education costs at private colleges probably won't rise quite as rapidly as they did in the 1980s.

- *Risk management (insurance):* To protect yourself in the least expensive way from the possibility of large losses.

  Planning for the 1990s: Put more emphasis on the quality of the insurance carrier.

- *Estate:* To provide for those you care about in the most efficient way possible.

  Planning for the 1990s: Watch the tax rates. They will make it more difficult to leave money to others.

Last is the goal many people consider the ultimate one:

- *Financial independence:* To build sufficient assets to support yourself without having to work forever. For some this can mean that one day they will be able to choose career activities without worrying about the amount of income those activities generate. For many others, financial independence means funding for a comfortable lifestyle at retirement without fear of running out of money.

  Planning for the 1990s: Achieving this goal will likely require more effort but will still be attainable.

These goals are all admirable; but you shouldn't include them in your planning unless they relate to you and your situation. Construct the ladder that is relevant to you. Don't worry yet about how much each goal will cost. We will discuss how to reconcile goals and resources in Step 6 and the appendices.

Filling in the steps of the Money Ladder will help you to understand yourself. Think about your goals and your life. You don't have to make lifelong decisions at a young age. Your goals are likely to change as you grow older. When you are in your twenties and thirties, review your long-range goals in all of the financial areas but, unless you are very structured, concentrate only on those areas that are of immediate concern. Your focus is likely to be on lifestyle and perhaps marriage, home, and family.

Even though you are more concerned with short-term considerations, try to fully contribute to all available pension options, or else you will be sacrificing an important tax advantage. Make sure you have adequate insurance coverage and a will. When you reach your late thirties or early forties, it is time to begin structuring and funding your full Money Ladder.

Step 2. Organize Your Goals. Identify what is important to *you*. Be honest, or your results won't be useful. We have found that thinking in terms of three different degrees of success for *each* category of goals can help relieve your financial pressures and give you incentive to climb the ladder.

Your *minimum goals* are those that have to be met because you are not willing to go below them. If they are not achieved, you will have too many financial "hurts" to be comfortable. Once these are under control—and they can be, for almost everyone—move on to your *satisfactory goals*. Satisfactory goals are those you feel are within your eventual grasp and which you would be pleased to achieve. If you don't reach them, you probably will be disappointed. Finally, identify what we call your *higher goals*. These goals are more of a stretch; if you reach them, you will be delighted. In the real estate area, for example, your minimum goal might be to own or rent an apartment in a very modest community; the goal you would be satisfied with might be to own a house in a better neighborhood; and your higher goal might be to own a larger house in one of the nicest sections of town or a vacation home.

Roy and Eileen, a couple in their fifties, spoke to us about their retirement goals. Roy mentioned that his basic financial goal was to have enough money to live "comfortably," which he defined as paying his bills on time and eating in a restaurant once a month. He looked grim as he said it. Eileen kept quiet but had a disapproving expression on her face. We moved to other topics, and later, when the couple felt more comfortable with us, Roy admitted he would really like to eat out more often and spend more on entertainment. Eileen, speaking up for the first time, added she would like to visit her two children who were a plane trip away, once or twice a year. When we asked them for a blue-sky scenario, they mentioned eating out a few nights a week, more frequent vacations, and the possibility of a small apartment in Florida for the winter months. It was clear that they had described their minimum, satisfactory, and higher goals.

Only when your goals work together will they form a solid foundation that allows you to safely plan to achieve your satisfactory and higher goals.

Step 3. Prepare a List of Assets. Form your personal balance sheet by listing all your assets. Include the fair market value of your home, your jewelry, and your bank and brokerage accounts. Separate the items into those that are investment assets and those that are personal assets that you will not sell. Then deduct all your outstanding debts. The difference between your assets and your outstanding debts is your net worth. Focus on your investment assets. (See Table A-2 in Appendix A.) These assets are available to finance your goals currently or to generate income and savings for future goals.

Step 4. Estimate Your Savings. The best way to do this is to prepare a detailed, projected cashflow statement, including all sources of income and expense. Use estimates of last year's actual figures as the basis for the future items. Or, a quicker way to obtain your savings goal is to add up total deposits into savings and investment accounts, and withdrawals from these accounts for the past year. Since most people underestimate their expenses, try to be as accurate as possible about the total amount of expenses and savings. See Chapter 1 for more information on both approaches.

Step 5. Develop Cash Needs for Goals. Decide how much it will cost to achieve each of your goals. Set a target date for reaching the funding for those goals and estimate the yearly savings you will need to hit your target date. Table A-6 in Appendix A, a Worksheet of Savings Needed to Reach Goals, can be the organizing point for identifying costs. See Appendices A and B for calculating the projected annual cost for each goal.

Step 6. Compare Your Goals with Your Resources. Use your current assets (from Step 3) and realistic projected savings rate (from Step 4) to compute your total resources. If your minimally acceptable goals exceed your resources, you can (1) block the whole thing out of your mind—a popular method, but not recommended because a day of reckoning will arrive; (2) develop additional sources of income; (3) increase your investment return; or (4) cut back on your current cost of living, thereby saving more. If you expect your income to rise rapidly, you can also keep your cost of living level on an inflation-adjusted basis and save the difference. But we caution against "tomorrow planning" in which tomorrow never seems to come.

Recently, through a series of setbacks and living beyond their means one working couple—Matthew and Margaret, both close to retirement age—found themselves in a precarious situation. They found out their retirement savings would run out well before the average mortality date for their respective ages. They were shocked. At first Margaret tried to deny a problem existed, questioning our retirement planning program that had uncovered the problem. Finally, the couple agreed to let us set up a realistic savings plan for them which, with a few extra years of working, a higher-paying job for Margaret, and a cutback in nonessentials, placed them on a more secure footing.

It is up to you to decide whether you want to remain at your present level on the Money Ladder or to move up by generating more job or investment-related income, or by initiating tighter restrictions in your standard of living to accumulate more savings. This is also the time to reappraise your goals based on your calculation of what each will cost you. You must decide upon the right balance of current lifestyle and future goals based on your needs.

Your minimum goals on the ladder should be thought of as a safety net. You want to ensure that you don't go below them. However, you will probably want to target to at least achieve your satisfactory goals. This should represent a secure, comfortable life for you. After all, *you* decide what is satisfactory. Keep all your goals in mind when deciding where to position yourself on the ladder. If you do decide to move up, you could save for all your higher goals, or you could combine some of your satisfactory and higher goals.

For example, Lois and Herb thought at first they wanted to fund for all their higher goals. When they saw how much savings were required they decided it was premature to consider these higher goals until their promotions occurred. But they also found out that one of their higher goals, a small vacation home, would cost less than they thought and decided to include it in their planning.

Step 7. Finalize Your Ladder. At this point you should have an idea of your goals and how much money you will need to execute your plan. Use the practical example in the question "Can you provide a practical example of putting it all together?" later in this chapter and its overall solution in Appendices A and B to help you.

Your ladder should be more than just numbers; it should include all your financial needs and both near- and long-term targets. For example, you should determine the amount of insurance you need and the date by which you will buy it. In addition, factor in quality-of-life targets such as vacations, remodeling your home, or eating out more often. Finalize the exact mix of your goals and the savings you are going to put away for each. The Money Ladder Goals Achievement Worksheet, Table A-7 in Appendix A, shows how to finalize your position on the ladder. Write down your goals and plan for achieving them. Keep this list in a convenient place so you can refer to it.

Step 8. Implement the Recommendations. For many people, putting the plan into effect is the hardest step. You want to do it, but you never get around to starting; or you begin, but you give up easily. You would be surprised at the number of people who pay large fees for financial advice and specific recommendations and then never take action. We provide you with an implementation schedule in Table A-8 in Appendix A.

Jason and Gloria paid thousands of dollars for a comprehensive financial plan. We offered to help implement our recommendations, but since our plans contain specific advice and names of investments, the couple said they felt comfortable doing it themselves. When we called six weeks later, they told us they had intended to start but hadn't gotten around to it yet, despite the fact they had two children and no life insurance or wills. We got the feeling that if no one pushed them, Jason and Gloria might never implement the plan. When we threatened to call every few weeks until they took action, they finally began the process. Some weeks later they sent us a nice note thanking us for being persistent and keeping after them.

A planner who takes pride in his or her work does not want to see good advice end up in somebody's desk drawer, and neither should you.

To help you take action, here are some suggestions:

1. Put in specific dates to execute your plans, and keep to them.

2. Set up separate investment accounts for each goal and pledge not to withdraw money from them except in extreme emergencies.
3. Keep a list of your goals and enter any actions you take that bring you closer to them. Check these at the end of every month to make sure you are on target.

For those who never stick to plans, we know it is difficult, but have you noticed how many people never seem to be able to afford major outlays or to retire without living on a very tight budget? You can avoid finding yourself in those situations with a good plan and a little determination.

For those who are very structured and have accumulated substantial savings but are afraid of the slightest mishap, lighten up. No figures can be exact, and given your personality you are not likely to have problems in this area. If you've worked hard for what you've accumulated, you deserve to enjoy yourself a little more now.

If you're seriously behind your goals, put your credit cards in a drawer. Keep going when you pass attractive store windows. Don't tune in the shopping channels on TV. Say no to all telephone solicitations. But do reward yourself occasionally for sticking to your plan. That can give you incentive to follow your plan and improve your morale. Whenever possible, increase *both* your quality of life and your savings accounts.

Step 9. Review and Update. Review your plan at least once a year and whenever there are major changes in your life. You can review by comparing your progress to your goals and judging how close you are getting to your desired accomplishments. How are you doing in terms of your projected time frame? Should you accelerate your savings program, or can you afford to take it a little easier? The numbers and your degree of satisfaction will give you the answers.

Can you provide a practical example of putting it all together?

This example illustrates our approach to financial planning and its benefits:

Doug and Linda came into our office wearing jeans. Linda was a social worker, Doug a copywriter. They looked young, so we were surprised to learn that they were both around 40 years old. They had one small child.

We often find that one spouse is more financially oriented and accurate, and the other less organized and sometimes more emotional. In this case, Linda was the more precise partner. She brought financial documents going back several years, and explained them to us in great detail. She also told us her goals. Linda wanted at least one more child, and she wanted to stay home and take care of her children herself. She also wanted to make sure she had enough money to send the children to college. She recognized that we would have to take a look at her near-term and longer-term financial resources to determine what was possible and what was not. Already, Linda's ladder was taking shape. Linda perceived her goals, and knew that there were some conflicts.

Doug was unhappy with his work situation. In fact, he wanted to change his career to something more creative. He wasn't too sure what that would be, but thought that writing scripts for movies could be interesting. From Doug's standpoint, projecting future income would be difficult. What he wanted was a series of options based on possible future levels of income. Doug needed to balance his goals for security with his unhappiness at his job.

Both Doug and Linda were concerned about having enough money for a comfortable retirement. They were satisfied with the way they were living now. In filling out our firm's questionnaire, they rated improving current standard of living as their lowest priority.

Doug and Linda were earning $50,000 and $25,000 a year respectively from their regular jobs and additional part-time work. They owned a home that was heavily mortgaged; their net equity was about $70,000. They had no other debt outstanding. They had about $38,000 cash in the bank, and stock mutual funds totaling $45,000. Their net worth of about $173,000 and job-related income of $75,000 qualified them as a fairly high-income family countrywide, but only as middle income in the New York metropolitan area, where it costs a great deal more to live than in most places in the country.

From our questionnaire and some follow-up interviews, we were able to get a fairly accurate reading of Doug and Linda's income and expenses. In working up their plan it became obvious that their goals exceeded their current resources and projected future resources. They wanted to save more than their income and cost of living allowed. Something had to give for their goals to fit together well.

Our firm has a weekly staff meeting in which we discuss current clients. The purpose is to get everyone's input in arriving at particular solutions to client problems. Our meetings resemble those on TV's *L.A. Law* and can get just as heated.

In this case, our firm was split into two groups. Those who sympathized with Linda and her desire to raise at least two children felt that Doug should give up any thoughts about a creative career that carried no assurance of a solid income. The other side said that no one should have to work at a job that he or she dislikes, and asked why Linda couldn't modify her position—the dual-income couple is standard today. We postponed our decision on what the couple could afford until we could gauge the exact impact of our other recommendations.

From a cashflow standpoint, Doug and Linda were generating net savings of about $16,000 a year, a good sum, to be used for meeting their goals. We recommended some tax planning strategies, including donating clothes to charities and deducting job-related miscellaneous expenses, which had the effect of reducing their taxes, thereby increasing their cashflow.

After looking at their real estate, we recommended refinancing their mortgage when interest rates declined 2 percent from their 10½ percent mortgage. That recommendation was contingent on their staying in their current home, which they weren't 100 percent sure they wanted to do. This would save them about $1500 annually after tax. We strongly encouraged them not to sell at the then-depressed prices for real estate, but we also told them to stop putting large amounts into fixing up the property. We believed that the increase in sales price as a result of home improvements would not cover their outlay in costs.

In the insurance area, we calculated that Doug would need about $300,000 of whole life insurance (their preferred type of life insurance) to provide financial independence for his family should he die prematurely, while Linda would need only $11,000 for the same reason. We also recommended that Doug buy private disability insurance to augment his poor corporate policy and that they bring their disability coverage up to 70 percent of their incomes—$35,000 and

$17,500 a year, respectively, 60 to 70 percent being the maximum granted by most insurance carriers. We noted that this would take cash away from Doug's career development and saving for the future.

By our calculations, Doug and Linda would need about $6000 a year in savings to reach their goals of retiring at age 65 and having a modest but comfortable lifestyle in retirement. The amount put away would have to grow with inflation (assumed to be 5 percent) over subsequent years.

We gave Doug and Linda alternatives in the education area. Annual college planning savings for tuition required to educate two children at private colleges would amount to $11,000 a year and at public universities $5000 to $6000 a year with the amount saved also rising by 5 percent a year thereafter.

We recommended pension plans both for Doug's independent income from moonlighting on a free-lance basis, and Linda's part-time income for patients she counseled after hours. As we discussed in Chapter 9, payments to a pension provide a current tax deduction and compound tax free until withdrawal. The pensions were important factors in keeping the couple's annual savings needs down.

From an investment viewpoint, Doug and Linda were both fairly conservative. We advised them to put 60 percent of their savings in stocks and 40 percent in bonds. After we reviewed their portfolio, it became apparent that it had little structure and there were several stocks and mutual funds that we felt they should sell. We recommended a diversified portfolio of specific no-load mutual funds to implement our target asset allocation.

Our near-term target investment asset allocation differed somewhat from the longer-term one because of our economic concerns at the time. Our longer-term target asset allocation consisted of short-, intermediate-, and long-term bonds, domestic smaller capitalization companies, large-company growth and income funds, and international bonds and stock funds. The effect was, by our calculations, to raise Doug and Linda's projected return to 10 percent a year, approximately 7 percent after tax, or about 2 percent over the anticipated long-term inflation rate. At the same time, we moved to reduce their risk by diversifying them more fully. They did not want to take additional risk to further increase their return.

In the estate planning area, we recommended that they make wills and include guardians for their child and any future offspring. We also recommended powers of attorney made out to each other in the event of illness. We referred them to a specific lawyer.

When we were finished with our preliminary recommendations, we were still left where we suspected we would be: too many demands on too few savings dollars. From our standpoint, the couple's current standard of living left little room for cutting back. We felt that whole life insurance of $300,000 for financial independence was expensive and unnecessary considering their goals and strong savings pattern. We recommended term insurance instead. (If they followed our plan, they would eventually outgrow the need for any life insurance.) Even so, there was still a projected negative net cash-flow.

It was apparent that Doug would not be able to leave his current job for an uncertain future. Instead, we recommended that he schedule three weeks a year for film writing, adding one additional week each year thereafter. That would allow him to get out of his so-called rut and explore possible new opportunities. It also kept him from making a rash move that could hurt the couple's other plans. We estimated that this lifestyle choice would cost about $2800 after adjustment for taxes.

We told Linda that her wish to permanently give up her salary was not economically feasible. Instead, we suggested that she expand her consulting business, which she could run out of her home. When her children were old enough to go to school, she should consider returning to a full-time job or developing her own business further. If she worked at home, she would be able to drop the children off at school and pick them up, and she could be at home when her children were at home. Linda would also save considerable money on child care if she worked at home. For education we indicated that they could afford their satisfactory goal of their children attending a state university and living away from home.

Now, finally, the numbers fit. They even had about $1900 a year left over for unexpected needs or to begin work on their home. Appendices A and B show you Doug and Linda's financial data and how we arrived at our conclusions.

Obviously, we didn't draw these recommendations from thin air. We had substantial discussions with the couple, worked their figures out carefully, and considered both Doug and Linda, who wanted to satisfy each other's needs. In other words, we helped them refine their goals. Our recommendations, based on Doug and Linda's goals, represented compromises made by both husband and wife, yet they retained the essence of what each wanted.

When we presented Doug and Linda's comprehensive financial plan to them, they were enthusiastic; this was a plan that they could live with comfortably. The road map we designed for their future and our blending of their goals with our specific financial and investment recommendations were what they had been looking for. The pieces of this couple's ladder had been reshaped to fit together. They could climb toward their goals steadily once the plan had been assembled. Our work enabled them to begin to move up the ladder from their minimum goals to their satisfactory ones. If Doug's new career worked out, they would be on their way to realizing their higher goals.

We agreed that the next review of Doug and Linda's financial situation would take place in a year. After that time, we could establish how progress toward each goal was proceeding. To assist you in doing your own planning, we provide a completely filled out ladder of Doug and Linda's needs and goals in Appendix A.

Is there anything else I should know?

First, congratulations! If you have read through the book, you are more likely to achieve your financial goals than the average person. In fact, if you take the information in these pages and put it to use, we will give you our last value-oriented money planning award.

Think positively. You can reach most of your goals even if you are starting late. Many of our clients have achieved the comfortable stage of financial independence and others are well on their way. You can do it too by investing some energy in improving your current financial situation and planning your future. Think of the ways to save you have discovered—reducing taxes, increasing investment income, selecting the proper insurance—and how you can best put this added money to work for you.

Review the parts of the book and the answers you found most useful and follow the advice that fits your situation.

Most important, take action now!

Appendix A
Constructing Your Own Financial Plan

This appendix uses a case study approach to show you how to construct your own financial plan. Based on the Money Ladder's step-by-step approach given in Chapter 13, it provides the calculations for a completed plan using the example of Doug and Linda, also discussed in Chapter 13.

Before you start, you may want to review the steps of a plan covered in Chapter 13.

Steps 1 and 2. Establish and Organize Your Goals. If you have already worked out your goals, fine. If not, look at Steps 1 and 2 concerning goals in Chapter 13. Table A-1 gives Doug and Linda's goals. It is followed by a blank worksheet (Table A-1*a*) for you to complete.

Table A-1. Money Ladder: Goals Identification Worksheet for Doug and Linda's Plan

Section	Minimum	Satisfactory	Higher
Financial independence	20% decline in lifestyle in retirement	Same lifestyle in retirement as currently enjoyed	More travel and eating out in retirement
Estate	Establish wills and set guardian	No further change	No further change
Disability insurance	Minimum coverage 50% of recommended amount	Full coverage	No further change
Life insurance	Full-term insurance coverage	No further change	No further change
Education	Two children at city university living at home	Two children at state university, living away from home	Two children at private university, living away from home
Debt	Refinance current mortgage at rate 2% lower	As is	As is
Real estate	As is	As is	Major home improvements
Investments	Return of 2% over inflation (10% pretax and 7% after-tax growth rates)	No further change	No further change
Taxes	As is	Save $1200 in taxes	Save $1700 in taxes
Lifestyle	As is	Doug has time off for career	Doug has more time off; Linda has household help

Table A-1*a*. Money Ladder: Goals Identification Worksheet for Your Finances

Section	Minimum	Satisfactory	Higher
Financial independence			
Estate			
Disability insurance			
Life insurance			
Education			
Debt			
Real estate			
Investments			
Taxes			
Lifestyle			
Other			
Other			

Step 3. Prepare a List of Assets. Make a list of your assets on the Personal Balance Sheet in Table A-2. Doug and Linda's figures appear in the left column.

Step 4. Estimate Your Savings. Prepare a detailed accounting of your income and expenses for the year. Chapter 1 gives advice on working out this "personal cashflow statement" and other budgeting advice on an itemized basis. You can use your paycheck to determine your job-related income and how much tax you pay monthly. Estimate expenses from last year if your situation has not changed much. Calculate the net cashflow figure.

As a simpler approach or as a check on your net cashflow, look at how much your savings and retirement accounts have grown over the past year. Compare your current statement with one of 12 months ago. Subtract the old statement from the current one to find the difference over the year. Remember that the savings figure includes income from your investments. If a large part of your savings figure comes from the investment income shown in the cashflow statement, this means that you are saving little of your salary.

If the simple amount from your bank statements and the itemized figures are not the same, you may have to check your expense figures. If you actually saved less than you thought, you probably have left out some expenses. Think about whether you had a one-time expense that reduced your savings.

In Table A-3 we give you a personal cashflow statement we developed for Doug and Linda. It is followed by columns for you to fill in.

Table A-2. Personal Balance Sheet

	Doug and Linda	Your finances
ASSETS:		
Cash and money-market accounts	$33,000	______
Bank accounts	5,000	______
Brokerage accounts and mutual funds	45,000	______
Cash value of insurance policies	0	______
Other	0	______
Total investment assets	$83,000	______
Real estate		
Home	$240,000	______
Other	0	______
Retirement and pension accounts	0	______
Equity in business	0	______
Personal possessions	15,000	______
Cars, boats	5,000	______
Other	0	______
Total noninvestment asssets	260,000	______
Total Assets	$343,000	______
LIABILITIES:		
Home mortgage	$170,000	______
Second mortgages	0	______
Student loans	0	______
Car and other loans	0	______
Credit card	0	______
Total Liabilities	$170,000	______
NET WORTH (total assets – liabilities)	$173,000	______

Table A-3. Cashflow Statement

	Doug and Linda		Your figures	
	Monthly	Annually	Monthly	Annually
CASH INFLOWS:				
Salary	$4,833	$58,000	______	______
Bonus			______	______
Business income	1,417	17,000	______	______
Interest	333	4,000	______	______
Dividends	42	500	______	______
Other (Alimony, etc.)		______	______	______
Total Cash Inflows		**$79,500**		______
CASH OUTFLOWS:				
Continuing Monthly Payments				
Rent or mortgage	$1,520	$18,240	______	______
Real estate taxes	42	500	______	______
Utilities	125	1,500	______	______
Debt			______	______
Other		______	______	______
Total Monthly Payments		**$20,240**		______
Other Monthly Cash Expenses				
Food and beverages—eating in	$400	$4,800	______	______
Household care	50	600	______	______
Household furnishings	83	1,000	______	______
Clothing	125	1,500	______	______
Transportation	333	4,000	______	______
Health care	142	1,700	______	______
Insurance	100	1,200	______	______
Education and training	10	120	______	______

Table A-3. Cashflow Statement (*Continued*)

	Doug and Linda		Your figures	
	Monthly	Annually	Monthly	Annually
Eating out and entertainment	100	1,200	______	______
Vacations	167	2,000	______	______
Personal care	20	240	______	______
Contributions and gifts	42	500	______	______
Credit card not counted above	42	500	______	______
Miscellaneous	75	900	______	______
Total Monthly Expenses		**$20,260**		______
Total Living Expenses		**$40,500**		______
Taxes				
Social security tax	$586	$7,038	______	______
Federal income tax	753	9,036	______	______
State and local income tax	528	6,327	______	______
Total Taxes		**$22,401**		______
Total Outflows		**$62,901**		______
NET CASHFLOW (SAVINGS)				
(Total inflows – total outflows)		**$16,599**		______

Step 5. Determine How Much to Save for Each Goal. You can estimate the cost for many of your goals using the techniques described throughout the book. Using a simplified approach, we will guide you through an estimation of your annual savings need for each goal.

In Appendix B we will offer you a more detailed way of establishing your needs. You can use Appendix B to mathematically determine more precise estimates for your personal situation. There we also work out the numbers for Doug and Linda so you can see how it is done. In each appendix our examples show Doug and Linda's satisfactory goals—the level they chose to save for currently. Note that both appendices provide only estimates of need. For more accurate calculations, you can see an advisor. However, we believe that the figures obtained should be helpful in your own planning. Once you have determined the figures, you can copy them onto the Money Ladder Savings Worksheet.

Most of the items in Appendix A are easy to calculate. The hardest thing to determine is your after-tax investment return; even that isn't really difficult. You can estimate your own rate of return. Review Chapters 3 and 4, particularly the question "What return should I target for my investments?" in Chapter 4. A simpler way to get your estimated return is given in "Determining Your Investment Return" later in this Appendix, where we also explain how to obtain a blended investment return by adjusting your after-tax return for the benefit of any investments in a pension fund.

One more thing: Throughout this book and in these two appendices, we have, for planning purposes, generally built in payments (required savings) that grow by the level of inflation. We believe that keeping savings in line with growth in income is generally the best way to do long-term planning. If you plan to save a flat $5000 a year for retirement for 25 years and inflation averages 5 percent a year, your $5000 a year will be equal to only $2500 a year in 14 years. By allowing your savings to rise with projected inflation, you will be putting away $10,000, not $5000, a year in 14 years and likely not feel any more of a pinch than you do today.

To simplify matters, you can use the following estimates for each goal:

Financial Independence. If you have questions, review Chapter 9. Determining how much to save for retirement involves a little math. We have two ways for you to figure out how much you should be putting away. The more precise way is given in Appendix B. You may also use the simplified method below.

Table A-4 gives you the amount you need at retirement today to cover various costs of living through age 90. But these figures are not for everyone. They assume that one spouse did not work, so the couple will get a maximum of $1500 per month in social security (1½ times 1992 near maximum social security payments). If you are *single* but have the same living cost as indicated in Table A-4, *add* the adjustment factor given in Table A-5. However, if *both* you and your spouse are expected to get full regular social security benefits, *subtract* the adjustment from the amount needed at retirement.

Table A-4. Retirement Needs at Age 65

Living costs during retirement	Amount needed at retirement
$ 15,000	$ 55,000
20,000	125,000
25,000	215,000
30,000	305,000
35,000	415,000
40,000	545,000
45,000	600,000
50,000	765,000
60,000	985,000
70,000	1,210,000
80,000	1,430,000
100,000	1,870,000

Table A-5. Social Security Adjustment

Living costs during retirement	Adjustment to amount needed at 65
$ 15,000	$ 90,000
20,000	105,000
25,000	110,000
30,000	115,000
35,000	115,000
40,000	115,000
45,000	115,000
50,000	115,000
60,000	115,000
70,000	115,000
80,000	115,000
100,000	115,000

How Much to Save for Retirement. Doug and Linda, the couple with whom you are familiar from Chapter 13, are retiring in 26 years. They plan to live on $35,000 per year after retirement (about 85 percent of their current cost of living). Doug will get full social security benefits, while Linda will get 50 percent of that amount. They have $83,000 in investment assets today. Looking at Table A-4, we see that the couple would need a total of $415,000 to retire if they were 65 today. Since they will be receiving approximately 1½ times full social security benefits, they do not have to refer to Table A-5.

Schedule A-1. How Much to Save for Retirement

	Doug and Linda's plan	Your finances
1. Amount needed today	$415,000	______
2. Social security adjustment	$0	______
3. Adjusted amount needed (subtract line 2 from line 1)	$415,000	______
4. Number of years until retirement	26	______
5. Inflation rate	5%	______
6. Multiplier from Table B-1 in Appendix B (look under inflation rate and years to retirement given above)	3.56	______
7. Amount in future (multiply line 3 by line 6)	$1,477,400	______
8. Investment assets today	$83,000	______
9. Number of years to retirement	26	______
10. Blended after-tax investment return (see Tables A-9 and A-10 and the introduction to Step 5)	8%	______
11. Multiplier from Table B-1 (using figures on lines 9 and 10)	7.40	______
12. Assets at retirement (multiply line 8 by line 11)	$614,200	______
13. Remaining amount to save for (subtract line 12 from line 7)	$863,200	______
14. Amount in thousands (divide line 13 by 1000 and round)	$863	______
15. Number of years until retirement	26	______
16. Blended after-tax investment return (see line 10)	8%	______
17. Number from Table B-3 in Appendix B (using figures on lines 15 and 16)	7.81	______
18. Amount to save in first year (multiply line 14 by line 17)	$6,740	______

In this case, the couple will have to save $6740 (see Schedule A-1), then 5 percent more each year for the next 26 years to have enough for a retirement at the end of that time. Their living costs will be the equivalent of $35,000 today.

Estate. Many people don't assign a high priority to passing on large assets to their children or other heirs except for their spouse. They are more concerned with having enough money for themselves and their spouse to live on. Often money issues between a husband and wife are handled in insurance and retirement planning. Some, however, will want to make sure they will have a sizable estate for their heirs. If you know the amount you would like to give, you can begin saving for this amount now. Chapter 10 gives guidelines for trusts and passing funds on to your heirs.

Since Doug and Linda do not have any current desire to leave money to their children, we will use an example (Schedule A-2) of another couple, age 65, who want to leave $140,000 in real dollars to be divided by their two children. They assume they will live 25 more years and that estate taxes and other costs will come to $10,000.

In this case, you would have to save $4978, then 5 percent more each year for the next 25 years to have $508,000 in the future. This is equivalent to $150,000 today.

Note that this worksheet can be used for saving for any large outlay.

Disability Insurance. The most coverage you can get is about 60 to 70 percent of your current income, depending on your situation. By default, your highest disability goal cannot be bigger than this. Your insurance agent can give you costs on various amounts of coverage. Review Chapter 5 for more information about disability, especially the question "Is disability insurance necessary?"

Life Insurance. Chapter 5 gives you a simple way to figure out insurance needs. Look at the answer to "How much life insurance is enough?"

Using the chapter's guide, you might choose to have coverage equal to four times each individual's yearly salary. Add double your salary for each child who needs to be raised and educated. Then subtract the current amount of investment assets from each person's required sum. Let's use our figure of four times yearly salary for both husband and wife and two times salary for each child. In the case of Doug and Linda, that would come to $317,000 for Doug (4 times his income, plus 2 times for two children for a total of 8 times his

Schedule A-2. How Much to Save for a Future Expense

	Example	Your finances
1. Amount to give if it were today	$140,000	______
2. Estimated estate settlement costs	$10,000	______
3. Total amount to provide for (add lines 1 and 2)	$150,000	______
4. Number of years until outlay	25	______
5. Inflation rate	5%	______
6. Multiplier from Table B-1 (using figures on lines 4 and 5)	3.39	______
7. Amount in future (multiply line 3 by line 6)	$508,500	______
8. Amount in thousands (divide by 1000 and round)	$508	______
9. How many years until outlay	25	______
10. After-tax investment return	7%	______
11. Number from Table B-3 (using figures on lines 9 and 10)	9.8	______
12. Amount to save in first year (multiply line 8 by line 11)	$4,978	______

income of $50,000, or $400,000 minus $83,000 of assets) and $117,000 for Linda (8 times $25,000 minus $83,000).

Your goal may be less than the full maintenance of the family's current standard of living; you can reduce your insurance need by as much as you see fit. Insurance agents can give you costs for various levels of coverage.

If you choose to complete Appendix B, you will be able to develop a more accurate calculation.

Education. Table 6-2 gives you amounts to save each year for different costs and children's ages. Select the figures that are right for you.

Debt. Chapter 2 covers refinancing of home mortgages and personal debt. If you choose to repay personal debt, this can reduce your annual expenses. Compare the amount of the new annual payment with the old one. That is what we did to figure the interest savings on refinancing Doug and Linda's mortgage. Their total monthly payments at 10½ percent were $18,240 for a year. The total at 8½ percent is $15,900.

Real Estate. If you are considering a real estate purchase, ask the lending institution how much your monthly mortgage payment would be. Also take into account any taxes, maintenance fees, and so forth. You may also want to save for a down payment on a small vacation home. In this case, Chapter 1 gives you a simple way to figure out how much to save per year to get the amount you need. Look at the answer to, "How should I plan for major expenses?" in Chapter 1. For a more accurate method use Schedule A-2, "How Much to Save for a Future Expense," in this appendix.

Investments. Normally, the investment return you use will be reflected in the amount to save for each goal—the higher the return, the less you will need to save. We have placed the return on the Money Ladder Goals Identification Worksheet to illustrate the number used in figuring out how much to save. Some people will project steady increases in returns as they move up the ladder from minimum to satisfactory and higher goals. They may be willing to take additional risk as they move further up or may hope for higher returns for the same amount of risk.

Others may choose to target declines in investment returns as they step up the ladder. They could have lower risk itself as a satisfactory or a higher goal, preferring the security of a safer investment if they don't need the extra return. You may want to simplify, using the same return you feel comfortable with in all the scenarios as Doug and Linda did. In any event, be realistic and don't use a return that will provide you with an uncomfortable level of risk. See the last question of Chapter 4, "What return should I target for my investments?" and Table A-4 in this appendix for estimating your return.

Taxes. You can save on taxes through pension contributions, home mortgage interest, tax-advantaged investments, and payments to a qualified advisor or preparer to find tax advantages for you. Set a goal for yourself and work to find ways to reduce your tax burden to reach your goal. Chapter 8 is the place to start.

Lifestyle. If your goal is to improve your lifestyle, estimate how much more you will spend annually. Similarly, if you want to cut back, estimate your savings for the year. The last question in

Chapter 1—"What about quality-of-life considerations?"—addresses your cost of living.

Once you have figured out the costs, place them on your Yearly Savings Needed Worksheet, Table A-6*a*. The figures for Doug and Linda are in Table A-6.

Step 6. Compare Your Goals with Your Resources. It is time to figure out how realistic your goals are. In the Goals Achievement Worksheet we integrate the cost for each goal with available resources in a format that allows you to calculate how far up the ladder you can go.

As you move up the ladder, enter the additional cost for each item rather than the total. At the end of each section, subtract the total cost from your remaining savings. For example, you have total savings of $10,000 and it takes $7000 to fund your minimum goals. This means that you have $3000 remaining to use on your satisfactory goals.

If you feel that any of the goals or costs are out of line, now is the time to make changes. You are refining and customizing your personal financial plan.

A comparison of goals and resources for Doug and Linda appears in our Goals Achievement Worksheet, Table A-7.

Table A-6. Money Ladder: Yearly Savings Needed to Reach Goals for Doug and Linda's Plan

Goal	Minimum	Satisfactory	Higher	See Chapter	Where to find calculations
Financial independence	$2,548	$5,997	$9,627	9	Retirement Worksheet in Appendix B
Estate	–0–	–0–	–0–	10	Schedule A-2, Appendix A
Disability insurance	$1,390	$2,780	$2,780	5	Disability Worksheet in Appendix B
Life insurance	$428	$428	$428	5	Life Insurance Worksheet in Appendix B
Education	$2,700	$5,424	$10,900	6, Table 6-2	Education Worksheet in Appendix B
Real estate	–0–	–0–	$7,100	7	Our estimate
Debt	–$1,500 after-tax savings	–0–	–0–	2	Our estimate
Investments	10% pretax, 7% after-tax return	10% pretax, 7% after-tax return	10% pretax, 7% after-tax return	4	Our estimate
Taxes	–0–	–$1,200	–$1,700	8	Our estimate
Lifestyle	–0–	$2,800	$5,100	1	Our estimate

Table A-6*a*. Money Ladder: Savings Needed to Reach Goals for Your Finances

Goal	Minimum	Satisfactory	Higher	See Chapter	Where to find calculations
Financial independence				9	Retirement Worksheet in Appendix B
Estate				10	Your estimate
Disability insurance				5	Disability Worksheet in Appendix B
Life insurance				5	Life Insurance Worksheet in Appendix B
Education				6, Table 6-2	Education Worksheet in Appendix B
Real estate				7	Your estimate
Debt				2	Your estimate
Investments				3,4	Your estimate
Taxes				8	Your estimate
Lifestyle				1	Your estimate

Step 7. Finalize Your Ladder. Look again at your Goals Achievement Worksheet. Do you fall close to your satisfactory goals, with a modest amount remaining like Doug and Linda? If you have a large amount remaining, you may have set your sights too low, even after taking your higher goals into account. You may want to upgrade your goals.

On the other hand, you may have fallen short. If your goals are not unrealistic, this means that you will have to earn or save more or face the prospect of living at your minimum level in the future.

Step 8. Implement and Move Up the Ladder to Your Satisfactory and Higher Goals. As we mention in Chapter 13, for your efforts to be worthwhile, you have to act on your plan. You have worked out your goals and how much to save to reach each of them. All you need is a timetable stating clearly the actions needed and the dates by which you will handle them. In Table A-8*a* we provide you with a worksheet for this. First, in Table A-8 we will show you our recommendations for implementing Doug and Linda's goals.

Table A-7. Money Ladder: Goals Achievement Worksheet for Doug and Linda's Plan

	Doug and Linda	Your finances
TOTAL SAVINGS	$16,599	______
MINIMUM GOALS:		
Financial independence	$ 2,548	______
Estate	0	______
Disability insurance	1,390	______
Life insurance	428	______
Education	2,700	______
Debt	−1,500	______
Home	0	______
Tax	0	______
Lifestyle	0	______
Total for Minimum Goals	$ 5,566	______
Funds Remaining (subtract total for goals from total savings)	$11,033	______
SATISFACTORY GOALS:		
Additional Amounts:		
Financial independence	$3,449	______
Estate	0	______
Disability insurance	1,390	______
Life insurance	0	______
Education	2,724	______
Debt	0	______

Table A-7. Money Ladder: Goals Achievement Worksheet for Doug and Linda's Plan (*Continued*)

	Doug and Linda	Your finances
Home	0	______
Tax	–1,200	______
Lifestyle	2,800	______
Total for Satisfactory Goals	$9,163*	______
Funds Remaining (subtract total for goals from funds remaining)	$1,870	______
HIGHER GOALS:		
Additional Amounts:		
Financial independence	$ 3,630	______
Estate	0	______
Disability insurance	0	______
Life insurance	0	______
Education	5,476	______
Debt	0	______
Home	7,100	______
Tax	–500	______
Lifestyle	2,300	______
Total for Higher Goals	$18,006	______
Additional Funds Needed (subtract total for goals from funds remaining)	$–16,136	______

*Level at which Doug and Linda chose to stop.

Table A-8. Money Ladder: Implementation Worksheet for Doug and Linda's Plan

Section of plan	Goal	Savings amount	Time frame
Financial independence	Save for same lifestyle as currently enjoyed	$5997 per year	Begin now
Estate	Establish wills and set guardian	None	Make appointment with lawyer within two weeks
Disability insurance	Get maximum coverage	$2780 per year	Begin research of policies within three weeks; conclude within six weeks
Life insurance	Get full term insurance coverage	$428 per year	Begin research of policies within three weeks; conclude within six weeks
Education	Save for two children at state university, living away from home	$5424 per year	Begin saving now
Real estate	No change	–0–	—
Debt	Refinance mortgage	$1500 after-tax savings per year after refinancing costs in first year	Refinance when rates drop to 2% under their rate of 10.5%
Investments	Diversify assets; increase pretax return to 10%	Will reduce amount needed for goals	Begin diversifying now with full reallocation within one month
Taxes	Increase deductions, start pension contributions	Save $1200 per year	Do this tax year
Lifestyle	Doug takes three weeks off for career	Will cost $2800 per year	Begin this year

Table A-8a. Money Ladder: Implementation Worksheet, Your Finances

Section of plan	Goal	Savings amount	Time frame
Financial independence			
Estate			
Disability insurance			
Life insurance			
Education			
Real estate			
Debt			
Investments			
Taxes			
Lifestyle			

Determining Your Investment Return. You don't have to be an investment professional to estimate your after-tax investment return. Don't be concerned about yearly fluctuations. Your figure should be a longer-term projection. Develop your own estimate using the information given in Table A-9. Alternatively, you can select one of our estimates in the following table. If you have large commission costs or tend to make weak buy-and-sell decisions (we prefer buying and holding for longer-term growth), reduce the rates indicated by 1 percent or more. In any event, it is better to be conservative than to overestimate your future investment return.

Table A-9. Estimating Your After-Tax Rate of Return

Investment makeup	After-tax investment return, %
Mostly taxable bonds, CDs, and money-market accounts; little or no growth investments such as stocks	4–5
Taxable bonds, CDs, and money-market accounts, but some growth investments or longer-term tax-free municipal bonds	6
A large portion in growth investments such as stocks or income-producing real estate	7
All growth investments having above-average risk, and a demonstrable past longer-term record of above-average returns relative to the market	8

Note: To get an approximation of your pretax investment return, divide the above figures by 0.72. Both pretax and after-tax investment return figures are not adjusted for inflation.

You will need to adjust the after-tax investment return selected from Table A-9 for any monies placed in a qualified pension plan—one that allows you to deduct amounts deposited in the plan from your salary, such as a 401(k). Use the adjustment factor in Table A-10 to get a blended after-tax investment return.

Table A-10. Estimating Your Blended Rate of Return (Includes Tax Benefit from Pension Plan)

Importance of pension contribution	Add to after-tax investment return, %
Aren't sure how much of required retirement savings will come from a pension but are contributing thousands of dollars a year to one	1
A moderate amount of retirement savings comes from a pension	1
Most of your retirement savings comes from a pension	2
All of your retirement savings comes from a pension	3

For example, since we knew that about half of Doug and Linda's retirement savings would come from a pension, we added 1 percent to their 7 percent after-tax investment return to arrive at a blended 8 percent figure.

Appendix B
Figuring Your Finances

This appendix provides you with a detailed method for calculating your needs in the areas of retirement, life insurance, disability insurance, and college planning for your children. A simpler estimation of your needs is given in Appendix A.

Schedule B-1. Retirement Needs

The retirement needs worksheet compares the amount you need for living costs from your date of retirement on, with your assets and projected income in retirement. It provides the amount of savings that will be required to meet any anticipated shortfall in funds available at retirement date.

	Doug and Linda	Your figures
Step 1. Retirement Sum Needed		
1. Current annual income (including investment income)	$79,500	______
2. Less current annual savings (net cashflow from Cashflow Statement)	$16,599	______
3. Less current taxes (from Cashflow Worksheet, tax return, or estimate at 28% times line 1)	$22,401	______
4. Current cost of living (subtract lines 2 and 3 from line 1)	$40,500	______

Schedule B-1. Retirement Needs (*Continued*)

	Doug and Linda	Your figures
5. Retirement adjustment (your estimate or 70 percent)	85%	______
6. Cost of living in retirement (multiply line 4 by line 5)	$34,425	______
7. Number of years to retirement	26	______
8. Expected inflation rate (your estimate or 5%)	5%	______
9. Multiplier (from Table B-1, using figures on lines 7 and 8)	3.56	______
10. Income needed in first year of retirement (multiply line 6 by line 9)	$122,553	______
11. Income as a fraction of $1000 (divide line 10 by 1000 and round)	123	______
12. Number of years to be funded (subtract your retirement age from 90 or other upper limit)	25	______
13. Estimated after-tax rate of return (see "What return should I target for my investment?" in Chapter 4 for developing your own figure and "Determining Your Investment Return" in Appendix A for estimates)	7%	______
14. Enter amount equal to $1000 per year (from Table B-2, using figures on lines 12 and 13)	$19,744	______
15. Total amount you will need to cover all retirement living expenses (multiply line 14 by line 11)	$2,428,512	______

Schedule B-1. Retirement Needs (*Continued*)

	Doug and Linda	Your figures
Step 2. Income Available During Retirement		
Type 1: Income that grows with inflation		
16. Projected social security benefit (annual amount in today's dollars; for figure, call your social security office)	$18,000	_______
17. Social security subject to tax (50% taxable if your income will be over $25,000 for single, $32,000 for married)	$9,000	_______
18. Overall tax rate (divide line 3 by line 1 or use 28% estimate)	28%	_______
19. Taxes on social security (multiply line 17 by line 18)	$2,520	_______
20. Social security benefit after taxes have been subtracted (subtract line 19 from 16)	$15,480	_______
21. Other inflating income	$0	_______
22. Overall tax rate (enter number from line 18)	28%	_______
23. Taxes on other income (multiply line 21 by line 22)	$0	_______
24. Other inflating income after taxes have been subtracted (subtract line 23 from line 21)	$0	_______
25. Total inflating income after taxes have been subtracted (add lines 20 and 24)	$15,480	_______
26. Number of years to retirement	26	_______
27. Expected annual inflation rate	5%	_______
28. Multiplier (from Table B-1, using figures on lines 26 and 27)	3.56	_______

Schedule B-1. Retirement Needs (*Continued*)

	Doug and Linda	Your figures
29. Income at retirement age (multiply line 25 by line 28)	$55,109	______
30. Income received as a fraction of $1000 per year (divide line 29 by 1000 and round)	55	______
31. Enter amount equal to $1000 per year (use figure from line 14)	$19,744	______
32. Total value of growing income (multiply line 30 by line 31)	$1,085, 920	______
Type 2: Annuities and other income that doesn't grow		
33. Projected pension annuity benefit (get figure from your employer or insurance company)	$0	______
34. Other flat income	$0	______
35. Total flat income (add lines 33 and 34)	$0	______
36. Overall tax rate (enter number from line 18)	28%	______
37. Taxes on other income (multiply line 35 by line 36)	$0	______
38. Other inflating income after taxes have been subtracted (subtract line 37 from line 35)	$0	______
39. Income received as a fraction of $1000 per year (divide line 38 by 1000 and round)	$0	______
40. Enter amount equal to $1000 (use figure from line 14)	$19,744	______
41. Total value of flat income (multiply line 38 by line 40)	$0	______

Note that since Doug and Linda have no annuities or flat income payments in retirement, Type 2 doesn't enter into the calculation.

Schedule B-1. Retirement Needs (*Continued*)

	Doug and Linda	Your figures
Step 3. Assets Available		
42. Current investment assets (from Personal Balance Sheet, Table A-2)	$83,000	______
43. After-tax investment return (from line 13)	7%	______
44. Years to retirement	26	______
45. Multiplier (from Table B-1, using figures from lines 43 and 44)	5.81	______
46. Value of savings at retirement (line 42 times line 45)	$482,230	______

If you are the main contributor to your pension and will be getting a lump sum at retirement, complete the following section. Since qualified retirement savings compound tax-free, with taxes only being paid as the money is taken out, use the rate of return adjusted for your pension contributions as described in Step 48.

47. Current retirement savings	$0	______
48. Your rate of return—before tax (If you are under age 50, use your before-tax return minus 1%; if you are 50 or over, use your after-tax rate of return. See "Determining Your Investment Return" in Appendix A)	9%	______
49. Years to retirement	26	______
50. Multiplier (from Table B-1, using figures on lines 48 and 49)	9.40	______
51. Value of savings at retirement (line 47 times line 50)	$0	______

Note that since Doug and Linda have no pension savings yet, this section doesn't enter into the calculation.

Schedule B-1. Retirement Needs (*Continued*)

	Doug and Linda	Your figures
Step 4: Evaluating Your Savings Needs		
Now let's see where you stand.		
52. Total amount you will need (enter amount on line 15)	$2,428,512	______
53. Value of growing income (enter amount on line 32)	$1,085,920	______
54. Value of flat income (enter amount on line 41)	$0	______
55. Value of personal savings (enter amount on line 46)	$482,230	______
56. Value of retirement savings (enter amount on line 51)	$0	______
57. Total amount available (add lines 53–56)	$1,568,150	______
58. Total additional amount needed at retirement (subtract line 57 from line 52)	$860,362	______

Step 5: How Much to Save

In saving for retirement, you have two options—placing your savings in a pension plan or in a regular account. The pension plan will accumulate faster than regular savings, because you get a current tax savings and your deposits grow tax-free. Since the government places restrictions on the size of your annual pension contribution, most people will want to save some money in each type of account. Below, you will calculate the amount to save if all your savings were in a regular account and the amount to save if it were in a pension. Then you determine how much you can legally save in a pension. The remaining amount you need to save, if any, will be regular savings.

Schedule B-1. Retirement Needs (*Continued*)

	Doug and Linda		Your finances	
	Regular savings	Pension savings	Regular savings	Pension savings
59. Total amount needed at retirement, in thousands (divide amount in line 58 by 1000; if line 58 is negative, you do not need to save more	860	860	______	______
60. Years to retirement	26	26	______	______
61. Rate of return (use after-tax rate of return for regular savings, before tax rate of return for pension savings)	7%	10%	______	______
62. Multiplier (from Table B-3, using figures from lines 60 and 61)	8.88	5.98	______	______
63. Amount to save each year from now to retirement if total needed were to be made up of either pension or regular savings only (multiply line 59 by line 62; this savings amount will have to increase by 5% a year)	$7,637	$5,143	______	______
64. Enter your maximum allowable annual pension contribution (ask your employer, plan administrator, or accountant)		$3,400		______
65. Percentage of savings need covered by maximum allowable pension contribution (divide line 64 by line 63—if the result is greater than 100%, skip to line 68 and place the pension savings figure from line 63 on line 68)		66%		______

Schedule B-1. Retirement Needs (*Continued*)

	Doug and Linda		Your finances	
	Regular savings	Pension savings	Regular savings	Pension savings
66. Percentage to save in **regular savings** account (subtract line 65 from 100%)	34%		____	
67. Amount to save in **regular savings** account (multiply line 63 by line 66)	2,597		____	
68. Total annual savings needed for retirement (add lines 64 and 67)		5,997		____

Schedule B-2. Life Insurance Needs

Life insurance needs are separated by various stages of life:

1. time until children leave the house
2. from that date to retirement date
3. from retirement date on

All three parts are added up and current investment assets are subtracted to arrive at the amount needed. Note that this worksheet requires you to fill out the previous retirement worksheet first. That is why we start with stage 3—the retirement stage—at line 69.

	Doug	Linda	You	Spouse
Step 1. Retirement Portion				
69. Expense amount (enter amount on line 52)	$2,428,512	$2,428,512	____	____
70. Adjustment factor for one less person (enter 70% or your estimate)	70%	70%	____	____
71. Adjusted amount for living expenses (multiply line 69 by line 70)	$1,699,958	$1,699,958	____	____

Schedule B-2. Life Insurance Needs (*Continued*)

	Doug	Linda	You	Spouse
72. Value of growing income (enter amount on line 53)	$1,085,920	$1,085,920	_____	_____
73. Survivor's social security and other growing income in retirement (call your local social security office)	$12,000	$12,000	_____	_____
74. Total joint social security and other growing income (from line 16)	$18,000	$18,000	_____	_____
75. Percentage that will remain (divide line 73 by 74)	67%	67%	_____	_____
76. Reduced amount for social security and growing income (multiply line 72 by line 75)	$727,566	$727,566	_____	_____
77. Value of flat income (enter amount on line 54)	$0	$0	_____	_____
78. Reduction of annuity and flat income for one person (enter 50% or your estimate)	50%	50%	_____	_____
79. Reduced value for flat income (multiply line 77 by line 78)	$0	$0	_____	_____
80. Remaining amount to be covered by insurance (subtract lines 76 and 79 from line 71; if negative, enter 0)	$972,392	$972,392	_____	_____

Schedule B-2. Life Insurance Needs (*Continued*)

	Doug	Linda	You	Spouse
81. Number of years to retirement	26	26	_____	_____
82. Your after-tax rate of return (see line 13)	7%	7%	_____	_____
83. Divisor (from Table B-1, using figures on lines 81 and 82)	5.81	5.81	_____	_____
84. Equivalent amount today (divide line 80 by line 83)	$167,365	$167,365	_____	_____
Step 2: Portion from Now to Time Youngest Child Reaches 18				
85. Current living expenses (enter figure on line 4)	$40,500	$40,500	_____	_____
86. Adjustment of living costs for one person (enter 80% or your estimate)	80%	80%	_____	_____
87. New living costs (multiply line 85 by line 86)	$32,400	$32,400	_____	_____
88. Remaining income after death of spouse	$25,000	$50,000	_____	_____
89. Overall tax rate (enter number from line 18)	28%	28%	_____	_____
90. Taxes on remaining income (multiply line 88 by line 89)	$7,000	$14,000	_____	_____
91. Remaining income after taxes have been subtracted (subtract line 90 from line 88)	$18,000	$36,000	_____	_____

Schedule B-2. Life Insurance Needs (*Continued*)

	Doug	Linda	You	Spouse
92. Estimated social security benefit for spouse and child of deceased worker (call your local social security office)	$10,020	$6,600	_____	_____
93. Total after-tax income (add lines 91 and 92)	$28,020	$42,600	_____	_____
94. Income to be replaced by insurance (subtract line 93 from line 87)	$4,380	$–10,200	_____	_____
95. Income needed as a fraction of $1000 (divide line 94 by 1000 and round)	4	–10	_____	_____
96. Years from now to year youngest child is 18	18	18	_____	_____
97. Your after-tax rate of return (see line 13)	7%	7%	_____	_____
98. Amount equal to $1000 per year (from Table B-2, using figures from lines 96 and 97)	$15,118	$15,118	_____	_____
99. Amount needed (multiply line 95 by line 98)	$60,472	$–151,180	_____	_____
Step 3: Portion from Time Youngest Child Reaches 18 to Retirement				
100. Current living expenses (enter figure on line 85)	$40,500	$40,500	_____	_____
101. Adjustment of living costs (enter 80% or your estimate)	80%	80%	_____	_____
102. New living costs (multiply line 100 by line 101)	$32,400	$32,400	_____	_____

Schedule B-2. Life Insurance Needs (*Continued*)

	Doug	Linda	You	Spouse
103. Number of years from now to time youngest child reaches age 18	18	18	______	______
104. Expected inflation rate	5%	5%	______	______
105. Multiplier (from Table B-1, using figures on lines 103 and 104)	2.41	2.41	______	______
106. Living costs when youngest child is 18 (multiply line 102 by line 105)	$78,084	$78,084	______	______
107. Remaining after-tax income after death of spouse (enter amount on line 91)	$18,000	$36,000	______	______
108. Multiplier from line 105	2.41	2.41	______	______
109. Total income when youngest child is 18 (multiply line 107 by line 108)	$43,380	$86,760	______	______
110. Income to be replaced by insurance (subtract line 109 from line 106)	$34,704	$–8,676	______	______
111. Income needed as a fraction of $1000 (divide line 110 by 1000 and round)	35	–9	______	______
112. Years from year youngest child is 18 to retirement	8	8	______	______
113. Your after-tax rate of return (see line 13)	7%	7%	______	______

Schedule B-2. Life Insurance Needs (*Continued*)

	Doug	Linda	You	Spouse
114. Amount equal to 1000 per year (from Table B-2, using figures on lines 112 and 113)	$7,356	$7,356	_____	_____
115. Amount needed when youngest child is 18 (multiply line 111 by line 114)	$257,460	$–66,204	_____	_____
116. Years until youngest child is 18	18	18	_____	_____
117. Your estimated after-tax rate of return	7%	7%	_____	_____
118. Divisor (from Table B-1, using figures on lines 116 and 117)	3.38	3.38	_____	_____
119. Amount needed today (divide line 115 by line 118)	$76,172	$–19,587	_____	_____

Step 4: Your Total Insurance Needs

Now you will add the subtotals from the three stages of life to arrive at your total need for insurance.

	Doug	Linda	You	Spouse
120. Total amount needed for now to year youngest child is 18 (from line 99)	$60,472	$–151,180	_____	_____
121. Total amount needed for year youngest child is 18 to retirement (from line 119)	76,172	–19,587	_____	_____
122. Total amount needed for retirement (enter number from line 84)	167,365	167,365	_____	_____

Schedule B-2. Life Insurance Needs (*Continued*)

	Doug	Linda	You	Spouse
123. Total amount needed for education today (enter figure from College Planning Worksheet, Schedule B-4)	72,000	72,000	_____	_____
124. Total amount needed for funeral expenses, estate settlement, and emergency fund (use $25,000 or your estimate)	25,000	25,000	_____	_____
125. Total amount needed today (add lines 120 through 124)	401,009	93,598	_____	_____
126. Current investment assets (from line 42)	83,000	83,000	_____	_____
127. Total insurance needed (subtract line 126 from line 125)	318,009	10,598	_____	_____
128. Cost of insurance on line 127 (per quotation from insurance agent)	428	0	_____	_____

Note that Linda's need was felt to be too small to cover, so she will not need to purchase life insurance.

Schedule B-3. Disability Insurance Needs

This schedule takes your living costs, adjusts for any change due to disability, and figures out the amount of income needed. If you have paid the premiums, the amount received is not subject to taxes. If your employer paid the premiums, the payments are taxed and you should use the larger figure on line 20 to determine disability needed. Otherwise, you should use line 17. Insurance companies generally provide coverage to a maximum of only 60 to 70 percent of your earned income. They don't want you to have an incentive to stay out of work by providing you with a higher after-tax income from disability payments than from your job. In the case of Doug and

Schedule B-3. Disability Insurance Needs (*Continued*)

Linda, the disability insurance needs calculated below is about 70 percent of the nontaxable figure. Because your living costs and savings needs are projected to grow at 5 percent, your disability coverage should also grow at 5 percent annually.

	Doug	Linda	You	Spouse
1. Current living expenses (from line 4 of Retirement Worksheet)	$40,500	$40,500	_____	_____
2. Adjustment of living expenses for disabled person (use your estimate or 100%)	100%	100%	_____	_____
3. Adjusted living expenses (multiply line 1 by line 2)	$40,500	$40,500	_____	_____
4. Spouse's after-tax income remaining (from line 91 of Life Insurance Worksheet)	$18,000	$36,000	_____	_____
5. Amount needed for current living costs (subtract line 4 from line 3; if negative, enter zero)	$22,500	$4,500	_____	_____

In addition to the amount needed for your ongoing expenses on line 5, you will still have to set aside money for the goals on your Money Ladder. Enter each of the figures from the Money Ladder Savings Needed Worksheet at the level (minimum, satisfactory, or higher goals) you are saving for:

	Doug	Linda	You	Spouse
6. Amount to save for retirement	$5,997	$5,997	_____	_____
7. Amount to save for estate	$0	$0	_____	_____
8. Disability insurance costs (estimate cost figure only for spouse who is not disabled)	$900	$1,500	_____	_____

Schedule B-3. Disability Insurance Needs (*Continued*)

	Doug	Linda	You	Spouse
9. Life insurance costs	$428	$428	_____	_____
10. Amount to save for education	$5,400	$5,400	_____	_____
11. Real estate costs	$0	$0	_____	_____
12. Debt costs or savings	$–1,500	$–1,500	_____	_____
13. Tax costs or savings	$–1,200	$–1,200	_____	_____
14. Lifestyle costs or savings	$0	$2,800	_____	_____
15. Other savings goals	$0	$0	_____	_____
16. Total income needed for goals (add lines 6 through 15)	$10,025	$13,425	_____	_____
17. Total income needed for living costs (copy number from line 5)	$22,500	$4,500	_____	_____
18. Total disability income needed if the income received is not taxable (add lines 15 and 16)	$32,525	$17,925	_____	_____
19. Estimated tax rate (from line 18 of insurance worksheet)	28%	28%	_____	_____
20. Divisor (subtract line 9 from 100%)	72%	72%	_____	_____
21. Total disability income needed if the income received is taxable (divide line 17 by line 19)	$45,174	$24,896	_____	_____
22. Cost of insurance on line 20 (per quotation from insurance agent)	$1,786	$994	_____	_____

Schedule B-4. College Planning Needs

This schedule gives you the yearly amount you need to set aside—growing by 5 percent annually—to fund college costs for your children.

	Doug and Linda's		Your	Your	Your
	First child	Second child	first child	second child	third child
1. Child's age	3	0	____	____	____
2. Years to college	15	18	____	____	____
3. College inflation (use 7% or your estimate)	7%	7%	____	____	____
4. Multiplier (from Table B-1, using figures on lines 2 and 3)	2.76	3.38	____	____	____
5. Cost of four years of college today	$36,000	$36,000	____	____	____
6. Cost when college begins (multiply line 5 by line 4)	$99,360	$121,680	____	____	____
7. Years to college	15	18	____	____	____
8. After-tax investment return (see "What return should I target for my investments?" in Chapter 4 and "Determining Your Investment Return" in Appendix A)	7%	7%	____	____	____
9. Divisor (from Table B-1, using figures from lines 7 and 8)	2.76	3.38	____	____	____
10. Amount needed today (divide line 6 by line 9)	$36,000	$36,000	____	____	____

Schedule B-4. College Planning Needs (*Continued*)

	Doug and Linda's		Your	Your	Your
	First child	Second child	first child	second child	third child
11. Total amount needed (add across total children's costs on line 10)	$72,000		_____		
12. Total amount needed when college starts as fraction of $1000 (divide line 6 by 1000, round)	99.4	121.7	_____	_____	_____
13. Multiplier (from Table B-3, using figures from lines 7 and 8)	29.41	20.55	_____	_____	_____
14. Amount to save each year (multiply line 12 by line 13)	$2,923	$2,501	_____	_____	_____

Table B-1. What a Dollar Will Be Equal To in the Future

Number of years until due	Rate of return or rate of inflation										
	3%	4%	5%	6%	7%	8%	9%	10%	11%	12%	15%
1	$1.03	$1.04	$1.05	$1.06	$1.07	$1.08	$1.09	$1.10	$1.11	$1.12	$1.15
2	1.06	1.08	1.10	1.12	1.14	1.17	1.19	1.21	1.23	1.25	1.32
3	1.09	1.12	1.16	1.19	1.23	1.26	1.30	1.33	1.37	1.40	1.52
4	1.13	1.17	1.22	1.26	1.31	1.36	1.41	1.46	1.52	1.57	1.75
5	1.16	1.22	1.28	1.34	1.40	1.47	1.54	1.61	1.69	1.76	2.01
6	1.19	1.27	1.34	1.42	1.50	1.59	1.68	1.77	1.87	1.97	2.31
7	1.23	1.32	1.41	1.50	1.61	1.71	1.83	1.95	2.08	2.21	2.66
8	1.27	1.37	1.48	1.59	1.72	1.85	1.99	2.14	2.30	2.48	3.06
9	1.30	1.42	1.55	1.69	1.84	2.00	2.17	2.36	2.56	2.77	3.52
10	1.34	1.48	1.63	1.79	1.97	2.16	2.37	2.59	2.84	3.11	4.05
11	1.38	1.54	1.71	1.90	2.10	2.33	2.58	2.85	3.15	3.48	4.65
12	1.43	1.60	1.80	2.01	2.25	2.52	2.81	3.14	3.50	3.90	5.35
13	1.47	1.67	1.89	2.13	2.41	2.72	3.07	3.45	3.88	4.36	6.15
14	1.51	1.73	1.98	2.26	2.58	2.94	3.34	3.80	4.31	4.89	7.08
15	1.56	1.80	2.08	2.40	2.76	3.17	3.64	4.18	4.78	5.47	8.14
16	1.60	1.87	2.18	2.54	2.95	3.43	3.97	4.59	5.31	6.13	9.36
17	1.65	1.95	2.29	2.69	3.16	3.70	4.33	5.05	5.90	6.87	10.76
18	1.70	2.03	2.41	2.85	3.38	4.00	4.72	5.56	6.54	7.69	12.38
19	1.75	2.11	2.53	3.03	3.62	4.32	5.14	6.12	7.26	8.61	14.23
20	1.81	2.19	2.65	3.21	3.87	4.66	5.60	6.73	8.06	9.65	16.37
21	1.86	2.28	2.79	3.40	4.14	5.03	6.11	7.40	8.95	10.80	18.82
22	1.92	2.37	2.93	3.60	4.43	5.44	6.66	8.14	9.93	12.10	21.64
23	1.97	2.46	3.07	3.82	4.74	5.87	7.26	8.95	11.03	13.55	24.89

Table B-1. What a Dollar Will Be Equal To in the Future (*Continued*)

Number of years until due	Rate of return or rate of inflation										
	3%	4%	5%	6%	7%	8%	9%	10%	11%	12%	15%
24	2.03	2.56	3.23	4.05	5.07	6.34	7.91	9.85	12.24	15.18	28.63
25	2.09	2.67	3.39	4.29	5.43	6.85	8.62	10.83	13.59	17.00	32.92
26	2.16	2.77	3.56	4.55	5.81	7.40	9.40	11.92	15.08	19.04	37.86
27	2.22	2.88	3.73	4.82	6.21	7.99	10.25	13.11	16.74	21.32	43.54
28	2.29	3.00	3.92	5.11	6.65	8.63	11.17	14.42	18.58	23.88	50.07
29	2.36	3.12	4.12	5.42	7.11	9.32	12.17	15.86	20.62	26.75	57.58
30	2.43	3.24	4.32	5.74	7.61	10.06	13.27	17.45	22.89	29.96	66.21
31	2.50	3.37	4.54	6.09	8.15	10.87	14.46	19.19	25.41	33.56	76.14
32	2.58	3.51	4.76	6.45	8.72	11.74	15.76	21.11	28.21	37.58	87.57
33	2.65	3.65	5.00	6.84	9.33	12.68	17.18	23.23	31.31	42.09	100.70
34	2.73	3.79	5.25	7.25	9.98	13.69	18.73	25.55	34.75	47.14	115.80
35	2.81	3.95	5.52	7.69	10.68	14.79	20.41	28.10	38.57	52.80	133.18
36	2.90	4.10	5.79	8.15	11.42	15.97	22.25	30.91	42.82	59.14	153.15
37	2.99	4.27	6.08	8.64	12.22	17.25	24.25	34.00	47.53	66.23	176.12
38	3.07	4.44	6.39	9.15	13.08	18.63	26.44	37.40	52.76	74.18	202.54
39	3.17	4.62	6.70	9.70	13.99	20.12	28.82	41.14	58.56	83.08	232.92
40	3.26	4.80	7.04	10.29	14.97	21.72	31.41	45.26	65.00	93.05	267.86
45	3.78	5.84	8.99	13.76	21.00	31.92	48.33	72.89	109.53	163.99	538.77
50	4.38	7.11	11.47	18.42	29.46	46.90	74.36	117.39	184.56	289.00	1083.66

Table B-2. Amount Equal To Receiving Income for a Fixed Number of Years; Income Begins at $1000, then Increases by 5 Percent Annually

Number of years payments are received	Rate of return or rate of inflation 3%	4%	5%	6%	7%	8%	9%	10%	11%	12%
1	$1,019	$1,010	$1,000	$991	$981	$972	$963	$955	$946	$938
2	2,059	2,029	2,000	1,972	1,944	1,917	1,891	1,866	1,841	1,816
3	3,118	3,058	3,000	2,944	2,889	2,836	2,785	2,735	2,687	2,640
4	4,198	4,097	4,000	3,907	3,817	3,730	3,646	3,566	3,488	3,413
5	5,299	5,146	5,000	4,860	4,727	4,598	4,476	4,358	4,245	4,137
6	6,421	6,205	6,000	5,805	5,619	5,443	5,275	5,115	4,962	4,816
7	7,565	7,274	7,000	6,741	6,496	6,264	6,045	5,837	5,640	5,452
8	8,732	8,354	8,000	7,668	7,356	7,062	6,786	6,526	6,281	6,049
9	9,921	9,444	9,000	8,586	8,199	7,838	7,500	7,184	6,887	6,609
10	11,133	10,544	10,000	9,496	9,028	8,593	8,188	7,812	7,461	7,133
11	12,368	11,655	11,000	10,397	9,840	9,326	8,851	8,411	8,003	7,625
12	13,628	12,777	12,000	11,289	10,637	10,039	9,490	8,983	8,517	8,086
13	14,912	13,910	13,000	12,173	11,420	10,733	10,105	9,530	9,002	8,518
14	16,221	15,053	14,000	13,049	12,188	11,407	10,697	10,051	9,462	8,923
15	17,555	16,207	15,000	13,916	12,941	12,062	11,268	10,549	9,896	9,303
16	18,916	17,373	16,000	14,776	13,681	12,699	11,818	11,024	10,307	9,659
17	20,302	18,549	17,000	15,627	14,406	13,319	12,347	11,477	10,696	9,993
18	21,716	19,737	18,000	16,470	15,118	13,921	12,858	11,910	11,064	10,306
19	23,157	20,937	19,000	17,305	15,817	14,507	13,349	12,323	11,412	10,599
20	24,626	22,148	20,000	18,132	16,503	15,076	13,822	12,718	11,741	10,874
21	26,124	23,370	21,000	18,952	17,176	15,629	14,279	13,094	12,052	11,132

Table B-2. Amount Equal To Receiving Income for a Fixed Number of Years; Income Begins at $1000, then Increases by 5 Percent Annually (*Continued*)

Number of years payments are received	Rate of return or rate of inflation									
	3%	4%	5%	6%	7%	8%	9%	10%	11%	12%
22	27,650	24,605	22,000	19,764	17,836	16,167	14,718	13,454	12,347	11,374
23	29,207	25,851	23,000	20,568	18,484	16,691	15,141	13,797	12,625	11,600
24	30,793	27,109	24,000	21,364	19,120	17,199	15,549	14,124	12,889	11,813
25	32,410	28,379	25,000	22,153	19,744	17,694	15,941	14,437	13,138	12,012
26	34,059	29,662	26,000	22,935	20,356	18,174	16,320	14,735	13,374	12,199
27	35,740	30,957	27,000	23,709	20,957	18,642	16,684	15,020	13,597	12,374
28	37,453	32,264	28,000	24,476	21,546	19,096	17,035	15,291	13,808	12,538
29	39,200	33,584	29,000	25,236	22,125	19,538	17,373	15,551	14,007	12,692
30	40,981	34,916	30,000	25,988	22,693	19,967	17,699	15,799	14,196	12,836
31	42,796	36,262	31,000	26,734	23,250	20,385	18,013	16,035	14,375	12,971
32	44,646	37,620	32,000	27,472	23,796	20,791	18,315	16,261	14,544	13,098
33	46,533	38,991	33,000	28,203	24,333	21,186	18,606	16,476	14,703	13,217
34	48,455	40,376	34,000	28,928	24,859	21,569	18,887	16,682	14,855	13,328
35	50,416	41,774	35,000	29,645	25,376	21,942	19,157	16,878	14,998	13,433
36	52,414	43,185	36,000	30,356	25,883	22,305	19,417	17,065	15,133	13,531
37	54,451	44,610	37,000	31,061	26,381	22,658	19,668	17,244	15,261	13,623
38	56,528	46,048	38,000	31,758	26,869	23,001	19,910	17,415	15,382	13,709
39	58,645	47,501	39,000	32,449	27,348	23,334	20,142	17,578	15,496	13,789
40	60,803	48,967	40,000	33,133	27,818	23,658	20,366	17,733	15,605	13,865
45	72,239	56,513	45,000	36,460	30,040	25,148	21,370	18,411	16,064	14,178
50	84,829	64,429	50,000	39,633	32,062	26,443	22,202	18,949	16,413	14,405

Table B-3. Amount Necessary to Save per Year to Get $1000 at End of Period (Payments Grow by 5 Percent Annually)

Number of years payments are made	Rate of return									
	3%	4%	5%	6%	7%	8%	9%	10%	11%	12%
1	$1,000.00	$1,000.00	$1,000.00	$1,000.00	$1,000.00	$1,000.00	$1,000.00	$1,000.00	$1,000.00	$1,000.00
2	480.77	478.47	476.19	473.93	471.70	469.48	467.29	465.12	462.96	460.83
3	308.18	305.24	302.34	299.48	296.66	293.87	291.11	288.39	285.71	283.05
4	222.23	219.07	215.96	212.90	209.89	206.92	204.00	201.13	198.31	195.52
5	170.93	167.70	164.54	161.44	158.39	155.40	152.47	149.60	146.78	144.02
6	136.95	133.73	130.59	127.51	124.51	121.57	118.69	115.88	113.14	110.46
7	112.85	109.69	106.60	103.59	100.66	97.81	95.03	92.32	89.68	87.11
8	94.93	91.84	88.84	85.92	83.08	80.33	77.65	75.06	72.54	70.10
9	81.12	78.11	75.20	72.38	69.65	67.01	64.46	61.99	59.60	57.29
10	70.18	67.27	64.46	61.75	59.13	56.60	54.17	51.82	49.57	47.39
11	61.33	58.52	55.81	53.20	50.70	48.29	45.97	43.75	41.63	39.59
12	54.04	51.33	48.72	46.22	43.83	41.53	39.34	37.24	35.24	33.33
13	47.95	45.34	42.83	40.44	38.15	35.97	33.89	31.92	30.04	28.25
14	42.80	40.28	37.88	35.59	33.41	31.34	29.37	27.51	25.75	24.08
15	38.39	35.97	33.67	31.48	29.41	27.44	25.58	23.83	22.18	20.62
16	34.59	32.27	30.06	27.97	26.00	24.13	22.38	20.73	19.18	17.73
17	31.29	29.06	26.95	24.95	23.07	21.31	19.65	18.10	16.65	15.30
18	28.40	26.26	24.24	22.34	20.55	18.88	17.31	15.86	14.50	13.25
19	25.86	23.80	21.87	20.05	18.36	16.77	15.30	13.93	12.67	11.50
20	23.61	21.64	19.79	18.06	16.44	14.94	13.55	12.27	11.09	10.01
21	21.61	19.72	17.95	16.30	14.76	13.35	12.04	10.84	9.74	8.73

Table B-3. Amount Necessary to Save per Year to Get $1000 at End of Period (Payments Grow by 5 Percent Annually) *(Continued)*

Number of years payments are made	Rate of return									
	3%	4%	5%	6%	7%	8%	9%	10%	11%	12%
22	19.82	18.01	16.32	14.74	13.29	11.95	10.71	9.59	8.56	7.63
23	18.22	16.48	14.86	13.36	11.98	10.71	9.55	8.50	7.54	6.68
24	16.77	15.11	13.57	12.14	10.83	9.63	8.54	7.55	6.66	5.86
25	15.47	13.88	12.40	11.04	9.80	8.67	7.64	6.71	5.88	5.14
26	14.30	12.77	11.36	10.06	8.88	7.81	6.85	5.98	5.21	4.52
27	13.23	11.76	10.42	9.18	8.06	7.05	6.14	5.33	4.61	3.98
28	12.25	10.85	9.57	8.39	7.33	6.37	5.52	4.76	4.09	3.51
29	11.37	10.03	8.80	7.68	6.67	5.77	4.97	4.26	3.63	3.09
30	10.56	9.27	8.10	7.03	6.08	5.23	4.47	3.81	3.23	2.73
31	9.81	8.58	7.46	6.45	5.54	4.74	4.03	3.41	2.87	2.41
32	9.13	7.96	6.89	5.92	5.06	4.30	3.64	3.06	2.56	2.13
33	8.51	7.38	6.36	5.44	4.63	3.91	3.28	2.74	2.28	1.89
34	7.93	6.85	5.88	5.01	4.23	3.56	2.97	2.46	2.03	1.67
35	7.40	6.37	5.44	4.61	3.88	3.24	2.68	2.21	1.81	1.48
36	6.91	5.92	5.04	4.25	3.55	2.95	2.43	1.99	1.62	1.31
37	6.46	5.51	4.67	3.91	3.26	2.69	2.20	1.79	1.45	1.16
38	6.04	5.14	4.33	3.61	2.99	2.45	1.99	1.61	1.29	1.03
39	5.65	4.79	4.02	3.33	2.74	2.24	1.81	1.45	1.16	0.92
40	5.29	4.47	3.73	3.08	2.52	2.04	1.64	1.31	1.04	0.81
45	3.84	3.18	2.60	2.09	1.66	1.31	1.02	0.78	0.60	0.45
50	2.82	2.29	1.83	1.44	1.11	0.85	0.64	0.47	0.35	0.25

Appendix C
Tax Law Changes in the 1993 Tax Act

What are the recent tax law changes? Are there any tax strategies to deal with Clinton's 1993 tax act?

Introduction

The tax act of 1993 was devised to reduce our yawning budget deficit and to reverse the Reagan Administration's tilt toward higher income individuals. To make sure the impact on your situation is minimized, please note the following details of the plan and our comments:

Details

1. Effective January 1, 1994, charitable contribution rules have been tightened. In order to take a tax deduction, receipts must be obtained from the charity for all contributions of $250 or more. The acknowledgment must state the cash amount contributed and a description of any property donated. (An estimate of the value of the property contribution need not be given.) In addition, the charity must state whether it gave the donor anything of value and an estimate of that value. This receipt must be received by the date the taxpayer is obligated to file the return.

Comments

1. Remember, having a canceled check for $250 or more is no longer enough to qualify for a charitable deduction. But a canceled check alone will be enough if you make multiple contributions to the same charity, all under the $250 limit (subject to not abusing the

right). One money-saving recommendation, whatever the amount of your contribution, is to make your donation in stock or other qualifying assets in which you have large profits, instead of cash. By doing so, you will escape paying a capital gains tax on the sale of the stock.

Details

2. Effective January 1, 1994, charities must give each person who has made a contribution of over $75 in which the donor receives something in return from the charity, a receipt showing a good faith estimate of the value of the benefit.

Comments

2. Keep the checks under $75.00. But the days of taking large deductions for checks made out to charities for entrance fees and purchases at events such as auctions, or theater activities, are over.

Personal Tax Changes

Details

3. Two new tax brackets have been created—one of 36 percent—for joint taxable incomes over $140,000 ($115,000 single), and 39.6 percent for joint and single taxable incomes over $250,000. In addition, the relatively new 1.45 percent hospital insurance tax (2.9 percent for the business owner) is now based on your entire taxable income instead of the first $135,000. It is now possible once again for people in high tax areas like New York City to be taxed at over 50 percent on the next dollar they earn.

Comments

3. The extra amount payable for 1993 because of the new higher tax brackets can be divided into three parts and paid in equal amounts in April 1994, April 1995, and April 1996 respectively. We recommend delaying payment as allowed. In the meantime the amounts which will be due can be invested.

Details

4. The marriage penalty under the new tax law has been increased significantly. It now can cost thousands more for people

earning about the same amount to get married and file jointly over remaining single and filing individual tax returns.

Comments

4. When planning a fall marriage, consider postponement to the new year.

Details

5. For many people interest expense on loans of securities (margin loans) will now be deductible only to the extent of interest and dividend income. Previously, net long-term capital gains income (net gains on sale of assets) could also be included in calculating the amount of interest deductibility. Now if you use long-term capital gains income as a way to obtain a larger tax deduction for margin interest, you will be taxed at ordinary income rates for the capital gains used and lose the ability to use favorable capital gains tax rates.

Comments

5. Margin loans are still one of the only effective ways of receiving a tax deduction on a loan. They are particularly useful for those who don't own a home and therefore cannot get a tax deduction for home equity loans. Current borrowing rates are extremely low. Keep in mind that mutual funds are also marginable.

Be careful about using capital gains as a margin interest expense offset if you are in a high tax bracket. Often it will pay to forsake the tax deduction and keep favorable capital gains tax treatment.

Details

6. The 10 percent tax on purchases of luxury goods has been repealed except for passenger cars priced at over $30,000 for 1993. This $30,000 figure is indexed annually for inflation.

Comments

6. It looks to us like Detroit may have influenced the Administration since almost all luxury cars are imported.

Details

7. Estates and trusts are taxed at the same new higher tax rates as individuals and they move to higher income tax brackets sooner

than before. For example, the 28 percent tax bracket starts at taxable income over $1500 versus $3750 prior.

Comments

7. The attractiveness of trusts as *income tax* shelters has been further reduced. For many people the principal reason for setting up trusts will be non-income-tax-related, such as controlling when the funds are to be used by the beneficiary. An exception can be people in high tax brackets or those who wish to shelter the first $1500 in taxable income including being able to shelter the first $600 of your child's non-work-related income completely tax free. In addition, some trusts still can be an excellent *estate tax* shelter tool.

Details

8. Effective 1994, the maximum amount two wage earners or one wage earner and one full-time student can credit against their income for child care expenses for a child over one year old has been raised from $1434 to $2038 for one child and to $2527 for two children. The credit for children under one year old has been eliminated and the tax credit extended to childless low-income workers between the ages of 25 and 65.

Comments

8. Be sure to claim this deduction if your income and child spending pattern permits. If you own a business, and your child over 25 does not have a job and you do not claim him or her as a dependent, here is another reason why it could be beneficial to employ your child.

Details

9. People with adjusted gross income of over $150,000 will have to make estimated payments of 110 percent of the previous year's tax or 90 percent of the current year's tax, whichever is lower. Previously they generally were not able to use the prior year's estimate if their adjusted gross income exceeded $75,000 and their income was more than $40,000 higher than the previous year. Those making under $150,000 in AGI can use 100 percent of the prior year's tax payments and be assured of no penalty. (There will also be no penalty for

underwithholding caused by falling into the Administration's new higher tax rates.)

Comments

9. This rule should make things simpler for those people to whom it applies and make their accountants' lives easier.

Details

10. Beginning in 1994, the tax deductible amount of business entertainment will be reduced from 80 percent to 50 percent of the bill. You won't be able to deduct spousal business travel expenses unless he or she literally works for the corporation and the travel is for a business purpose for both of you.

Comments

10. President Clinton is just continuing what President Carter started. However, the net amount of cash spent for the meal will only go up by approximately 15 percent.

Details

11. The cost of club dues is no longer tax deductible.

Comments

11. Tell your club to replace future increases in dues with higher usage costs for activities and meals, which are partly deductible.

Details

12. Effective 1994, social security will be taxed at 85 percent of the amounts in excess of $44,000 joint and $34,000 single of "provisional income." [Provisional income is Adjusted Gross Income (income before most deductions) plus tax-exempt income (municipal income bond) plus ½ of social security.]

Comments

12. Grin and bear it. For most people the change won't exceed $1000 per year.

Details

13. More people will be subject to the alternative minimum tax and their rates will be higher.

Comments

13. The rules here can make your eyes glaze over. If you think you might qualify, speak to your accountant about this.

Investment Implications

How do these changes affect investment policy?

As we have stated, all other things being equal, investments that produce capital gains are now more attractive. That is because the top federal tax rate on capital gains income is 28 percent, well below the maximum 39.6 percent rate for ordinary income. But one must also take into consideration that shifts in the proportion of portfolio assets to stocks should be guided by the fundamentals and valuations as discussed in Chapters 3 and 4. Tax-deferred annuities are being highlighted by many salespersons. For most annuity policies the overhead costs and the lack of full investment choices will offset their tax benefits. Municipal bonds are, in our opinion, a more attractive investment. They are fully federal, state, and local tax free as opposed to a deferral with the annuity. Moreover, you can shift your assets at any time without penalty. Finally, the yields on municipal bonds are currently fairly high relative to taxable rates which is likely to result in muni bonds outperforming taxable ones.

Personal real estate is a highly attractive vehicle, since you can enjoy the tax deduction on depreciation and on monies borrowed. Prices on real estate are low now and increases in values are taxed only when sold. The tax act's shift to longer depreciable lives of 39 years on nonresidential real estate versus 31.5 years formerly (depreciation on residential property held as an investment was held level at 27.5 years) will not result in a material long-term difference in profitability. However, be careful of tax-advantaged income housing partnerships given new life under the tax act. The tax credit on these low-income housing investments can substantially reduce your cost, but it will only be beneficial if the investment provides income and a profit on sale—something most of these types of partnership have not historically done.

Finally, qualified pension plans of all types, including 401(k)s, are even more attractive now. They virtually are the only vehicles that provide a current tax deduction for contributions and income earned is tax deferred until withdrawn. From a financial standpoint, you should put the maximum you can in these plans even if you have to borrow (judiciously) to fund these payments. As much sense as pensions make now, they will be even more important as tax rates continue their long-range cyclical climb to higher levels.

New Long-Term Care Regulations

How can I plan for long-term health care under Clinton's new health care package?

Comments

While Clinton's health plan may help cover some long-term health care costs, for many, the days of making yourself poor prior to entering a nursing home are gone. In the past, the government would examine prior transfers to offspring or other parties over a 30-month period to determine Medicaid eligibility for government aid. It was simple for those people not bothered by the ethics of the situation to shift money two and a half years before entering a home or leave enough money to cover two and a half years of payments. The balance would go to the children or other beneficiaries outright or be put in a Medicaid Trust with income only to the elderly parents. The principal would be left to the beneficiaries upon death of the parents.

The full nursing home cost, amounting to as much as $100,000 a year in high-cost areas, would be borne by the government. Now the government will look back 36 months on outright gifts and apparently 60 months on amounts placed in a trust. The period of ineligibility for government aid if transfers are made within the three-year or five-year period will extend from one month to an entire lifetime depending on the amount transferred and nursing home costs in your area. Moreover, apparently the government will be reimbursed for any aid given from the remaining assets of the estate after the nursing home patient has passed away.

Comments

For many people this will end the attractiveness of long-term care induced estate transfers. This strategy always had as it weakness giving up control of your money. The average person will have to look more closely at the final version of Clinton's health plan. Interestingly, the Administration intends to make at-home care more attractive, perhaps because it can cost the government less money. Additionally, long-term health care insurance is likely to prove more attractive. A reassuring note is the fear of bankrupting yourself and leaving nothing to your spouse or children is generally overstated. The overwhelming majority of individuals—particularly males—don't spend their remaining days in a nursing home. The government will continue to pay for those who genuinely can't afford it themselves.

Further Readings

Chapter 1

Bailard, Biehl & Kaiser, Inc., *Personal Money Management,* 6th ed., Macmillan, New York, 1992.

Phillips, Carole, *Money Talk: The Last Taboo,* Arbor House, New York, 1984.

Quinn, Jane Bryant, *Making the Most of Your Money,* Simon & Schuster, New York, 1991.

Chapter 2

Doran, Kenneth, *Personal Bankruptcy and Debt Adjustment,* Random House, New York, 1991.

Jorgenson, Richard, *No Nonsense Credit,* Liberty Hall Press, Summit, PA, 1991.

Chapter 3

Graham, Benjamin, *The Intelligent Investor,* HarperCollins, New York, 1973.

Jones, Charles P., *Investments: Analysis and Management,* 3d ed., Wiley, New York, 1991.

Chapter 4

Altfest, Lewis J., "Bond Funds Versus Equity Funds: A Study of Performance," *The Journal of Financial Planning,* July 1990.

Business Week's Annual Guide to Mutual Funds, McGraw-Hill, New York, annual.

Cohen, Jerome, Edward Zinbarg, and Arthur Zeikel, *Investment Analysis and Portfolio Management,* 5th ed., Irwin, Homewood, IL, 1987.

Dreman, David, *The New Contrarian Investment Strategy,* Random House, New York, 1982.

Forsyth, Randall W., "Mutual Bonds: Portfolio Analysis of Selected Fixed-Income Funds," *Barron's,* December 24, 1990.

Gibson, Roger, *Asset Allocation,* Business One Irwin, Homewood, IL, 1990.

Gould, Carole, "Bond Funds, Expenses and Returns," *New York Times,* January 27, 1991, Section 3, page 23.

The Individual Investor's Guide to No-Load Mutual Funds, American Association of Individual Investors, Chicago, annual.

Chapter 5

Daily, Glenn S., *The Individual Investor's Guide to Low-Load Insurance Products,* International Publishing Corporation, Chicago, 1990.

Life Insurance: How to Buy the Right Policy From the Right Company at the Right Price, Consumers Union, Mount Vernon, NY, 1988.

Vaughn, Emmett J., *Fundamentals of Risk and Insurance,* 6th ed., Wiley, New York, 1992.

Chapter 6

Krefetz, Gerald, *Paying for College: A Guide for Parents,* The College Board, New York, 1992.

Leider, Robert, and Anna Leider, *Lovejoy's Guide to Financial Aid,* 3d ed., Monarch Press, Simon & Schuster, New York, 1989.

Leider, Robert, and Anna Leider, *Don't Miss Out: The Ambitious Student's Guide to Financial Aid,* 15th ed., Octameron Press, Alexandria, VA, 1991–1992.

Margolin, Judith P., *Financing a College Education,* Plenum, New York, 1989.

Peterson's College Money Handbook, Peterson's Guides, Princeton, NJ, 1992.

The Student Guide: Five Federal Financial Aid Programs, U.S. Department of Education, U.S. Government Printing Office, Washington, DC.

Chapter 7

Changing Times Staff, *Buying and Selling a Home,* Kiplinger Books, Washington, DC, 1990.

Haigh, Timothy, and Daniel Singer, *Real Estate Investment Advisor,* Probus, Chicago, 1988.

Greer, Gaylon, and Michael Farrell, *Investment Analysis for Real Estate Decisions,* 2d ed., Longman, Chicago, 1988.

Irwin, Robert, *Tips and Traps When Selling a Home,* McGraw-Hill, New York, 1990.

Jaffee, Austin, and C. F. Sirmans, *Fundamentals of Real Estate Investment,* 2d ed., Prentice-Hall, Englewood Cliffs, NJ, 1989.

Chapter 8

Block, Julian, *Julian Block's Year-Round Tax Strategies,* Prima Publishing, Rocklin, CA, 1992.

The Ernst & Young Tax Guide 1992, Wiley, New York, 1992.

Chapter 9

Leonetti, Michael, *Retire Worry Free: Financial Strategies for Tomorrow's Independence,* Dearborn Trade, Chicago, 1989.

Matthews, Joseph, *Social Security, Medicare and Pensions,* 5th ed., No Lo Press, Berkeley, CA, 1991.

Chapter 10

Leimberg, Stephan R., Stephen N. Kandell, Herbert L. Levy, Ralph Garo Miller, Morey S. Rosenbloom, *The Tools and Techniques of Estate Planning,* 8th ed., National Underwriter, Cincinnati, 1990.

Plotnick, Charles K., and Stephan R. Leimberg, *How to Settle an Estate,* Consumer Reports, Yonkers, NY, 1991.

Shenkman, Martin, *The Estate Planning Guide,* Wiley, New York, 1991.

Chapter 11

Gates, Philomene, *Suddenly Alone: A Woman's Guide to Widowhood,* HarperCollins, New York, 1990.

Saltman, David, and Henry Schaffner, *Don't Get Married Until You Read This: A Layman's Guide to Prenuptial Agreements,* Barron's Educational Series, New York, 1989.

Zipp, Alan S., *Handbook of Tax and Financial Planning for Divorce and Separation,* Prentice-Hall, Englewood Cliffs, NJ, 1985.

Chapter 12

Caregiving Tips, The National Council on the Aging, Washington, DC, 1988.

Family Home Caring Guides, The National Council on the Aging, Washington, DC, 1987.

Guide to Health Insurance for People with Medicare, U.S. Department of Health and Human Services, Washington, DC, 1992.

Levin, Nora Jean, *How to Care for Your Parents: A Handbook for Adult Children,* Storm King Press, Washington, DC, 1987.

Wexler, Nancy, *Mama Can't Remember Anymore: How to Manage the Care of Aging Parents,* Wein & Wein, Thousand Oaks, CA, 1991.

Index